CORRUPTION

WHAT EVERYONE NEEDS TO KNOW®

CORRUPTION
WHAT EVERYONE NEEDS TO KNOW®

RAY FISMAN
MIRIAM A. GOLDEN

OXFORD
UNIVERSITY PRESS

OXFORD

UNIVERSITY PRESS

Oxford University Press is a department of the University of Oxford. It furthers the University's objective of excellence in research, scholarship, and education by publishing worldwide. Oxford is a registered trade mark of Oxford University Press in the UK and certain other countries.

Published in the United States of America by Oxford University Press
198 Madison Avenue, New York, NY 10016, United States of America.

Library of Congress Cataloging-in-Publication Data
Names: Fisman, Raymond, author. | Golden, Miriam A., author.
Title: Corruption : what everyone needs to know /
Ray Fisman, Miriam A. Golden.
Description: New York : Oxford University Press, [2017] |
Series: What Everyone Needs to Know
Identifiers: LCCN 2016042678 | ISBN 9780190463984 (Hardcover) |
ISBN 9780190463977 (Paperback)
Subjects: LCSH: Corruption.
Classification: LCC JF1081 .F57 2017 | DDC 364.1/323–dc23 LC record available
at https://lccn.loc.gov/2016042678

1 3 5 7 9 8 6 4 2

Paperback printed by LSC Communications, United States of America
Hardback printed by Bridgeport National Bindery, Inc., United States of America

CONTENTS

FIGURES

PREFACE

We wrote this book together through pure happenstance; really, a lucky accident. An editor at Oxford University Press approached each of us independently about the possibility of taking on this volume. Ray was interested in writing a book on corruption, but wanted to find a coauthor. Miriam wanted to take on this book project, and happened to meet Ray just as she was considering the idea. Writing it together has allowed us to bring a much greater range of knowledge and literatures to bear than would have been possible if this book had been authored by only one of us, or even by two people from a single discipline. And it has been a lot more fun—a fact that we hope is evident in the pages to come.

We are two scholars who have each studied corruption for many years. Miriam, a political scientist, has conducted field research and collected original data on various aspects of corruption in Italy, India, and Ghana. Ray, an economist, spent much of his youth traveling the world trying to understand corruption firsthand in Indonesia, India, and elsewhere. (Today he studies the same issues from the comfort of his home in Boston.) We bring different disciplinary perspectives to this volume. Before we began writing together, Ray had thought more about the economic consequences of corruption, for instance, and Miriam, more about how political parties become corrupt. The similarities in our approach are greater than any differences, however. We are both committed to close and careful review of the best evidence available, and both interested in how new research techniques—especially experimental research—can be brought to bear on the questions that concern us. Finally, we are both cautious about drawing overly strong conclusions that go beyond what the data and evidence support—cautious but not, as we will confess momentarily, immune to the temptation.

Why did we write this book?

Authors in the social sciences today face a dilemma: most research is presented in peer-reviewed articles subject to ever more exacting standards. In itself, that's great, and we are fully supportive of the thorough and rigorous vetting of research that peer review imposes. The dilemma is that an article by its very nature presents the results of a single, narrowly focused piece of research—when what we, as scholars and as citizens, also want is an overview of how these various results fit together. The article format permits research results to accumulate but not add up as answers—except to questions that can be shoehorned into a single piece of research. In other words, articles force us to think small, write short, and ask narrow questions, when sometimes—although by no means always—we need to think a little bigger, write a little longer, and try to answer broader questions.

We think that the study of corruption has arrived at a juncture where it will especially benefit from a book-length overview. A substantial amount of research into corruption in the last two decades has generated some meaningful but narrowly focused results. Many of these are isolated to the study of a single country or even a particular region of a single country, or they offer a specific framework of analysis or study a highly specific aspect of corruption. This prompts us to seek the space to reflect more broadly—and to speculate somewhat more daringly—than is feasible or reasonable in article-length research papers. That is, we want to be able to say some things we are not certain are true, but that are plausible and indeed even implied by the most scientifically scrupulous research. Perhaps the last volume to try to do this was James Scott's *Comparative Political Corruption*,[1] a wonderful book that is, however, now more than four decades old. Of the many other book-length studies of corruption available, Susan Rose-Ackerman's *Corruption: A Study in Political Economy*[2] stands out for its innovative use of microeconomic tools and breadth of insight. But that volume is also nearly forty years old. Since then, new ways to measure corruption have been devised, and as a result, we know a good deal more about corruption than we did forty or fifty years ago. We also have new tools of analysis at our disposal, particularly those that come out of new ways of thinking about causal inference, and we have new methods of data collection and analysis. Finally, the world has changed since then as well. Corruption may not be worse, but it is more visible and has assumed somewhat different characteristics. Public opposition to corruption has become much more pronounced and, as a result, we also know a good deal more about the strengths and weaknesses of various anticorruption tactics and techniques of intervention. We hope that our book fills the gap that these changes have produced.

We have sought to indicate, in what follows, the degree of confidence that we ascribe to various statements and arguments. In the main, we have high confidence in evidence-based results, often arising from experimental (or quasi-experimental) work. We also have confidence in the accuracy of descriptive analyses of systematic and well-constructed observational data. But there is much we think is also probably true, which arises out of our years of thinking about the issues we treat and decades of working with less-than-perfect (for now) empirical evidence. Finally, there are some parts of what you will read in this work that are neither true nor false in an empirical sense. They are, instead, frameworks that we have found to be useful for organizing our thinking about various aspects of corruption.

Who are our intended readers?

The primary audience for this book is ordinary people (including university students) who are curious to know more about corruption than what they might chance upon in the news. We also hope that this volume serves as a useful primer on corruption for academics, policymakers, and others who may have an interest in the topic as it intersects with their work lives and professional responsibilities. In our writing, we have focused on communicating with those who come to this book without rigorous social scientific training, since we trust that our graduate students and colleagues will be able to read something written for a broader audience, and we know that a broad audience is not interested in reading academic work whose point is hidden behind jargon or algebra.

We also write with an international audience in mind, employing examples from a range of countries and circumstances that, we hope, make the ideas we discuss tangible and relevant to readers across the globe. We would like to provide readers in high-corruption countries with some analytic tools for understanding the interactions and transactions they observe in their everyday lives. For readers in nations where corruption is less of a pressing concern, we hope to provide a better appreciation for the difficulties confronted by their less fortunate counterparts in the rest of the world.

Are there electronic resources that complement this book?

We provide some accompanying electronic resources on our homepages. (Miriam's is www.golden.polisci.ucla.edu and Ray's is sites.bu.edu/fisman.) Color versions of some of the figures are posted there, as well as the underlying data, so readers may reanalyze the material on their own if they wish.

ACKNOWLEDGMENTS

Our first thanks go to Andrew Gelman for taking the trouble to introduce us. Without his introduction, we would not have become coauthors, and this particular book would not have been written.

We would like to acknowledge our students and colleagues who took time out of their busy schedules to read the manuscript, thereby improving this book immeasurably. Jasper Cooper, Marko Klašnja, Paul Lagunes, Pablo Querubín, Joshua Tucker, and Matthew Stephenson spent most of a day with us in New York to discuss the entire manuscript, in a meeting that played a crucial role in thinking through the project. At the University of California at Los Angeles (UCLA), Ruth Carlitz, Eugenia Nazrullaeva, Manoel Gehrke Ryff Moreira, Alexandra Petrachkova, Arseniy Samsonov, and Luke Sonnet also read the entire manuscript and made useful suggestions. Others who generously read the entire manuscript and provided comments were James Alt, Catherine de Vries, Luis Garicano, Lucio Picci, and Shanker Satyanath.

Miriam thanks the UCLA undergraduates enrolled in PS169 in fall 2015, who read first drafts of many chapters, and Luke Sonnet, who assisted.

Miriam acknowledges the John Simon Guggenheim Memorial Foundation for financial support when this book was conceived and begun, and the Academic Senate of the

University of California at Los Angeles for assistance while completing it. The manuscript was finalized while in residence at the lovely Nuffield College, University of Oxford.

Edson Smith and Andy Lin of the UCLA Institute for Digital Research and Education designed the figures. Manoel Gehrke Ryff Moreira produced the graphics.

Finally, at Oxford University Press, we were bolstered by the enormous enthusiasm of Scott Parris and the editorial support of David McBride and David Pervin.

CORRUPTION

WHAT EVERYONE NEEDS TO KNOW®

1

INTRODUCTION

1.1 What is the purpose of this book?

Well over half of the world's inhabitants live in countries where corruption is relatively common, according to standard survey data. In other words, most people on earth live in places where they must contend with the fundamental dilemma of corruption—whether to pay a bribe to receive a government benefit or service they need and to which they may well be entitled, or to take the moral high ground and go without. Ordinary citizens are often well aware that they are the victims of corruption, but feel powerless to do anything about it. Our purpose in this volume is to provide an understanding of the dilemma corruption presents to people trapped in it and to others who are likely appalled by it.

We have both spent much of our professional lives—which together stretch to over five decades—thinking about corruption. This book represents our joint effort at capturing our understanding of this complicated, multifaceted, and immensely important phenomenon in a nontechnical and readily accessible form. Our aim is not only to summarize our own insights but also to provide the reader with an overview of existing knowledge on political corruption, knowledge that's emerged from the work of a great many scholars. Thus, we aim to help readers (and ourselves) better understand where, why, and how corruption occurs.

We aspire to do more than simply educate our audience. In addition to telling you what we know about corruption, we aim to provide a framework for thinking about how to reduce it.

On balance, we take the view that corruption carries negative social consequences: it harms economic efficiency, increases social inequities, and undermines the functioning of democracy. (This overall conclusion probably doesn't come as a surprise, but many of the details that we uncover in the pages that follow are likely unexpected.) But corruption isn't immediately and directly harmful to everyone—and that's what makes it such an intractable problem. Even if corruption carries negative consequences for society as a whole, individuals become involved in corrupt transactions precisely because they benefit from them. The corrupt politician or public bureaucrat benefits by misusing his public office. The benefit usually includes—but is not limited to—financial gain. Ordinary citizens living in corrupt environments are trapped by corruption when they pay bribes, knowing full well they are wrong to do so, because the alternatives—not being able to see the doctor, get a driver's license, or receive much-needed government permits—are worse. In the short run, individuals benefit from corrupt activities even when in principle they dislike them, making corruption immensely difficult to remedy.

In the last chapter of this book, we discuss some specific ideas about how to fight corruption. But to get there we first need to spend some time (in what constitutes the bulk of the book) understanding the nature of the problem: Where is corruption most common? Who is involved? What kinds of activities are most susceptible? We also need to better appreciate the processes that produce it: how does partisan electoral competition promote (or reduce) corruption? Why don't democratic elections reduce or eliminate it?

1.2   Why does corruption matter?

The simplest way to think about corruption is to imagine a public official taking a bribe in the course of doing his job. (In the next chapter, we'll complicate this view, but not by much.) This might be a single small bribe, perhaps a trivial amount used to grease a palm. Or it might be a stream of large payments, such as millions of dollars from a multinational corporation in exchange for a government contract to build new fighter jets. We could add up every bribe paid—from petty amounts all the way up to grand corruption—but we still wouldn't capture corruption's total impact. That's because, when bribes are commonplace, it leads to many changes in the way a society is organized. Many types of political and economic distortions occur that harm the public good and that lead to yet more corruption. Companies that pay bribes and win contracts drive their honest competitors out of business, thereby changing the nature of the market. The public officials on the receiving end write more rules with the express purpose of taking yet more bribes, thereby complicating the regulatory environment. Government jobs attract candidates who want to take bribes rather than serve the public, leading to less scrupulous officials. Political authorities become dependent on bribes to fund their reelection campaigns. They proliferate government jobs in order to put in place more civil servants who will pass portions of bribes up to the politicians who appointed them, leading to bloated government payrolls. Governments budget for more roads than necessary, in order to extract more bribes, thereby reshaping public investment. All those roads require more cement than would otherwise be used, again distorting the market. The public suffers as a result: there is less money for healthcare and education, and inequitable access distorted by having to pay bribes for services to which everyone is legally entitled.

The cost of corruption is thus not limited to the sum of the bribes paid to public servants. Corruption is far more corrosive of government and the economy—a bribe's impact is magnified through its undermining effect on political and market institutions. The vast misallocation of public and human resources that results from widespread corruption impedes the functioning of government and the economy. (For this reason, organizations across the globe often consider systemic corruption as an indicator of broader failures of governance.)

The indirect effects of corruption are undoubtedly larger—far larger—than the direct cost of bribes and monies embezzled or misappropriated. In this book, we examine who pays bribes or embezzles funds and why, with the goal of understanding why it's so hard to put a stop to corruption—even when everyone (or almost everyone) involved wishes otherwise. We now turn to providing a basic framework for understanding how corruption—despite its damaging effects—can be so persistent.

1.3 What is our framework for understanding corruption?

We conceptualize corruption as an equilibrium in the specific sense that social scientists use the term. That is, corruption happens as a result of interactions among individuals in which, given the choices others make, no one person can make herself better off by choosing any other course of action. Our presentation of corruption-as-equilibrium is by no means novel—scholars have framed the problem in these terms for decades. But this way of thinking about corruption is especially useful to provide an appreciation for why corruption (which we will define more precisely in the next chapter) is so resistant to remedy. We lay out our basic framework here because we refer back to it repeatedly throughout the book.

Roughly speaking, there are four types of participants in corrupt activities: elected public officials (i.e., politicians), government bureaucrats, businesses, and ordinary citizens. At least superficially, it's easy to see why each of these groups chooses to engage in corruption. The incentives of politicians and bureaucrats—the first two types of participants on our list—are particularly obvious. Elected public officials benefit from corruption when they abuse their positions by extorting bribes from businesses in exchange for government contracts or favorable legislation. Civil servants, likewise, benefit from corruption when they augment their salaries with money from bribes that they take from citizens in exchange for delivering public services or deliberately neglecting to enforce regulations. Businesses profit from lucrative government contracts won through bribery or connections, and lower their expenses by bribing their way around regulations. And private individuals? They benefit from getting to see a doctor at a public hospital, having their water line turned on, or avoiding a parking ticket.

But if you think about bribe payers as a group, it's very far from clear that corruption is good for them. After all, private individuals are usually paying bribes for government services to which they're entitled by law—and why should they have to pay for what's rightfully theirs?

The same can often be said of businesses. When they sell their services to governments—contracting to build schools or to provide training, for example—the benefits of paying kickbacks for firms as a group are unclear, because the winning company's gains represents other companies' losses. All companies might well be better off if they could agree to abstain from paying bribes. The same number of contracts would still come up for bid, and the winners wouldn't have to budget in the extra expense of bribery.[1] Why, then, don't businesses and regular citizens band together and refuse to pay?

To structure our thinking about this question, we turn to classic work that Thomas Schelling, winner of the Nobel Prize in Economics, laid out in a highly readable set of essays.[2] Schelling was interested in what he called *contingent behavior*: behavior that depends on what others are doing. Much of how we behave is contingent, including whether we wear jeans or a ball gown to a dinner party; whether we drive a car to work or take a bus; and whether we eat lunch in the cafeteria at noon or at 2 o'clock. We make each of these decisions after having considered what we expect others to do. Likewise, whether we choose to engage in or denounce corruption is contingent on how we expect others to behave. In a society where corruption is common, few dare to speak out against it on their own. Not only would denunciations lead to social disapproval and perhaps even physical danger, they don't do much good unless others join in. That is, you need a critical mass of disapproval to be effective. Similarly, if everyone you know pays a bribe to get a doctor's appointment, you conclude that if you want to see a doctor, you had better save up your bribe money. In both cases, deciding whether to pay bribes or denounce them hinges on how many others participate in or speak out against corruption.

To be clear, the behaviors that people see around them and the choices that they themselves make are not necessarily what they believe are best, what they see as moral, or even what they want. We find considerable evidence, which we present in chapters to come, that the vast majority of people in most countries disapprove of corruption.[3] Yet in situations where corruption is common, individuals often see no option but to participate. Conversely, in situations where corruption is uncommon, individuals who offer bribes are easily exposed and, as a result, generally don't offer bribes in the first place. Anyone trying to bribe a doctor for more personal attention or better treatment in Chile—a middle-income but very low-corruption country—exposes himself to shame, ridicule, and perhaps a few months in prison. Anyone *not* offering a bribe to see a doctor in Romania risks going without healthcare entirely.

Corruption is thus what is called a *multiple equilibrium* phenomenon: in some countries corruption is endemic, while in other, apparently similar countries, corruption rarely comes up in day-to-day life. The difference, we argue, reflects in large part what everyone expects everyone else to do. If others pay bribes, you'll go along with them. If everyone denounces bribery, you'll do that instead. To repeat, this is not because individuals necessarily have more relaxed moral compasses in high-corruption settings, but because it's too costly if their behavior deviates from the norms or expectations of those around them. As a result, countries at similar levels of economic development and with similar political institutions may end up with vastly different degrees of corruption, depending on these shared expectations.

One way of grasping the idea of corruption-as-equilibrium is to consider how the benefits of giving or taking bribes (versus the benefits of staying honest) change as ever more members of a society resort to bribery. We illustrate this idea in Figure 1.1.

In the diagram, we capture one plausible relationship between the expected honesty of others and the benefits of bribery (or honesty) for a single individual. In the figure, the "pay bribe" line depicts the benefits to an individual from paying bribes, which, as we discussed above, changes depending on how many others he expects will also behave corruptly. The "be honest" line similarly shows the benefits for someone who abstains from corruption, which again depend on what others do. Start at the far left of the graph, where everyone else is expected to be honest. What should you choose to do? It's actually quite hard to be corrupt under these circumstances, even if you want to be, as indicated by the low net benefits of engaging in corruption. There's a shortage of willing accomplices, which makes it difficult to find partners to collude with to get around the government's regulations or steal from its coffers. With no one else to cover for you, you are swimming alone in a sea of honest compatriots, meaning you face higher odds of getting caught (and perhaps harsher sanctions if you do). The benefits from adopting a "be honest" posture—labeled A—are considerably higher than the benefits of paying a bribe.

Move a little to the right—but just a little, so you're still to the left of point B, where the two lines cross. You're now

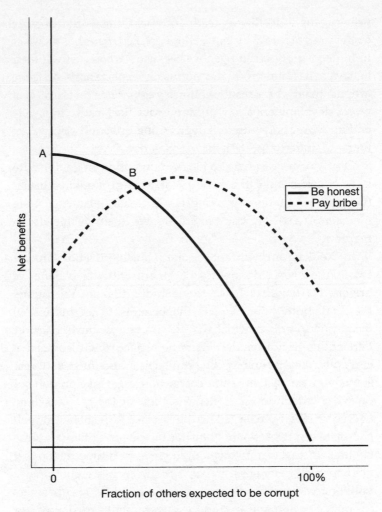

Figure 1.1 Diagram Depicting Corruption as a Multiple Equilibrium Phenomenon

Note: Figure adapted from Figure 1 in J. C. Andvig, The Economics of Corruption: A Survey, *Studi economici*, 1(43), 57–94.

in a setting where a few others—but not very many—will behave corruptly. The net benefits to corruption increase a bit. It's now a little easier to find partners in crime, and the benefits from remaining honest are a little lower—you might, for example, find that dishonest companies occasionally beat you out for government contracts, or that the kids of your corrupt neighbors buy their way into better schools. But as long as there aren't too many people trying this, it's still better to stay honest. Suppose that everyone thinks this way. Then, even if there's a little corruption to begin with, no individual wants to follow suit, and we make our way back to the left side of the graph, where no one's taking bribes. That is, when we are a little to the right, society is not in equilibrium: the few individuals engaging in corruption will want to switch to law-abiding behavior, given what others are doing. We thus return to the extreme left, where we are in equilibrium.

Suppose, though, that there is a big increase in how much corruption people believe is out there—now jump out past B, where the two lines intersect. To the right of B, no single individual finds it's worth it to stay honest—she'll find herself too often shut out of contracts, good schools, and even basic government services. And besides, if everyone else is doing it, the sense of wrongdoing diminishes. As a result, the few honest individuals resign themselves to going along with everyone else. Which, of course, moves us further and further to the right, until everyone expects everyone else to take bribes and takes bribes themselves.[4]

Observe that, as a result, there are only two stable situations in this description of the decision to take bribes: if we start to the left of point B, where the two lines intersect, we end up at the extreme left of the figure, as fewer and fewer individuals find it worthwhile to act corruptly. Here we are in a virtuous cycle. If we start to the right of point B, the opposite happens—ever more individuals decide that the benefits of corruption exceed those of honesty. We end up in a vicious cycle. Each of these endpoints, where either no one or everyone engages in corruption, constitutes an equilibrium.

One important aspect of the corruption-as-equilibrium model is that people get stuck in a situation where they willingly pay bribes, given everything they believe is going on around them, even when they prefer to be in a situation where no bribes are paid. Perhaps corruption is good for a select few oligarchs or well-placed and unscrupulous government officials who are raking in millions in profits and bribes. However, for everyone else, corruption is a *second best* strategy; it is never what citizens, businesses, or even (bribe taking) government officials would most prefer.

We've already explained why this would be the case for ordinary citizens and businesses. Regular people have to pay bribes for government services or contracts that, in an alternative (corruption-free) universe, they would receive without a bribe. For businesses, bribery is yet another cost of doing business, and one that makes transactions with government more expensive and more uncertain. Even for government officials on the receiving end of these payments, it isn't obvious that the corrupt equilibrium is preferred to the honest one. Put yourselves in the shoes of a doctor or police officer—would you rather earn a pittance of a salary, with the expectation (indeed, the requirement) that you make ends meet by extorting patients or students? Or would you prefer to earn a decent living and hold a position of respect in your community? If you enter politics, would you prefer to compete on an even footing with other candidates via legally funded campaign contributions, or (like everyone else) embezzle from government coffers to finance your reelection bid? Do you want to use your campaign funds to illegally buy votes because that's what your competitors do, or use your money to advertise your campaign on television? We'd argue that the low-corruption equilibrium is better for just about everyone.

The way we've depicted it, corruption does not depend on coercion: bribers *could* refuse to pay without risking physical harm. If you don't bribe a traffic cop who deliberately targets you for an undeserved ticket, you end up with a fine, not a beating. Yet it doesn't seem quite right to put on an equal footing bureaucrats who collect bribes and citizens who pay bribes for government services to which they are legally entitled. The government officials who take bribes are *extorting* citizens or businesses. That is, there is a threat—perhaps only implicit—underlying these transactions, an inequality of authority and power. That's why it is common to accuse politicians who accept bribes of misusing or abusing their official positions. They are entrusted with public authority and are supposed to follow certain rules, particularly in their dealings with the public. When they fail to do so, by threatening to withhold a public service from a deserving citizen, they can get away with it precisely because of the unequal status between public official and citizen.

One implication of this observation is that, while it's true that corruption represents an equilibrium from which an individual benefits, not everyone benefits equally. Bribe-takers benefit more than bribe payers, in general, because of the greater authority of the former. So while it's difficult to alter a high-corruption equilibrium, support for changes aimed at reducing corruption is far more likely to come from those who pay bribes than from those who take them.

Where do these expectations of bribery and corruption come from? It is a bit of a mystery why some countries end up with everyone expecting that everyone else pays bribes (and hence following suit) while other countries attain the bribe-free equilibrium.[5] In this volume, we do not pretend to offer a complete explanation for why countries at roughly similar levels of economic development may exhibit vastly different degrees of corruption. We cannot provide a complete accounting of why, for example, Chile is full of honest government officials whereas Venezuela—another Latin American nation, which at least until very recently was slightly wealthier than Chile—ranks as one of the world's most corrupt. We will, however, discuss circumstances that make it more likely that one or the other outcome prevails.

We are tentatively hopeful that demands for—and expectations of—honest government are rising in the world today. We cannot predict exactly when and where anticorruption crusades will take off. But we believe that our framework for understanding the problem of corruption can help us draw some conclusions that will allow anticorruption movements to emerge. That is the goal—an ambitious one—that we set out for ourselves in writing this book.

1.4 How can a corrupt country shift to a low-corruption equilibrium?

The preceding discussion implies that individuals who engage in corruption are not necessarily less ethical than those of us who happen to have been born in low-corruption countries. One implication of this is that appeals to morality are unlikely to be successful in getting individuals to change their delinquent ways. It makes more sense to think of people in corrupt societies as trapped in tough situations where they do what's in their individual best interests, despite the social cost of doing so. Of course, in any society, there are some individuals whose moral thresholds are so high and so firm that they resist the temptation to blindly follow the norm, and who therefore resist participation in corrupt activities, whatever the risk to themselves. But the more common corruption is in a society, the fewer, the more isolated, and the more at risk these individuals are.

To appreciate why it's so difficult to switch from one equilibrium to another—even one that everyone might prefer—consider a seemingly straightforward change in social behavior like, say, a shift from driving on the left to driving on the right. Just ask residents of the South Pacific island of Samoa, who made the switch in 2009, what was involved. Most Samoans agreed that in the long run, left-sided driving would make sense: it would synchronize the island's cars and driving norms with nearby Australia, making it easier and cheaper to import vehicles.[6]

But you can't change driving practices by convincing one motorist at a time to switch sides: unless *everyone* changes at once, the left- and right-driving norms will very literally collide. So prior to the change, which took place to much blaring of sirens and ringing of church bells at 6 a.m. on September 7, 2009, there were months of intensive public outreach to let *everyone* know that the norm was about to change. (Despite some forecasts of disaster, everything went smoothly.)

Samoans had it relatively easy in making this switch. The shift in driving norms could be nudged along by accompanying changes in the formal rules of the road. It was also easy enough to see how things were going on September 8 and take corrective measures as needed. Anticorruption reformers have a much harder time exploiting the complementary lever of legal enforcement or checking on how their efforts are translating into real changes. Corruption is, when done right, hidden from view. And it exists precisely because rules aren't being followed in the first place. Even if most citizens of highly corrupt countries see bribery as a problem that needs addressing, it's hard to refuse to bribe a cop, or to raise a fuss if one is elicited, unless you know that others are on board with making the same change.

That is, what matters isn't whether you deem corruption to be unethical and immoral. How you'll act depends on how you think *everyone else* feels about corruption and what you believe everyone else will do about it. No one wants to be the first to storm the ramparts, lest they find themselves facing down the enemy alone. For corruption to be tackled effectively, people who are opposed to it have to coordinate their efforts. This is what makes corruption so hard to change.

How can a society escape from the vicious cycle of paying and taking bribes? Sometimes—not often, but sometimes—corruption does unravel. As we write this in the autumn of 2016, almost all members of Brazil's political elite have been exposed as deeply involved in large-scale corruption, as the world watches, astonished, by the daily revelations of the so-called Petrobras scandal. The country is in the midst of the largest corruption scandal ever to beset a democratic nation. After decades during which corruption was business as usual, there is the sudden threat of legal and political retribution. In November 2016, for example, the ex-governor of the state of Rio de Janeiro was jailed for siphoning off tens of millions of dollars from public construction contracts, an event that would have been unimaginable just a few years ago. How did this happen, and why so fast?

In chapter 8, we detail the unraveling of Italian corruption in the early 1990s, which had been, until the Petrobras investigation, the most extensive political corruption scandal ever to affect a contemporary democracy. The downfall of Italy's political elite was similarly swift, with corruption revelations resulting in the sudden collapse of the entire array of political parties that had governed the country for the preceding fifty years. We use the example to emphasize some features that, at least in that instance, appear necessary to the sudden and unexpected uprising of voters against a long-ruling and corrupt political elite. And we document the perhaps surprising finding that, using measures that capture change over time, the shift in Italy's culture of corruption has been permanent, despite Italy's continued reputation as an unusually corrupt wealthy nation.

These types of sudden shifts in behavior were studied by the eminent economist Thomas Schelling (whose work on contingent behavior provided the structure for our earlier discussion of corruption equilibria). Schelling called them "tipping points." He used the tipping point model to investigate the dynamics of racial segregation in U.S. housing. It helped to explain why, for example, neighborhoods that were predominantly white might suddenly "tip" and become black in a matter of a few years once a critical mass of African Americans moved in, even if most people (both black *and* white) did not actively want to live in segregated neighborhoods. This occurs because members of both races want to avoid being in the minority.[7] In Schelling's example, racial segregation could emerge even when individual members of a community do not desire it.

It's one thing to recognize the importance of tipping points, and quite another to actually make one happen—that is, to trigger a change in social norms. We'll offer some ideas on how a corrupt equilibrium may be "tipped" in chapter 9, based in part on approaches that have proven successful in the past.

1.5   What are other frameworks for thinking about corruption?

Our view is that conceiving of corruption as an equilibrium offers a powerful way to both frame the problem and to think about what to do about it. The approach emphasizes that corruption is based on social expectations, and that changing those expectations will be crucial to fighting corruption. An equilibrium-based approach also offers insights into some of corruption's more puzzling aspects, such as why it's so resistant to remedy or why politicians who win elections on anticorruption platforms often end up just as corrupt as their predecessors. But this is not the only way to conceptualize the problem. Here we sketch out the arguments of some prominent alternative frameworks.

The first alternative views corruption as a product of poverty. The *modernization* argument, as it is called, posits that poor people demand more amenities than what a resource-strapped government can realistically provide. As a result, those with sufficient means resort to bribes to access the few hospital beds, slots at decent schools, and other scarce services provided by government. The rule of law is weak in poor countries, which makes it that much easier for government officials to accept the bribes that are offered. Under the modernization hypothesis, it is only when a sizable middle class develops that widespread corruption can be reined in.[8]

There are parts of this view that we agree with. It becomes increasingly difficult to sustain widespread corruption as a country develops a larger middle class, and certainly we do observe lower levels of corruption in wealthy societies. But this view is highly incomplete when it comes to explaining circumstances in the world's poor and middle-income countries. These, as we document in chapter 3, exhibit widely varying levels of corruption. In some, bribery is commonplace, while in others corruption levels are comparable to those found in the world's wealthiest nations. Thus, while the modernization thesis fits with what we observe in rich countries, it falls short in explaining the patterns we observe in most of the world.

The second broad view of corruption sees it as a form of what is called *rent-seeking* by public officials and their private sector counterparts. This perspective was once particularly common to economists, many of whom contended that government intervention in the economy via licensing and regulation presents opportunities for businesses to profit from preferential treatment by bureaucrats. These profits are referred to as "rents"—as opposed to the profits that accrue when an enterprise creates new wealth—and may be shared with government officials who in turn extract payments when they dispense rent-creating licenses or trade protection. A classic example is helpful in clarifying the definition of rents, and also the nature of rent-seeking. Consider a landowner who puts a toll booth on the bridge over a river on his property. The landowner hasn't done anything to make the river or bridge more productive by demanding tolls—its sole purpose is to extract payments from those crossing the bridge, something that used to be free. Imagine, furthermore, that an enterprising businessman then pays the landowner for the right to collect tolls. This adds another layer of rent-seeking, since the toll collector isn't improving the bridge either.[9] Taxi medallions, liquor licenses, import permits—all these serve as examples of common ways that governments create what many would consider unnecessary rents, which businesses may then acquire through bribery, influence, or—more innocuously—through luck.

Again, there are parts of this view that we agree with. Government intervention in and regulation of economic activities do indeed offer opportunities for corruption. However, we do not see these opportunities as the *causes* of corruption.

There are countries where governments regulate many aspects of economic life—including the Scandinavian nations, which are typically deemed the world's least corrupt— but where government officials do not ordinarily take advantage of the opportunities to extort citizens for bribes in the process of enforcing the rules. Government intervention in the economy is a necessary but not sufficient condition for corruption to occur. Moreover, many regulations are useful for society at large. We don't want to live in a society without rules governing, say, safety standards for building contractors or mining companies. These rules ensure that buildings and mines are constructed so multistory office blocks don't collapse nor mines bury workers.

A third view comes from the political science literature, which contends that nondemocratic regimes—what are also called authoritarian regimes, or dictatorships—are often corrupt, whereas democratic political institutions offer mechanisms to rein in illegal behavior by public officials. The logic underlying what we will call the *regime* perspective is impeccable. Rulers who are not subject to elections have the opportunity to use the vast resources of the state as they wish; and why not use this power to line one's own pockets while in office? By contrast, rulers subject to elections are forced to operate according to the will of the people—voters surely will not elect and reelect those who steal from the public purse. This view underlies the concept of electoral accountability: so long as voters can throw the rascals out— that is, eject politicians whose performance in office is less than adequate—elected public officials will serve the interests of those they represent.[10]

The problem with the regime view is that as far as corruption and political malfeasance are concerned, it's simply inaccurate. As we document in the chapters to follow, and especially in chapter 8, voters do not throw corrupt politicians out of office when free and competitive elections permit them to do so. Even officials widely known to be corrupt are usually reelected. Thus, democratic political institutions are insufficient to drive out corruption, and indeed, they are not even necessary.

Some unelected leaders choose to run their governments honestly despite the absence of electoral sanctions. We devote considerable space to this puzzle later in the book, with a particular focus on the obstacles that prevent elections and voters from reducing corruption.

Finally, there is the *institutional* view, whose best-known proponents are economist Daron Acemoglu and political scientist James Robinson.[11] Acemoglu and Robinson emphasize a broad set of economic institutions, like property rights and market orientation, which define whether countries grow rich or stagnate. These institutions are in turn determined by a political process in which different groups in society jockey for power and resources. Let's say that a traditional ruling elite retains political power. Its kleptocratic leader will have rigged the country's basic institutions to fleece the country of its resources. These resources, in turn, provide the dictator with the means required to stay in power, regardless of the wishes of the broader population.

This institutional explanation for underdevelopment emphasizes the importance of history in determining a country's current circumstances, as in our example above, where concentrated power and self-serving government institutions tend to propagate themselves. Acemoglu and Robinson's arguments have been extremely helpful in explaining how many harmful institutions survive, as well as when they are most apt to change. We see our approach as broadly consistent with their framework, but we are much more focused on the specifics of corrupt interactions rather than the general sweep of history.

Overall, our take on all these frameworks is that, while there are useful elements in each, some of which we will incorporate in the discussions to come, none is adequate for understanding some of corruption's most important features. Relative to these approaches, we focus more squarely on the central role of *informal* institutions—individuals' beliefs, expectations, and norms of behavior—in understanding corruption. After all, every country in the world has written laws—that is, legal institutions—that formally penalize government officials who are caught stealing from public coffers or demanding bribes to deliver public services. To understand corruption, we need to understand better why individuals follow these rules—or flout them.[12]

1.6 What will you read in the chapters to come?

How much corruption is there, really? Before we decide that we want to devote our time and energies to dealing with corruption, we should first have some idea of its prevalence. Is it, as anticorruption zealots claim, ubiquitous in much of the world? Or, despite a few high-profile cases and stories of failed states, is it a more modest problem? We begin in chapter 2 by clarifying what exactly we mean when we talk about corruption, and also how we go about measuring it. What makes this a difficult—and also interesting—exercise is that corruption, when done right, leaves no traces. In chapter 3, we'll present evidence on the prevalence of corruption around the world, drawing on many sources and methodologies, including everything from surveys of everyday citizens to the videotape collection of one infamously corrupt Peruvian official.

We'll conclude that corruption is a global phenomenon that operates on a vast scale. But should we necessarily even label it as a problem? Until recently, many scholars (and many organizations, including the World Bank) saw anti-corruption efforts as a distraction from the "real" problems holding back economic development. According to that view, combating corruption might even be counterproductive for economic growth. As we'll see in chapter 4, thinking has changed—there's now a near-consensus that corruption is bad for business, bad for economic growth, and erodes citizens' trust in political institutions. It makes Chinese coal mines more dangerous, chokes off new business creation in Ukraine, and is responsible for uncounted deaths when government employees water down vaccines in Uganda.

This leads us back to the questions—which we began to address in this introduction—of who takes bribes and why, given the negative societal consequences of doing so. In chapter 5, we'll delve more deeply into the benefits that politicians and businesses extract from corrupt interactions, by exploring how Indian politicians' assets grow while in office, and analyzing the bets that investors make on the stock exchanges in Jakarta and elsewhere. We will also revisit the question of why it is so very hard for businesses to band together to overcome corruption, which will take us on a brief detour to a discussion of the well-known prisoners' dilemma. It will also require a more serious reckoning of the notion of a "culture of corruption," which will force us to confront, in chapter 6, whether certain social groups—based on religion, ethnicity, or history—are more predisposed to corruption than others. Our discussion of culture and norms will also bring us squarely back to the idea of corruption-as-equilibrium, and why it's so amazingly difficult to effect change.

Corruption is the result of more than just individual decisions. Societal institutions affect opportunities that each individual has for corruption. In chapter 7, we explore the ways that democratic political systems and political parties function, in order to understand whether changes to political institutions can remedy corruption. In line with our emphasis throughout on the importance of informal norms and practices, we conclude in this chapter that political institutions only prevent corruption when everyone follows the rules—which is precisely what is absent where corruption flourishes.

This leads us to what we, as individuals or collectively as societies, can do about corruption. We set the stage for this discussion in chapter 8, with some corruption success stories of recent vintage, including the Clean Hands campaign that purged the Italian Parliament in the 1990s, and the successful clean up of police corruption in the Republic of Georgia in the early 2000s. Our focus in this chapter is on the importance of voter coordination in retaliating against corrupt politicians.

Beyond showing up to vote on election day, what can *we* do? There aren't any silver bullets for ending corruption. Nor is that goal even possible. But guided by recent successes—and failures—we hope to come up with some overarching principles that may help us fight corruption more effectively. In chapter 9, we'll discuss technological innovations (including the ever-expanding role of social media in combating corruption) that have had both great successes and misfires. We'll examine whether higher salaries for government officials can reduce corruption—or whether they make the problem even worse. And we'll tell the unlikely story of how a former philosophy professor brought order to the lawless streets of Bogotá with the help of theater students and decks of cards. Anticorruption schemes come in many forms, and we hope our book can help our readers think about which ones fit best with their circumstances—and perhaps even devise new ones of their own.

1.7 What did we learn in chapter 1?

- Corruption has potentially very high costs, extending far beyond the sum of bribes paid and funds embezzled, because of the ways that corruption distorts economic and political institutions.
- Given prevailing circumstances, an individual benefits from participating in corruption—it thus constitutes an equilibrium.
- Individuals decide whether to participate in corruption based on their expectations of what others will do, and corruption hence constitutes a norm.
- Despite the immediate benefits of participating in corruption, individuals do not necessarily like it, and most would prefer to live in a society where corruption is not the norm.
- Corruption is a multiple equilibrium phenomenon, in that countries that are similar in other ways may exhibit vastly different degrees of corruption because of different expectations and norms that emerged in the past.

2

WHAT IS CORRUPTION?

Before we can consider the causes and consequences of corruption, or what to do about it, we need to have a common understanding of what we mean when we talk about corruption. This necessarily precedes our discussion of how we measure the extent of corruption in different countries—a topic we'll also take up in this chapter. After all, to measure something you need to know what it is that you're measuring.

As we'll see, corruption eludes a simple binary definition. It may be perpetrated by politicians or bureaucrats, whether on their own or in league with businesses or citizens; it may involve billion-dollar contracts or pocket change, or jobs or votes. Corrupt acts may be illegal, but need not be (although we will stress the legal dividing line). Corruption appears in many distinct forms and displays many shades of gray. Let's start, then, by addressing the question "what is corruption?" before proceeding in later chapters to consider where corruption is most prevalent, why it exists, why we care whether corruption is high or low, and what to do about it.

2.1 How do we define corruption?

In providing a definition, it's helpful to start with a few examples that represent unambiguous instances of corruption. In 2011, the health minister of Uttar Pradesh, the most populated state in India, was charged in what came to be known as the National Rural Health Mission Scam, which involved the embezzlement of an estimated 100 billion rupees (US$1.5 billion) in funds that were to be used for health facilities for the state's rural poor. The following year in America, Illinois governor Rod Blagojevich was indicted for scheming to sell one of his state's open seats for the U.S. Senate (vacated by Barack Obama) to the highest bidder.

These are epic instances of corruption that leave little room for interpretation or differences of opinion. Embezzling billions of dollars in public funds or selling what is supposed to be a freely elected public office are included in any definition of corruption.

Corruption also operates on a more modest scale—and largely out of the public eye. In 2014, a dozen building inspectors in New York City were charged with accepting bribes from contractors in exchange for ignoring work code violations. The stakes were hundreds or thousands of dollars, not billions, but we'd still all agree that the inspectors were corrupt. In fact, corruption extends all the way down to the petty shakedowns that motorists experience daily in cities scattered across the globe—such as bribing a traffic cop to avoid a ticket, which was likely issued for no good reason at all. In these cases, the sums of money are trivial, amounting perhaps to as little as a few dollars. But again, both examples are uncontested illustrations of corruption. No one would reasonably argue that these activities—assuming they occurred as described—could be considered legitimate behavior by public officials.

What unites these examples is that they all involve exploiting public office for private gain. In many instances, corruption involves an exchange between a public official and a private citizen—as when a contractor bribes a building inspector or a driver pays off a traffic cop. In other cases, public officials act on their own, as when they embezzle government funds. But, according to our definition, corruption always involves a public official who exploits his or her office to further his or her personal—rather than the public's—interests.

There are others who broaden the definition of corruption to include exploitative behaviors by those employed in the private sector as well. For example, if you go to the web page of Transparency International (TI), the best-known anticorruption organization on the planet, you'll find the following definition: "the abuse of entrusted power for private gain."[1] This formulation encompasses the self-serving acts of corporate executives, who are entrusted to run companies in their shareholders' best interests. It's certainly true that business leaders may act in morally repellant ways, exploiting their power to extract million-dollar paydays despite poor performance, or wasting shareholder value on corporate jets and other indulgences. But we'd argue that policing this type of misbehavior is better left to corporate governance activists than anticorruption crusaders. Our definition of "corruption" focuses on the public sector, not the private.[2] (Note, however, that our definition extends to private sector interactions with the public sphere, such as when a corporation pays bribe money to public officials to gain an economic advantage.)

We take a broad view of what constitutes private gain. Most obviously, politicians accept (or extort) cash bribes, using the money to buy cars, take vacations, or entertain their escorts. Politicians can (and very often do) also find jobs or assign contracts to family members. The politician herself may not be richer for it, but if she cares about her children, her siblings, and her cousins, she's benefiting, although in an indirect way.[3] The benefits we'd call corrupt extend to the candidate's partisan interests. Consider, for example, the widespread political corruption in Italy that developed in the decades after World War II (later exposed by the Clean Hands judicial crackdown that we discuss in chapter 8). It was common in the 1980s and early 1990s for low-level functionaries in the Italian Socialist Party to take large-scale bribes for public works contracts, 5 percent of which was passed up the chain of command to party headquarters in Rome. The party used the money to help fund its electoral campaigns. In other cases, a candidate's financial resources may be deployed to buy votes directly: in 1880, a candidate for office in Elmira, New York, could buy a vote for somewhere between $10 and $27—and many people did not think that there was anything wrong with the practice. Votes can be "bought" with sticks as well. In the 2014 presidential elections in Hungary, a significant fraction of voters in poor rural locations who were on the welfare rolls reported threats by campaign workers that their benefits would be cut off if they voted the "wrong way," despite being fully aware that the ballot was secret.[4] All of these forms of private gain are encompassed by our definition of corruption.

2.2 Is corruption necessarily illegal?

In *Comparative Political Corruption*, James Scott argues that there are three standards that we might use to define whether a public official's action is corrupt: the standard of public interest, the standard of public opinion, and the standard of the law.[5] Scott goes on to observe that in most cases, the three coincide. Take the Uttar Pradesh health minister's embezzlement of public funds that we discussed in the preceding section. The rural poor got less access to healthcare, so the public interest was harmed. Indians were, unsurprisingly, alarmed and upset by the scandal, so it ran counter to public opinion on the appropriate use of public office. Subsequently, the health minister was arrested because embezzling state funds is illegal. Regardless of which definition of corruption is applied in this case, the health minister's action was obviously corrupt.

In almost all of the examples that we consider in this book, behavior we classify as corrupt will fail by all three standards. There is no country we know of where it is legal for a public official to accept a bribe in exchange for awarding a public contract; and there is no country where it is legal for public health clinics to treat only voters who support a specific political party. These are both unequivocally illegal and illegitimate activities.

The legal demarcation of corruption has become stricter and more standardized internationally with the passage of time. In nineteenth-century America, it wasn't illegal for members of the United States Congress to accept bribes. In biblical times, it was *expected* that supplicants would bring an offering to a judge as payment for hearing a dispute. But most of the activities that are deemed corrupt today—embezzlement, handing out government jobs and contracts to family members, vote buying, the theft of public resources—are illegal in pretty much every democratic regime in the world. Nondemocracies are another matter, but even in many of these, there is a well-defined boundary between the public sphere and private benefits, and clear restrictions on appropriate behaviors by (most) public officials.

Some of the cases we look at are interesting precisely because they aren't quite so black and white. Take, for example, behaviors that aren't illegal but that somehow don't seem right to most people. Was it corrupt for U.S. Treasury Secretary Timothy Geithner to become president of Warburg Pincus (a company he'd been charged with regulating) in 2013, just over a year after leaving office? He waited out the legally mandated twelve-month period before taking a job in the financial services industry, so there was nothing illegal in his decision. But many saw it as payback for favorable treatment during his years of public service. Then again, as former president of the Federal Reserve Bank of New York (not to mention his term as treasury secretary), Geithner was eminently qualified to advise Warburg on investment decisions, so there was not necessarily any quid pro quo, just the recruitment of a financial expert who happened to work in government. It is thus hard to know whether Geithner exploited his time in office at the public's expense, or whether Warburg Pincus simply made a good hiring decision. But even if Geithner did nothing illegal and if the public wasn't harmed by his actions, many aspects of his behavior strike most ordinary Americans as corrupt.

The focus on legality can also lead to different interpretations of the same behavior in different countries. In the United States, it is illegal for an elected member of Congress to simultaneously sit on the board of a private company. In Italy, the equivalent is perfectly legal. So was it corrupt for Giovanni Agnelli, carmaker Fiat's major shareholder, to simultaneously serve as senator in his country's legislature? Anticorruption zealots might contend that Agnelli's appointment harmed Italians' already anemic trust in their government, because his role as senator might have given his company privileged access to government favors or resources. But Agnelli did not break the law. (Fiat's stock price jumped when Agnelli took his government post, suggesting that investors expected the company to benefit. So his critics may have a point.)[6]

Sometimes, as these examples suggest, using a legal standard to decide what is corrupt generates legitimate confusion. But even greater difficulties arise if we use public opinion or public interest instead as the standard by which we judge the behavior of officials. Let's continue with the Geithner and Agnelli examples. How do we know that the public's interests are damaged by their movements between government service and the private sector? One may argue that the public is harmed because it leads public servants to favor future (or current) private sector employers while in office. On the other hand, one might just as plausibly argue that it would be needlessly constraining to keep public officials out of the private sector—we get more productive public servants *and* a more efficient private sector if we allow our best and brightest (like Geithner and Agnelli) to do both. There are thus reasonable disagreements about whether the actions of Geithner or Agnelli run counter to the public interest. As for public opinion, it seems to vary from place to place such that similar behaviors are interpreted in different ways: the

American press condemned Geithner, whereas Italians were largely untroubled by Agnelli's dual role.

Therein lie the challenges in relying on an unspecified notion of the public interest or on public opinion as the standard for deciding what's corrupt: views may legitimately differ on what's good or bad for the economy or society, and public opinions and attitudes may vary a great deal across countries, over time, or based on circumstance.

The same is true for legal definitions of corruption, but much less so in today's world. In countries around the globe, public servants are hemmed in by legal restrictions that clearly demarcate the roles and responsibilities of elected and appointed officials. Everywhere, public officials have to follow rules in awarding contracts, disbursing entitlements, and doing their jobs. There is less discrepancy between what is legal for the mayor of Buenos Aires and the mayor of Cincinnati, or between a legislator in Poland and one in India, than ever before, and most of the activities that we study in this book are patently illegal in all of these settings. We will therefore mostly refer to corruption as lawbreaking throughout this book since, for all its shortcomings, the legal definition will allow us to draw a bright line—and a fairly objective one at that— separating corrupt activities from those we simply don't like or personally disagree with.

Even with our legal definition, we'll still have to deal with differences in what's seen as corrupt over time or across countries. To take just one example, driving citizens to the polls is a standard way of getting out the vote in the United States, whereas it's illegal (and also considered unethical by the electorate) in many Latin American countries.

Thus, whether we use the law, public opinion, or some measure of public interest, we will inevitably face difficulties in applying a uniform standard across countries. That said, providing a consistent definition of corruption will be easiest if the standard we apply is that of the law.

2.3 How do we measure corruption?

Corruption researchers and anticorruption enforcers face a similar problem—both aim to document something that, if done right, is invisible to outsiders. Bribery is mainly a cash business. There are usually no records, no bank transfers, and no receipts issued—ideally, no paper trail whatsoever. (In the epic corruption scandal-in-progress surrounding the construction of adjustable barriers to protect the Italian city of Venice from rising seas, businessmen reportedly took care of the paper trail by keeping records on edible paper so any evidence could be eaten—one presumes accompanied by a glass of locally produced sparkling Prosecco—after the transaction was complete.) Precisely because their actions are illegal, participants seek to hide any evidence of their activities.

Where corruption relies on electronic bank transfers to move and launder money, the funds are sanitized so the movements don't alert authorities. In cases of large-scale, high-level corruption—commonly referred to as "grand corruption"—officials routinely use shell companies to move money out of the country. Experimental evidence shows that it is surprisingly easy to set up even anonymous shell companies, despite the fact that doing so is illegal. Corporate service providers are supposed to require notarized identity documents from clients, making anonymous shell corporations impossible to establish. To see just how easy it was in practice, three political scientists sent more than 7,000 email solicitations to 3,800 corporate service providers in 181 countries, posing as potential clients attempting to set up anonymous shell corporations.[7] Even when an email purported to come from a government procurement official working in a highly corrupt and impoverished country— meant to tip off the recipient that the request might involve funds of dubious origin—corporate service providers were just as likely to agree to a meeting as those receiving an email from a (fictitious) prospective client located in a low-corruption nation.

A 2016 leak of more than eleven million records from the Panamanian law firm Mossack Fonseca revealed just how effective corrupt politicians (and businesses) have been in moving money around without alerting the press or investigative authorities. The so-called Panama Papers gave citizens of many nations direct evidence of long-suspected corruption of public officials. For example, the leaked documents exposed three Nigerian oil ministers, senior employees of the national oil company, and two state governors already under investigation for money laundering for having set up offshore shell companies that they'd used to buy yachts, private jets, and real estate in Manhattan and Beverly Hills.[8]

Enforcement authorities and investigative journalists also occasionally catch bribe givers and takers in the act. As a result, we know that the clichéd handoff of suitcases stuffed with unmarked bills has played out many times in reality. (Indeed, the 500 euro note is now being abolished because it made it too easy to load a small briefcase with a very large amount of illegally obtained currency.) In the late 1970s in the United States, for example, the Federal Bureau of Investigation (FBI) created a phony company called Abdul Enterprises to solicit favors—including assistance in laundering money—for a fictitious Middle Eastern oil sheik. Undercover FBI agents taped themselves offering cash to politicians, and the resulting Abscam operation led to judicial convictions of five congressmen, a U.S senator, and numerous local officials. In India, where the government has rarely taken on the task of catching politicians in the act, the magazine *Tehelka* pulled off an Abscam-like exposé in 2001. A pair of *Tehelka* journalists posed as representatives for a nonexistent London-based company, innocuously called West End, hoping to sell night-vision cameras to the Indian army. The reporters caught senior government officials and army officers on tape taking bribes or discussing how bribe payments were to take place.

To capture how much corruption there is in a particular place at a point in time, we have to go beyond media reportage of anecdotes or even the massive revelations generated by the Panama Papers. Most corruption is, we surmise, successfully kept secret, making news stories a particularly unreliable measure of its actual extent or frequency. And we certainly can't rely on legal prosecutions of corrupt officials as a measure of corruption, since doing so assumes that the judiciary is willing and able to identify and prosecute.[9] In fact, where corruption is most common, the judiciary is least likely to have the independence to investigate government officials.

So is the absence of anticorruption enforcement an indication that a country's officials are squeaky clean (so there are no cases to investigate) or so thoroughly embroiled in corruption that even the enforcers are themselves on the take? Conversely, does a full docket of anticorruption cases represent a judiciary earnestly dealing with corruption, or are the cases created to give the public the (false) impression that the government is dealing with the problem? You can see why it's so hard to interpret legal prosecutions as a measure of corruption.

If you ask government officials themselves, their answers are unlikely to be entirely truthful: they often have reason to deny allegations of malfeasance. Consider, for example, the three decades that President Suharto (who, like many Indonesians, goes by just a single name) ruled Indonesia, during which time his family is thought to have amassed a multibillion-dollar fortune. To this day, family members continue to reject accusations of corruption during the Suharto years, and have sued anyone who claims otherwise. (In one high-profile case, former President Suharto won a hundred-million-dollar lawsuit against *Time* magazine for claiming that he'd stolen $73 billion during his years in office.) We cannot expect criminals to expose themselves by publicly confessing their misdeeds, but if they don't do so, we cannot use their own words to assess their malfeasance.

As a result, we're forced to measure corruption indirectly. One way to do so is to ask others—such as political experts or those doing business in the country—how often public officials engage in bribery and embezzlement. The main advantage of this approach is that it is possible to administer a survey for any country you wish, generating a roughly comparable index of corruption that can be used to rank countries around the world. It is likewise possible to use surveys to rank states, regions, or provinces within a country, or to rank branches of the civil service within a government. We'll make frequent use of Transparency International's Corruption Perceptions Index (CPI), which is an average of a number of global corruption surveys conducted by various organizations focused on government accountability and business climate.[10]

Transparency International's Corruption Perceptions Index is, as the name emphasizes, a perceptions-based measure rather than one that necessarily reflects anyone's actual involvement in corrupt transactions. An alternative way to collect information on corruption is using experience-based surveys. These may ask corporate employees to provide estimates of, for example, the fraction of a government contract's value that's paid in kickbacks, or the fraction of revenues that's spent each year on bribes. (An example is the World Bank's World Business Environment Survey, which covers firms in about eighty countries.) Experiential surveys of ordinary people are also used to measure the petty shakedowns and extortions of daily life. They ask questions like "Were you asked for a bribe by a government official in the last year?" Some surveys include more specific questions, such as, "Were you asked for a bribe at a public health facility in order to receive treatment? Were you pressured to vote a certain way with the threat that public services would be withheld if you failed to comply? Have you paid a bribe to a public official in the last year?" The United Nations has collected information of this sort on a regular basis, using instruments such as the International Crime Victimization Survey.

There are benefits to using the data generated by each type of respondent and each type of data. A single expert might be able to assess the extent of corruption in many countries or regions, ideally using a uniform benchmark to define what constitutes a bribe. Likewise, a businessperson who works in many locations around the world is implicitly calibrating responses to a common standard. This allows perceptions-based surveys to sidestep, to some degree, the concern that what constitutes a bribe differs across countries. But perceptions-based surveys are also more vulnerable to *mis*perceptions resulting from, say, a crackdown that puts bribery in the headlines, even while actual corruption may be on the decline. And both perceptual and experiential survey measures can be deliberately distorted up or down depending on the motives of the respondent. Those opposed to current public policies may wish to besmirch the government's reputation by telling surveyors how terribly corrupt the country is, or they may be so fearful of retribution they say there's no corruption at all, even when it's rampant, despite the promises of anonymity made by the survey enumerators.

How do experiential measures compare with perceptual measures of corruption?

It is difficult to compare the data generated by reports from ordinary people about whether they paid bribes with expert surveys. Among other things, the two are rarely conducted simultaneously and seldom use easily comparable questions. One exception comes from the results of a study conducted between 1995 and 2003 in eight West African countries, by researchers Mireille Razafindrakoto and François Roubaud.[11] The pair administered two sets of surveys: one that asked ordinary people about *experiences* with corruption and another that asked experts for each country about their *perceptions* of ordinary people's experiences with corruption. The experts were asked what percentage of households they thought had paid bribes in the last year, in order to make the responses between experts and households as comparable as possible.

The researchers found a substantial and systematic discrepancy between expert perceptions and the actual incidence of bribe paying by the public. Across the eight countries, only about 13 percent of households reported having been forced to pay a bribe in the last year, ranging from 8.7 percent in Benin to 16.5 percent in the Ivory Coast. The country experts gave bribe estimates that were four times higher than what households reported, and failed even to get the ranking correct across countries. Experts rated Burkina Faso as least corrupt among the eight sample countries by quite a wide margin, estimating that bribe rates were 10 percentage points lower than the second-most-corrupt nation in the group. The household surveys suggested instead that Burkina Faso was among the most corrupt, with 15.2 percent of respondents reporting that they paid bribes.[12]

Why did the two approaches yield such different results? Perhaps households felt more intimidated by surveyors (though the researchers show that citizens were not shy about criticizing the government more generally), or held a narrower view of what constitutes a bribe relative to the experts. But it's almost certainly the case that the experts vastly overestimate the prevalence of bribery in ordinary people's lives. Even in high-corruption countries, in any given year less than 20 percent of the adult population pays a bribe or receives a handout aimed at buying their vote, a figure that's much lower than experts would have you believe.

Why can't we use objective measures of corruption?

In an effort to move beyond the "cheap talk" that characterizes survey responses, researchers in the emerging field of "forensic economics" are developing a range of techniques for studying otherwise hidden behaviors—including corruption—without directly asking about them.[13]

A 2005 paper by one of us (Miriam, in collaboration with economist Lucio Picci) provides an illustration of how forensic economists go about uncovering corruption, in this case in public construction in Italy.[14] To get an intuitive feel for our method, consider the 500-kilometer (300-mile) A3 coastal motorway in the country's South, from Naples to Reggio Calabria. The road was conceived in the mid-1960s as a way of connecting the underdeveloped region of Calabria to the rest of Italy. A first attempt at building the A3 led to an inadequate freeway that was prone to traffic jams, particularly in the summer. So in 1997, the Italian government announced a set of ambitious renovations, to be completed by 2003. At the time of this writing (August 2016), with over ten billion euros already spent, the road still isn't quite done. Thus, a great deal of money has been spent, with very little road infrastructure to show for it. Where did all that money go? According to the European Commission's Anti-Fraud Office, there were "widespread irregularities" in contracts for the A3. What sorts of irregularities? As anti-Mafia lawyer Roberto De Palma told the *Daily Telegraph* in 2012, "once the work begins, [a company paid to do public construction] will suddenly disappear, stealing the cash and leaving just a few pillars built in the soil."[15]

In the Golden-Picci study of corruption in Italian public construction, for each of Italy's 103 provinces, the authors compare the billions spent on public construction overall to the existing public infrastructure—the kilometers of roads and the number of schoolrooms, hospital beds, electricity lines, and so on. A province with a high expenditure-to-infrastructure ratio, we surmise, has likely had more public funds siphoned off by dishonest construction companies colluding with corrupt procurement officials. The results confirm the suspicion that southern Italy—home to the infamous A3, and the birthplace of the Mafia—has much higher "leakage" rates than the North. While this could also be because southern Italian contractors are more inefficient (rather than corrupt), Golden and Picci also find that private sector construction is actually cheaper in the South. So if the explanation for southern Italy's high leakage rate is inefficiency, southerners are reserving their laziness and incompetence for the work they do on government projects.

We'll mention various other indirect approaches to generating "real" measures of corruption in the course of this book. Researchers who develop these techniques have to be flexible in the method they use in any given scenario, so it's not possible to provide a complete account of their different approaches up front. For present purposes, we want to point out that these "objective" measures, however valuable, are necessarily tailor-made to each specific situation, which makes it impossible to use them to compare corruption across countries.

Overall, we need to be opportunistic in picking measures of corruption, and to use what's best for the particular purpose at hand. For comparing corruption worldwide, it's hard to beat surveys like Transparency International's CPI. There is simply nothing else that provides reasonably comparable measures for most of the world's countries. To call out corruption in Italian procurement, a case study on fund leakage will be less subject to the he-said-she-said disputes that come with perceptions-based surveys, and can provide a more tangible estimate of how much money is wasted as a result of misspent or stolen funds. Almost by definition, however, these types of objective measures can be calculated for only one country at a time, so we'll be able to use them only when we zoom in to examine corruption across Indonesian villages or in Italian provinces. When we step back to evaluate how corrupt Indonesia or Italy is compared to the rest of the world, we'll need to rely on TI's perceptions-based measure. But when we do so, we need to be aware of the problems that come with relying on opinions—rather than facts—about corruption.

2.4 How is political corruption different from bureaucratic corruption?

Corruption comes in many shapes and sizes. There are obviously differences in scale—*petty* corruption, like the bribe to avoid a parking ticket, versus *grand* corruption, as when a multinational pays millions to secure a government contract. We've also distinguished between corruption that involves a trade of favors (bribery) versus outright theft (embezzlement of government funds).

One particularly important distinction we'll come back to repeatedly hinges on the perpetrators: government bureaucrats versus elected officials. (While this distinction, strictly speaking, applies only to democratic political regimes, where politicians are elected, we may similarly distinguish between the corruption of rulers versus civil servants in nondemocracies.) The different ways that these officials are selected—and what they do once in office— has consequences for the types of corruption they tend to engage in, and also for devising strategies for making them stop.[16]

Bureaucrats are government employees who work in offices of public administration, such as schools, hospitals (which are usually public), and public agencies—everything from the diplomatic corps to the department of transportation. They are teachers, orderlies, police, tax collectors, and regulators who ensure that everything from construction sites to hotels follow appropriate laws. In theory, civil servants get their jobs because they have appropriate expertise or qualifications, or fulfill some other merit-based criteria. Teachers are employed because they have teaching certificates or credentials, and nurses because they have medical training. In most countries, judges are bureaucratic appointees who owe their jobs to their legal expertise. Civil service jobs are often awarded on the basis of entrance examinations, which, in many countries, are quite rigorous and competitive.

These jobs are shielded from political influence, at least in principle (more on that in a moment). Teachers, nurses, and others shouldn't be fired each time the government changes hands. Civil servants and appointed public officials are, in principle, nonpartisan and politically neutral—and if they aren't, we can already see at least a hint of corruption marring the appointment process.

In contrast to bureaucrats, politicians are elected or, in a nondemocratic political system, come to acquire power either through force or inheritance. Politicians include presidents, prime ministers, legislators, mayors, and city council members.

Lying somewhere between politicians and bureaucrats is a layer of what are called "patronage appointments," officials assigned on the basis of partisanship and loyalty to the government. (Some of these positions are nominally bureaucratic, and some are explicitly political.) When a new government takes office, it makes new patronage appointments. In most countries, heads of executive branch agencies—everything from the director of the Public Sector Pension Investment Board in Canada to the director-general of Belgium's Royal Higher Institute of Defence—are patronage appointments, as are the more obviously political appointments of ambassadors and various diplomatic attachés. There is a much thicker layer of patronage appointments in the United States than in other democracies, leading to a lot more churning of government appointments—as well as residences in the Washington, D.C. area—every time a new president moves into the White House. But even in the United States, patronage appointments are a small fraction of the public-sector workforce overall.

We say that patronage appointments lie somewhere between bureaucrats and politicians because they display a mix of the characteristics of the two. They are partisan, not meritocratic, but they are appointed rather than elected. (Despite being guided by partisan concerns, special expertise is required for many patronage positions.)

As you might guess, bureaucratic corruption involves the abuse of public office by bureaucrats, and political corruption involves the abuse of public office by elected officials. Why make the distinction?

The main reason is that the underlying incentives for bureaucratic and political corruption differ. Bureaucrats live off their salaries, which are often lower than those in comparable private sector jobs, and they expect to retain their jobs into an indefinite future. When they engage in illegal activities, it is almost always in exchange for cash, which they use to increase their earnings. Politicians, by contrast, need to compete in every election cycle if they want to retain their jobs, which (as far as we know) they almost always do.[17] They (or the political parties that nominate them) need to build up war chests to wage these political campaigns, and to elicit the support of groups that can mobilize voters and/or campaign on their behalf, like business lobbies or trade unions. In countries where most campaigning still takes place by political parties and candidates directly—rather than through television and robocalls—parties and candidates need to build an organization of activists and fervent supporters. All of this requires a lot of money.

In democratic countries, politicians, like bureaucrats, may abuse their positions to line their own pockets with cash. (In the opening section of this chapter, we gave a few examples.) But as the above discussion suggests, they also often engage in corruption to cover the costs of getting reelected. This occurs even in the world's wealthiest democracies, where corruption is otherwise relatively modest. It was the case in Germany, where in the late 1990s it was revealed that the Christian Democratic Union had been using a system of secret accounts to collect about two million Deutschmarks (well over a million U.S. dollars) in illegal campaign contributions from businesses that hoped to influence government decisions. Likewise, the Spanish ruling political party was discovered in 2013 to have used a parallel bookkeeping system for eighteen years that recorded illegal undeclared cash contributions to the party. (According to the former party treasurer, Luis Bárcenas, donors delivered the funds to party headquarters in suitcases and bags of cash.) And in Italy, the same had been true, as came out in the Clean Hands revelations in the early 1990s. (We discuss both the German and Italian examples in greater detail in later chapters.)

While distinct, political and bureaucratic corruption are often intertwined. Bureaucrats who commit illegal acts—taking bribes in exchange for doing their jobs or embezzling public funds—are sometimes organized into hierarchies by the politicians who helped secure their jobs. In these cases, the bureaucrats often have to hand over part of their bribe receipts to the political patron who appointed them. Low-level bureaucrats pass upward a portion of kickbacks they receive to local party operatives; the local party operatives, in turn, pass the funds to a higher level, until eventually senior elected politicians receive their share. For instance, in one south Indian state in the 1970s and 1980s, farmers who used water from government-owned canals in the dry season were often extorted for kickbacks by the government engineers operating the canal system (we discuss this example in greater detail in chapter 5). The engineers then used some of the illegally collected monies to pay the politicians who oversaw them. The value of choice postings was such that senior engineers typically paid fourteen times their annual salary to secure transfer to a desirable (i.e., lucrative) locale.

This case is typical in that large-scale bureaucratic corruption only endures over a long period of time when politicians are aware of it, and are even active participants in it. Bureaucratic corruption, in other words, does not just happen when politicians are looking the other way. It occurs when politicians permit it or fail to exercise adequate oversight to prevent it, all too often because they are themselves benefiting financially and politically.

While bureaucrats nominally enjoy insulation from political pressures, the preceding example also provides a sense of the many ways that politicians nonetheless may exercise influence over civil servants. In India, bureaucrats of all kinds are constantly shifted around the country—in part to reduce corruption that might come from, say, a labor inspector getting to know the managers at the particular business operations he's meant to regulate. But these transfers ironically offer a means by which bureaucrats can be punished: a politician can arrange to have a "cooperative" inspector moved to a big city while ensuring that one who doesn't share his spoils (or, just as bad, who is scrupulously honest) is transferred to a rural backwater.[18] Politicians may similarly be able to have bureaucrats demoted or even fired. Persistent systems of bureaucratic corruption are thus especially likely to emerge in settings where politicians exercise undue influence over bureaucratic appointments, promotions, postings, or salaries.

In any setting, there can be the occasional bad apple—the unemployment officer who takes bribes, the public works inspector who doesn't inspect, the dirty cop involved in extorting drug dealers. Occasional bad apples tend to get caught, however, because their peers and colleagues are not taking bribes and won't shield their dishonest coworkers from punishment. For bureaucratic corruption to become common, bureaucrats have to shield rather than denounce one another. Likewise, bureaucratic corruption becomes common only if politicians are also routinely disregarding or even encouraging it. Corruption thus develops into a system that unites bureaucrats and politicians in defrauding the public when many culprits collude in the process. And when bureaucratic and political corruption become deeply intertwined, the systemic corruption that results will be particularly hard to dislodge.

2.5 How is corruption different from corporate malfeasance?

Whenever we ask American business school students for examples of corruption, Enron almost always comes up among the first few answers. Recall that in the late 1990s, executives at the company sold the public on a storyline of Enron's transformation from an oil and gas production company into one that made a fortune off oil, gas, and commodities trading. *Fortune* magazine named Enron "America's Most Innovative Company" six years running. But in 2001, it finally came to light that Enron's profits were the product of an elaborate accounting fiction, and the company filed for bankruptcy later that year. Top executives Jeffrey Skilling, Kenneth Lay, and

Andrew Fastow were convicted of defrauding their shareholders, lining their own pockets in the process.

Skilling and his co-conspirators violated their shareholders' trust, personally benefiting at their expense. Their behavior was morally corrupt, and the Enron scandal was an epic case of corporate malfeasance, what we might call economic corruption. But this sort of behavior lies outside of what we will cover in the chapters that follow, because Enron is a private company and none of its executives were public officials.

That said, perpetrating economic fraud often requires the complicity of government officials. Without a free pass from regulators, Enron's shareholders might not have seen their savings disappear. In this particular case, although Enron (like most big companies) lobbied government for favorable legislation, there's no evidence of any illegal payment to public officials' campaigns or bank accounts. But other examples reveal conspicuous involvement of government officials in corporate corruption.

When Walmart established a program of "aggressive and creative" corruption to facilitate its rapid expansion in Mexico, the legal line was very clearly crossed. In paying local officials to illegally acquire the land it wanted for new construction, the company was in clear violation of the laws of both Mexico and the United States (the latter forbids companies from paying bribes in foreign countries, even if doing so is common there). These actions left Walmart shareholders shouldering the risk of the legal repercussions that emerged when executives' misdeeds were uncovered.[19] Bribery on an epic scale also fueled the Spanish construction boom of the 1990s and 2000s, with builders paying local government officials to look the other way as they put up endless apartment and hotel developments that blighted the country's landscape. Spaniards have suffered mightily as a result—gross domestic product (GDP) is still lower in 2015 than it was in 2007, and unemployment is well over 20 percent.

Thus, as with bureaucratic and political corruption, economic and political corruption are distinct, and do not always appear together. Corporate corruption can operate independently of political coverage, for instance. But very often the two support and reinforce each other, creating a larger ecosystem that benefits those in positions of power—whether private or public—at society's expense.

2.6 Is influence peddling a form of corruption?

As we observed in the preceding section, no public officials were implicated in Enron's collapse. But the scandal's postmortem also indicates how government and corporate interests intersect in myriad ways that, while formally legal, we find to be inappropriate or unpalatable, and can often lead to policies that run counter to the public's interest. So while it falls short of corruption by a legal definition, influence peddling—the intrusion of big business's money into public life—is the leading candidate for expanding our definition to include acts by public officials that run counter to public interest or public opinion, even if they are legal.

To push its agenda, Enron offered lavish campaign contributions, totaling US$1.1 million, to local candidates in the 2000 election cycle alone. The company spent even more employing a fleet of lobbyists, and it exploited personal connections to, among other things, convince former U.S. President George W. Bush to call the governor of Pennsylvania on the company's behalf. These efforts paid off—according to the Center for Public Integrity, Enron's "formidable lobbying machine gained favorable treatment from Congress, federal and state governments, and various regulatory agencies on no fewer than 49 occasions."[20] While Enron's agenda was presented at the time as an earnest effort to rid the energy industry of pointless and outdated oversight, in practice it allowed the company to take ever greater liberties in cooking the books.

Influence peddling by corporations via legal means is entirely common in the United States and elsewhere, with consequences potentially more dire than the collapse of Enron. Companies attempt to secure favorable public policies or the appointments of sympathetic officials by providing expertise, information, and lobbying. Auto makers lobby government to prevent the adoption of stricter emissions standards. Textile companies lobby government to erect trade barriers that insulate them from foreign competition. Such influence peddling is often deeply resented by the public, which perceives that businesses have special access to public officials and that the interests of corporations will thus be reflected in public policy, to the detriment of the public interest. Because of these close links between business interests and government policies, most U.S. citizens think of their country's political life as mired in corruption: in the court of public opinion, influence peddling is deemed corrupt, despite being perfectly legal.[21]

The so-called revolving door between business and government (and back again), which we have already mentioned earlier in this chapter, only exacerbates the sense that officials are in bed with corporate interests. Many ex-officials join lobbying firms or other businesses where, it appears to many, their main function is to wheedle their former coworkers into serving private sector interests at the expense of the public good.

Research by three International Monetary Fund economists goes so far as to place some blame for the global financial crisis that emerged in 2007 on lobbying by U.S. banks.[22] The study opens by relating the cases of Countrywide Financial and Ameriquest, two of the largest mortgage lenders in the United States, which, according to a 2007 *Wall Street Journal* article, together spent nearly $30 million on campaign contributions and lobbying between 2002 and 2006. What was the objective of all that lobbying? To defeat legislation that might have limited the reckless lending that led to the subprime mortgage meltdown, which in turn metastasized into the Great Recession. Both Ameriquest and Countrywide were among the largest issuers of the high-interest loans to poor Americans that propelled the crisis. The data analysis in the study shows that this pattern holds more broadly—banks with the greatest exposure to subprime lending were the most active donors and lobbyists in Washington in the years leading up to the crisis. While these efforts were not illegal, they almost surely damaged the public interest, and the public outcry that followed makes it clear that their behavior ran counter to what voters felt were appropriate ties between business and government.

Why not ban any interaction between businesses and government leaders, in the same way most countries have banned bribes? One reason is that government officials often *want* to talk to business representatives in making policies that affect the private sector. Who, after all, is better-informed about the effects of government regulation of business than businesses themselves? This expertise versus bias trade-off shows up in many settings. Who should the CEO of General Motors (GM) ask about the future of the minivan? The executive overseeing GM's minivan business is probably the best-informed—minivans are his business, after all—but entirely biased. His division will get more research resources and marketing muscle if he can convince GM's head that minivans are the future of the car business. The answer isn't to stonewall the minivan expert: you hear him out, cognizant of the fact that he's biased. Government officials, too, need information from businesses, but also need to keep in mind that the information they are receiving is hardly objective.[23]

Does this mean the current rules do a good job of balancing the benefits of lobbying-as-expertise against the biases in policies that influence peddling might create? At least in the United States, the available evidence suggests otherwise. One study that comes to this conclusion is based on analyzing lobbyists' responses when lawmakers switch congressional committee assignments.[24] If lobbyists were providing expertise, you'd expect them to keep working on the same issues, regardless of which congressman or senator serves on a committee—medical experts would lobby healthcare committees and military experts would lobby defense committees. But the research finds that when politicians switch committees, lobbyists often migrate with them. This suggests that the connections have somehow become personalized, in ways that go beyond technical or trade expertise.[25] So while the influence-as-expertise view is possible in theory, it appears that in practice, personal connections may be more decisive. This evidence supports the suspicions of the American public that lobbying is not simply a benign transfer of information—it involves personalized access and influence as well.

If we dislike the cozy ties between business and government, what should we do? Recent court rulings in the United States (the 2010 *Citizens United* decision by the Supreme Court, above all) have made it *easier*, not harder, for corporations to curry favor with politicians. So rather than hoping for more stringent enforcement, the laws themselves need to be changed to make undesirable kinds of business-government ties illegal, not just counter to public opinion.

How far should we go if political and legal obstacles were to evaporate? Tim Geithner had to wait at least a year before taking a Wall Street job. Why not two, or five, or ten? In France, the "revolving door" between public service and corporate employment requires at least a three-year wait, for instance. It's a question of trade-offs: the best, brightest, and most-qualified might avoid government jobs altogether if it meant they'd be banned from private sector employment in their areas of expertise for a decade afterward. We also may end up restricting the ability of other groups to influence government in the public interest in ways we might regret. In the United States, for example, the Sierra Club exists to lobby on behalf of mountain climbers and national forest users, and to protect nature areas—possibly from developers who are almost certainly lobbying the same officials with the opposite agenda.

The fact that we may not want to do away with influence peddling altogether doesn't mean we shouldn't be working to put more limits on it. Where the proper and most effective limits lie is a matter of debate, but in our view the public is not well served by the current system. Our opinion is shared by as much as 80 percent of the U.S. public, which would like to see the *Citizens United* decision revised through congressional action.[26] The fact that influence peddling isn't illegal doesn't mean that we think it's acceptable.

In summary, while influence peddling may not break any laws, it's not difficult to come up with examples of individuals holding high political office in the U.S. who subsequently trade on their experience in government for personal gain. These are cases in which public opinion holds behavior to be corrupt, even if the law does not. It may be that the laws need change when it conflicts with public opinion, not the other way around.

2.7 Do clientelism and patronage involve corruption?

Patronage and clientelism are modes of corruption where politicians are offered "bribes" with political support instead of cash. Supporters, in turn, are rewarded with jobs, gifts, or government resources.

As we have already noted in section 2.4, every government makes entirely legal and appropriate patronage appointments for jobs such as ambassadorships and heads of public agencies. These positions are handed out as rewards to loyalists and effective campaign fundraisers.[27]

Patronage may, however, seep down to levels of government and guide appointments where it was not intended to operate and where it is not legitimate (or strictly legal). Civil servants who are by law required to be appointed on the basis of a standard examination may get their jobs through partisan affiliation or government connections. There are multiple ways that parties have devised for working their way around the formal appointment process. In a 1935 publication that drew on research conducted in U.S. cities, political scientist V. O. Key enumerated five basic "methods of evasion of civil service laws"—ranging from budgetary sabotage to manipulating the selection process—all of which are still in use today.[28] In Italy, in the decades after World War II, the regular civil service examination and appointment process moved so slowly (the backlog averaged three years) that hundreds of thousands of bureaucrats were appointed on a "temporary" basis—perfectly legally—and then had their positions transformed by legislative initiative into permanent ones, thus bypassing standard protocol. Without the usual controls in place, 41 percent of Italian civil servants who were hired between 1956 and 1961 never sat for the merit examinations that were supposedly required. In the period from 1973 to 1990, the figure rose to nearly 60 percent. These civil service jobs were thus transformed—in a perfectly legal manner—into patronage appointments.[29]

There can be a fine line between political patronage for partisan ends and legitimate job creation for purposes of economic development. When the Kenyan government authorized 10,000 kilometers of new road construction to begin in early 2015, the country was in desperate need of better transportation infrastructure. The road construction will generate an estimated 137,000 jobs—jobs that are also sorely needed (the country's unemployment rate was 40 percent in 2008, the last year that reliable data were available). But if the last century's history is any guide, these benefits are unlikely to be shared equally by all Kenyans. A study published in 2015 found that "districts that share the ethnicity of the president receive twice as much expenditure on roads and have four times the length of paved roads built" during periods when democracy was weak.[30] We'd conjecture that districts dominated by members of President Uhuru Kenyatta's Kikuyu tribe will get more than their fair share of Kenya's new roads this time as well. Road construction in this instance is legitimate, but its placement may be partially driven by patronage considerations.

Clientelism is a distinct form of patronage in which a political actor (known as the patron) delivers something to a voter (known as the client) in exchange for a vote. There's nothing illegal or even wrongheaded about providing schools, roads, or other government amenities to voters. What distinguishes clientelism is that the rules governing who gets the benefits are not public, and the benefits are contingent on electoral support.[31] Sometimes the exchange is direct, immediate, and personalized. Paying someone a few dollars to secure a vote is a form of clientelistic corruption by the candidate. It's called "vote buying," and it's illegal in almost every country in the world that holds elections. More often, clientelism involves longer-lived relationships that lock voters and politicians into well-established networks of exchange. For instance, giving a supporter a patronage appointment in government binds the recipient to the politician, since the job will disappear if the patron is removed from office.

Clientelism distorts the distribution of government benefits and jobs when the main criterion is partisanship rather than need or merit, that is, when electoral constituencies or individual voters receive government monies or benefits because of their support for the governing party. This redirects resources away from areas or voters that are more deserving or in need. Clientelism crosses directly into corruption when citizens receive public benefits for partisan reasons in illegal ways—by, for example, providing welfare benefits only to supporters of one party, whether they qualify as poor or not, while striking impoverished citizens who support the "wrong" party from welfare rolls. Such practices were well documented in Mexico prior to the 1997 adoption of the Progresa/Oportunidades formula for poverty relief.[32] In Italy, disability benefits were similarly misused to support able-bodied but unemployed members of the political parties that controlled the government.[33]

It's worth reiterating that there's not necessarily anything wrong with officials building support by providing valuable amenities to voters. Politicians are *supposed* to be responsive to citizen needs, and the provision of basic public infrastructure often does just this. Similarly, there is (in most settings we are aware of) nothing illegal when a trade union helps get its members to the polls on election day, after having campaigned for the party that had promised to raise the minimum wage and make other policy changes in the interests of workers. Enduring support networks that link groups of voters to political parties are common, and often useful in improving the political knowledge of citizens and encouraging them to vote. But these examples are closer to performance-based evaluations of politicians and parties than they are to clientelism. The difference is that clientelism hinges on the promise of partisan loyalty in exchange for personal benefits.

To summarize, clientelism and patronage often but not necessarily involve corruption. It's illegal to ignore or manipulate government hiring rules to stack city hall with partisan supporters rather than qualified candidates. But if there are no such rules—and sometimes there are not—then we find ourselves in a murky gray area where our various definitions of corruption fail to overlap. While not illegal, these patronage practices run counter to the public interest and, for the many citizens who fail to benefit from them, undermine faith in the functioning of government.

2.8 Does electoral fraud involve corruption?

Politicians need not buy off voters with jobs or payoffs if they can simply rig the results. Electoral fraud involves illegal activities before, during, or after an election that are intended to alter the outcome. Examples include voter intimidation or vote buying; ballot stuffing or ballot-box theft; and tampering with results in the process of aggregating them.[34] Sometimes these activities are not corrupt—just illegal. When thugs affiliated with a minor political party enter a polling station, grab the ballot box, and throw it into a river, a public official—and hence corruption—is not necessarily implicated. But electoral fraud often does involve corruption, as when it is perpetrated by the party in power using the nominally nonpartisan employees of the office of election administration. Ballot stuffing or double voting often takes place with the complicity of officials in polling stations—election officials who are employees of an administrative unit of government that is sworn to uphold the law and observe partisan neutrality. The ruling party is often in a position to pressure these officials to produce votes.[35]

The corruption of elections amounts to the corruption of democracy—an untethering of the will of the electorate from the selection of government leadership. It's hard to know how often politicians just pad their victory margins by corrupting the electoral process, or whether they are, more troublingly, altering who emerges as victor. But there's no shortage of cases where both losing candidates and outside observers have contended that an election was forfeited due to fraud. In Venezuela's referendum on the recall of President Hugo Chavez in 2004, exit polls had Chavez losing by a 20-percentage-point margin. Miraculously, he won nonetheless. An analysis by Venezuelan economists found decisive statistical evidence of vote fraud (not surprisingly, outside observers and other witnesses weren't allowed near the election computers on the day of the recall vote).[36] But it's hard to make broad generalizations about the frequency or magnitude of fraud: in new democracies, it is commonplace for the losing party to issue claims of electoral irregularities, whether or not any have taken place. (This may, in turn, encourage the incumbent party to cheat as much as possible, knowing that accusations will be forthcoming regardless of what it does.)

Election fraud is intimately linked to other forms of corruption we've described in this chapter. It insulates officials from popular backlash; and it promotes the candidacies of individuals without sufficient scruples to run an honest election—which, we would assert, probably also means they lack a conscience to keep them from exploiting their offices for personal gain. Corruption may flourish in the absence of electoral fraud, but where fraud is present it is usually part of a larger system of persistent corruption.

2.9 What did we learn in chapter 2?

- Corruption consists of the exploitation of public office for private gain. The private benefits of corruption can come in many forms—votes or jobs, for example, in addition to cash.
- Measuring corruption is hard because, by definition, its perpetrators wish to conceal it. Thus, most corruption measures are the result of survey responses, which necessitates that we interpret them with considerable caution.
- Most often, we can think of corruption as *illegal* actions by public officials for private gain, but sometimes legal acts (e.g., the revolving door in Washington, D.C.) may be deemed corrupt as well. These cases are often less clear-cut, however.
- Bureaucratic and political corruption differ according to their perpetrators and also in how the proceeds are used. In particular, politicians often engage in corruption to raise funds for their political campaigns.
- Bureaucratic and political corruption are often intertwined, with politician-appointed bureaucrats participating in hierarchies of corruption, in which politicians collect bribes from lower-level officials to fund reelection campaigns.
- Corruption differs from clientelism, in which politicians deliver personal benefits to voters in exchange for their electoral support.
- Electoral fraud is a form of corruption that attempts to alter electoral outcomes.

3

WHERE IS CORRUPTION MOST PREVALENT?

Now that we have a common understanding of *what* corruption is, we can take tools developed in the last chapter for measuring corruption to explore where it's most common. We'll see early on that there is a positive relationship between country-level wealth and corruption, something that's unlikely to surprise the reader. However, when we explore the patterns linking income and corruption across countries more closely, we'll find that there are a number of nuances that *are* unexpected. Examining these relationships more deeply will help us in our larger objective of understanding *why* corruption is more common in some places than others.

3.1 Why is corruption more common in poor countries?

Let's back up a moment. Is it even true that corruption is more common in poor countries? Or is this conventional wisdom misplaced? Let's begin by examining a global map of corruption, presented in Figure 3.1, that depicts countries according to their scores on the 2014 Corruption Perceptions Index (CPI) from Transparency International (TI). (Recall that the CPI is a corruption ranking across countries based on expert opinion surveys.)

We have organized TI's corruption scores into quartiles, and in the map, we shade countries according to the quartile they

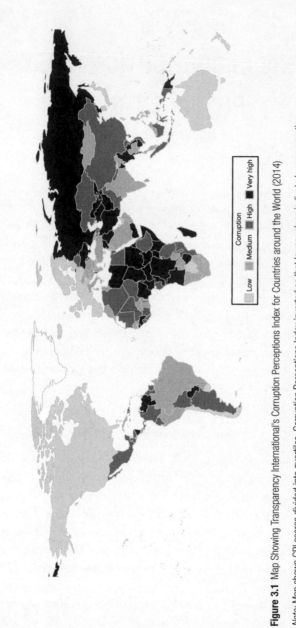

Figure 3.1 Map Showing Transparency International's Corruption Perceptions Index for Countries around the World (2014)

Note: Map shows CPI scores divided into quartiles. Corruption Perceptions Index inverted so that lower values indicate lower corruption.

fall into, from lightest (least corrupt) to darkest (most corrupt). The lightest-colored regions of the world include North America, Europe, and Australasia—which are also among the world's wealthiest areas. The darkest regions include parts of Africa, Asia, and the Middle East, areas that include many of the world's poorest nations.

Another way of visualizing the relationship between per capita national income and corruption is using a scatterplot. This allows us to see the relationship between the values of two variables—in this case, wealth and corruption—for countries around the world. Figure 3.2 shows a scatterplot with gross domestic product (GDP) per capita—a measure of a country's wealth—on the horizontal axis and the CPI on the vertical axis. (We discuss individually labeled countries in section 3.3 and elsewhere in the book.) The horizontal axis uses a logarithmic scale, which means the GDP figures get "squished" at higher levels: the distance on the graph between, say, US$1,000 and US$10,000 is the same as the distance between US$10,000 and US$100,000. We use a log scale because of the vast income disparities between poor and rich countries. If we didn't do this, the difference between a very poor country like Ethiopia (per capita GDP US$565 in 2014) and India (per capita GDP US$1,596) would be barely perceptible, despite the fact that India's income is nearly three times higher.

In 2014, the countries holding the top (least corrupt) ranks were Finland, Denmark, and New Zealand, with per capita incomes of approximately US$50,000, US$60,000, and US$40,000, respectively, while Afghanistan and Sudan (per capita GDP of US$659 and US$1,876 respectively) were the world's most corrupt nations, according to TI. (TI ranks Somalia and North Korea as even more corrupt, but we do not have GDP figures for these countries so we cannot include them in the figure.) More broadly, the graph shows a very clear negative relationship: corruption falls as we look across the figure to higher-income countries.[1] So, yes, corruption is worse in poor countries.

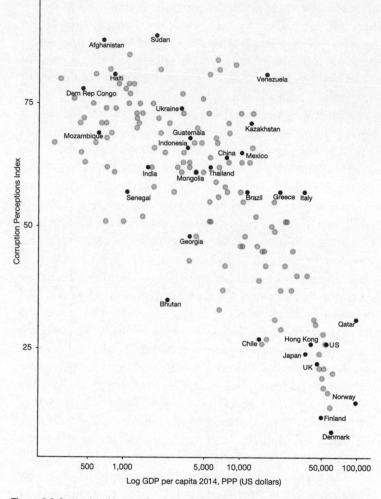

Figure 3.2 Scatterplot of Logged Per Capita GDP by Transparency International's Corruption Perceptions Index for 158 Countries (2014)

Note: Corruption Perceptions Index inverted so that lower values indicate lower corruption.

Does the cross-country relationship between corruption and income also characterize differences across states or provinces within individual countries? It turns out that it does, at least in the cases where we have data to explore this relationship. Figure 3.3, for example, shows state-level corruption ratings from Transparency International's India chapter for the twenty largest Indian states and union territories plotted against state-level income per capita in 2005, the most recent year for which we have the TI measure for Indian states. As with the cross-country evidence, corruption and poverty are intertwined. (Observe, however, the two outlier states, Kerala and Himachal Pradesh, which have found ways of staying pretty clean despite low incomes.)

The very strong correlation between corruption and poverty across countries—and across Indian states—leads to an obvious question: does corruption actually *cause* poverty?

When most people think about the relationship between corruption and poverty, that may well be the direction of causation they have in mind. There's no shortage of arguments and anecdotes to back up this view. In order to grow, economies require infrastructure like roads and electricity grids, which are usually provided by government. If public officials empty the public coffers through embezzlement, there will be less available to build schools and roads and to erect power lines. One very concrete and evocative illustration of the damaging effects of government theft comes from the hugely corrupt rule of Jean-Claude "Baby Doc" Duvalier in Haiti. During his reign in the 1970s and 1980s, Duvalier sold off the 150-kilometer rail link from Port-au-Prince to Verrettes to an investment consortium that carefully packed up the tracks and shipped them out of the country.[2] Duvalier, one presumes, deposited the proceeds into a Swiss bank account, leaving the public without even the funds derived from destroying Haiti's transportation infrastructure.

Corruption may also stunt economic development by scaring off businesses and their investment dollars. If you know that once your company is up, running, and generating profits, the fruits of your labor will be confiscated by bribe-seeking officials, why invest in the first place? Not surprisingly, it is generally the case that corruption depresses investment: in

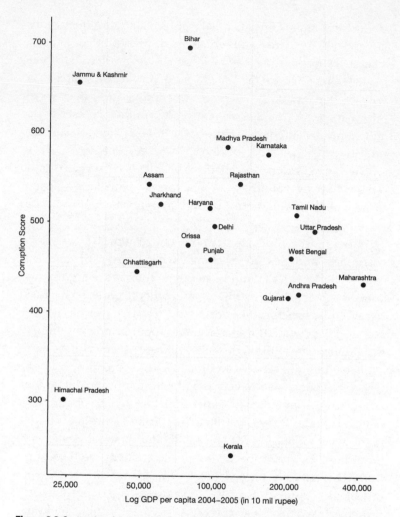

Figure 3.3 Scatterplot of Logged Per Capita GDP by TI India's Composite Corruption Score across 20 Major Indian States and Union Territories (2005)

Note: Corruption Composite Score based on proportion of household survey responses: (1) paying a bribe, (2) using influence, (3) not satisfied with quality of services from a government department, (4) which perceived that department was corrupt, (5) which thought corruption had increased in the department in past year, and (6) which thought there was no commitment by the department to reducing corruption. Corruption scores from Transparency International India, *India Corruption Study 2005* (New Delhi: Transparency International India, 2005), Table 1.5, 10.

the first serious study to investigate the relationship between corruption and growth, the investment channel is given pride of place in explaining the possible connection.[3] (We'll discuss a number of examples, as well as some of the details of how corruption impacts investment, in chapter 4.)

In mapping the cause-and-effect relationship between two variables, social scientists generally put the one that is doing the causing on the x-axis, and the one that is being affected on the y-axis. (We refer to the variable on the y-axis as the "dependent" variable that depends on or is affected by the "independent" variable on the x-axis.) In putting income on the x-axes in Figures 3.2 and 3.3, we are implicitly suggesting that poverty causes corruption, rather than suggesting that corruption causes poverty by reducing economic growth—despite the examples we have just provided.

There are in fact many credible arguments in support of the view that poverty causes corruption.[4] When government resources are scarce, the need to bribe public officials in order to get to the head of the queue may be that much greater. If there's little money to pay decent wages in the public sector, bureaucrats are easily tempted by corruption. And if, as a result of poverty, bureaucrats' supervisors are also underpaid and inadequately trained, there won't be proper monitoring to prevent officials from succumbing to temptation. Taking bribes to cover the basics, like healthcare and school fees, can be highly enticing, especially if no one is looking. A great deal of corruption is simply the result of scarcity of resources. Equivalently, rich countries can use their wealth to eradicate corruption, a point we return to shortly (in section 3.3). Controlling corruption costs money.

Finally, some other factor may be responsible for both poverty *and* corruption. Take southern Italy. For more than a century, the region has fought an ongoing battle with groups like the Sicilian Mafia and its Neapolitan counterpart, the Camorra. Perhaps the emergence of organized crime prior even to the establishment of the Italian Republic led to corruption—with crime bosses making politicians offers they couldn't refuse—and also undermined legitimate economic growth.

So which came first, corruption or poverty—or something else entirely? This sort of chicken-and-egg problem is typical of the challenges that confront social scientists in understanding how the world works. In physics or medicine, we might devise an experiment in a tightly controlled lab setting to understand what's causing what. If you want to know whether aspirin reduces heart attacks, give aspirin to one group of subjects and outwardly identical sugar pills to another group. After a few years, you'll know whether aspirin helps more than a sugar pill.

There is a movement afoot in the social sciences that takes a similar approach to understanding many types of social phenomena, from whether you can boost graduation rates by paying kids to go to school, to the effects of medical insurance on health. Some scholars are using this approach to try to crack the chicken-and-egg conundrum of corruption's causes and effects, and we will discuss some of these worthy efforts in the chapters that follow.[5] But experimenting with corruption in the real world is tough. We can't pay one group of government officials more than another, otherwise similar group and then offer both of them bribes to see what happens. That might tell us whether improving bureaucratic salaries decreased the temptation to take bribes. But it would also be unethical for us as social scientists to engage in the corruption of public officials by doing so.[6]

The ethical concerns raised by anticorruption experiments don't rule them out entirely. But even when we are able to undertake such experiments, we need to be cautious in interpreting the results. If stricter auditing of construction projects proves helpful in limiting corruption in Indonesia, it would be unwise to assume that it would necessarily have a comparable effect in, say, sub-Saharan Africa. The technical term for this issue— whether we can take the lessons learned in one study and apply them elsewhere—is "external validity."[7] Every society is complicated and dysfunctional in its own way, which is part of what makes it difficult to devise an experiment that is broadly applicable across a range of situations. To continue the medical analogy, we can learn only so much about what prevents heart attacks in women by running trials exclusively using men. We also need to run the experiment with women.[8] Moreover, very small, apparently innocuous details of specific anticorruption remedies—such as how we increase pay to bureaucrats, or how often and in what ways they are monitored—can dramatically affect outcomes. As a result, we may never get general, portable answers even to narrow questions, such as whether higher government salaries reduce corruption, let alone to the much broader matter of whether societies are poor because they're corrupt or corrupt because they're poor.

Then again, it's probably misguided to imagine that we could devise a perfect set of experiments to determine whether, even in a single society or particular set of circumstances, corruption causes poverty or vice versa. Because we'd end up discovering that both are true, leading to an endless cycle of corruption-causing-poverty-causing-corruption.

This brings us back to the question that introduced this section: why is corruption more common in poor countries? Corruption can (and does) happen everywhere. But it happens more often in poor countries, partly because poverty makes corruption more likely and partly because corruption worsens poverty. It's a complicated two-way relationship, and much of the remainder of this book is devoted to understanding the particular mechanisms that lead to the country-level poverty–corruption pattern we document above.

3.2　Why do some low-corruption countries remain poor?

Overall, as the data reported in Figure 3.2 show, there is a clear negative relationship between corruption and the level of national prosperity. But looking back at the scatterplot, there also remain large income disparities for countries at otherwise similar levels of perceived corruption. Mongolia (corruption rank of 80 out of 176 countries in 2014; GDP per capita of US$4,129 that year) is both less corrupt and a good deal poorer than both Mexico and Kazakhstan. But Mongolia is poor for other reasons. It has the economic misfortune of being one of a half-dozen landlocked Asian nations. This puts it at a major disadvantage in accessing global markets, given the historical importance of seaborne trade.

That is to say, the relative wealth or poverty of an individual nation depends on multiple factors, not only whether government officials at any one moment in time are corrupt, or even whether they are committed to growing the economy. When we focus on any single cause (or effect) of income, such as corruption, there will be a lot of variance in cross-country national income that remains unaccounted for. Given the many inputs into economic development—education, investment, trade policies, natural resources, war, simple bad luck—there are lots of ways that a perfectly honest government can find its citizens impoverished, even if political leaders genuinely desire otherwise.

There are even a few well-functioning and low-corruption countries that may have ended up with modest national incomes by choice. Consider the mountain nation of Bhutan, which, as illustrated in Figure 3.2, is the world's most unexpectedly honest nation, given its low per capita GDP. The country ranks as the least corrupt poor nation—its CPI score puts it almost on par with the United States—and it has deliberately restricted economic growth. A monarchy until 2008, Bhutan was blessed with an enlightened and well-meaning political leadership—so much so that the citizenry needed to be dragged kicking and screaming (by the king himself) to transition to democracy. Bhutan's leaders thumbed their noses at traditional measures of prosperity. Rather than chasing after economic development at all costs, the king measured progress through "Gross National Happiness," a measure based on contributors to well-being like health, education, community vitality, environmental quality, and even self-reported happiness. So who cares if Bhutan's income is just a third of neighboring China's—its citizens aren't choking on smog or working twelve hours a day in sunless sweatshops.

Unexpectedly uncorrupt but poor areas may emerge in regions within a single country as well. The southern Indian state of Kerala, which we mentioned earlier in this chapter, is often held up as an example of low incomes but high standards of living: health outcomes are comparable to those of developed nations despite a per capita income below the Indian average.[9] While unusual, Bhutan and Kerala illustrate that even very poor countries or regions may—with appropriate political leadership—reduce corruption to the levels typically found in much wealthier places.

The way we've presented these examples also raises the issue of whether we've once again got the question backward: instead of asking why some honest countries remain poor, perhaps we should ask how some poor countries have nonetheless managed to stamp out corruption. In fact, all the world's rich countries used to be poor—and most of them used to be very corrupt. Vote buying was once politics-as-usual in the United States, and the sale of public offices was common in Britain and France. Bribe taking by public officials has, at some point in history, been standard practice in most now-rich countries. Somehow they've all solved the chicken-and-egg problem of corruption and poverty. How did they pull it off?

3.3 How does corruption decline as countries get richer?

In many parts of India, a vote can be bought for a color television, a gold necklace, a sheep or cow, even a blender.[10] For a voter facing life-or-death economic circumstances, high-minded ideals like electoral democracy may seem hopelessly abstract and distant compared to the immediate offer of basic necessities or an otherwise unattainable indulgence. But this creates a system where politicians are elected based on which candidate is most willing and best able to bribe voters rather than on her competence or honesty. In fact, by electing the candidate most adept at bribery, voters are choosing precisely that person who is least bound by scruples and who expects to profit most from holding office—that's why she was willing to hand out so many blenders, televisions, saris, and sheep!

In even the world's poorest nations, ordinary people know when elected officials are corrupt—and they normally do not like it. Anthropologists who study small villages in poor nations report that villagers are acutely aware of the conspicuous displays of wealth of their leaders, and are attentive to how much leaders embezzled or extracted in bribes to finance such extravagances. In such environments, corruption is one of the most common topics of daily conversation.[11] Likewise, villagers are well aware of the need to pay a bribe for a government service to which they are nominally entitled. Because they are so poor—here we are talking about people living below or close to the US$2-a-day international poverty line—even very tiny payments can represent large fractions of their incomes. It's precisely because they have so little that their votes can be so cheaply bought. A color TV or a cow represents a very large financial offering for a very poor person. It's not that the world's poor don't value democracy, or that they don't understand their role in perpetuating a corrupt political class by voting into office the candidates who offer them the largest bribes. It's just that their circumstances force them into situations where, in the short term, they can't imagine doing otherwise. Most of us would do the same in their place.

It's precisely this lack of effective oversight by voters that can trap a country in a corrupt and impoverished equilibrium. The political candidates most eager to bribe voters are the ones most likely to be elected: across much of sub-Saharan Africa these days, all candidates are expected to provide handouts to the electorate, and all voters accept them. A candidate who fails to do so doesn't stand a chance. The most corrupt politicians—now elected—then proceed to enrich themselves at the country's expense. This is a variant on the idea of a poverty trap, which we've already invoked in describing corruption and poverty as a chicken-and-egg problem: impoverished citizens fail to elect public officials committed to government integrity; the politicians who are elected steal road- or school-building funds, or direct government contracts to incompetent builders in exchange for bribes; some of the funds thus embezzled are used to bribe voters; the citizenry remain sufficiently impoverished that their votes can be had for a toaster; and the process repeats. If only the country could jump-start economic growth, its political system could potentially flip from poverty trap to the virtuous cycle of greater wealth and better government.

Many now-developed countries provide case histories of this transition.[12] While we can make some general observations based on successful examples, at the same time it is important to keep in mind that the historical demise of corruption is a complicated and multifaceted process: depending on their individual circumstances, countries have taken very different paths to rooting out corruption.

Take, for example, the United States. As we observed in chapter 2, through the first half of the nineteenth century it wasn't illegal for members of Congress to accept bribes. After bribery was outlawed, it was at least another fifty years before any significant action was taken to curb chronic malfeasance by politicians in the nation's capital. During this time, the country's economy nonetheless grew at a torrid rate by the standards of the time, with per capita incomes increasing sevenfold in real terms between 1820 and 1900. Economic growth was driven in large part by the business enterprises of industrialists like Andrew Carnegie, Cornelius Vanderbilt, and John D. Rockefeller. These so-called robber barons amassed enormous wealth for themselves through whatever means necessary (often exploitative and nefarious ones), but at least they created the country's infrastructure in the process of building their fortunes, rather than dismantling it and shipping the proceeds out of the country in the manner of Haiti's Baby Doc Duvalier.

For the United States, it was the increasingly broad-based prosperity created by Carnegie and his ilk that laid the foundation for a robust anticorruption movement mounted by the country's sizable middle class. The middle class's newfound affluence, in turn, protected its members from the vote-buying practices that the country's urban political machines had long used to secure the support of poor immigrant communities. Anger over the methods deployed by the robber barons and their partners in government found a voice in the Progressive Movement, which sought to dismantle (or at least halt the spread of) the patronage machines that governed most U.S. cities east of the Mississippi.[13]

Increased prosperity also affects lawmakers and bureaucrats more directly: if government salaries rise with the broader economy, public officials may have less need to resort to bribery and embezzlement to make ends meet. (This isn't to excuse bribery, just to put it in the context in which it is often understood by its practitioners.) In addition to raising the incomes of government officials, economic prosperity creates more opportunities to amass wealth in the private sector, so the most avaricious individuals need not enter politics to become rich.[14]

In addition to providing the requisite resources to reduce officials' incentives to engage in corruption, greater economic prosperity can pay for tools to raise corruption's costs. Overhead cameras, reports filled out in triplicate, independent audits from certified accountants, biometric voter registration, dissemination of reports on the behavior of legislators, access to the Internet, and citizen exposés—all these monitoring technologies are expensive. Even if they pay off in only a couple of years in reduced corruption, poor countries often cannot afford to purchase these technologies, and even when they do, they may lack the trained personnel to operate the equipment properly. Good governance requires well-trained civil servants, and poor countries may have difficulties producing large numbers of these.

Costly forms of oversight also legitimately have their problems. One of us worked in Mozambique in the late 1990s for the World Bank. At the time, the country had hired a British company, the Crown Agents, to manage its customs business. Given the hopelessly low collection rate of import tariffs (and thus the hopelessly high rate of smuggling), the reformist government of Joaquim Chissano hoped that putting the Crown Agents in charge would essentially pay for itself. And in large part, this proved correct: tariff collection increased dramatically. Despite paying more taxes, large importers nonetheless were happy with the new regime: it was more transparent, streamlined, and less prone to corruption.

The companies that were pleased with the reforms all had the size and sophistication to deal with the many reporting requirements that a well-run bureaucracy like the Crown Agents requires. What about the small Mozambican firms—possibly operating entirely outside the formal economy— that had previously imported a few dollars' worth of spare parts a month or the occasional machine? They did fine in the old days, when you could slip a bribe to an official at the border. But they had neither the expertise to deal with the Crown Agents' bureaucracy nor the scale to make it worthwhile to hire someone to do it on their behalf. Under the Crown Agents' leadership, Mozambican border control became far less corrupt, while life became more difficult and less profitable for smaller, often informal, businesses.

Mozambique's experiences with the Crown Agents provides two narratives that can help to explain how corruption declines as countries get richer. Only richer countries have the funds to hire the Crown Agents or otherwise to pay the costs of monitoring and oversight. In addition, only the larger, more sophisticated businesses that exist in richer economies can afford to deal with the bureaucracy that anticorruption efforts require.

The transition from a situation of chronically high corruption to one of low-corruption thus involves many elements: companies that are more efficient and able to operate easily even without paying bribes; government officials who are well trained, well paid, and perform according to stricter professional norms; elected politicians who are more committed to anticorruption efforts; and voters who are less impoverished and thus less susceptible to vote buying or participation in election fraud. It's the complex interaction among these many factors that must ultimately undergo substantial change if a country is to reduce corruption and then sustain a low-corruption equilibrium. This historically has proven to be an uneven and lengthy process.

3.4 Why have some rich countries failed to stamp out corruption?

Even with increased prosperity, the transition to honest government is far from guaranteed. Any entrenched system, built on the interests of those in charge or those with a very strong interest in maintaining the status quo, will prove to be incredibly difficult to change. How else to explain the persistence of corruption in many developing—and even some developed—countries?

Let's turn back to Figure 3.2 and examine some more of the individually labeled countries. Many of these are countries with corruption levels that are much higher than what one might predict, given their national incomes. There's a story behind each one, usually unique to its circumstance. Afghanistan—not rich by any means, but more corrupt than its level of per capita income predicts—has been mired in poor governance due to endless wars and reconstruction. Venezuela, which—at least until very recently—was a solidly upper-middle-income nation, has had the twin misfortunes of "too much" oil and decades of political and economic mismanagement. Qatar, like other Persian Gulf oil kingdoms, is hugely rich but in a peculiar way. The country has not developed a robust manufacturing economy but depends instead on the global market for a single national resource: namely, oil.

Thus, even with national income growth, in some countries existing political elites (sometimes in collusion with economic powers) find ways to prevent or buy off the development of anticorruption movements that elsewhere spark campaigns and political competition to promote improvements. Viewing the glass as half-full, however, these misfortunes have arguably given such countries the most room to improve the way they're governed, and therefore the greatest opportunities to reduce corruption. Mexico, for instance, is somewhat more corrupt than its current per capita GDP of approximately US$10,000 would predict. It's also a country where there's a substantial anticorruption movement currently emerging, which is a natural result of a sizable middle class determined to bring corruption down to the levels expected of an upper-middle-income nation.

Mexico offers just one example of a corrupt and entrenched political elite that ends up exposed to grassroots and political opposition, which, as we'll discuss in greater detail in chapter 7, is more apt to develop as countries get richer. Corruption doesn't automatically decline with higher incomes—it takes effort. Dedicated anticorruption politicians and mass movements are essential ingredients in improving governance as economies develop. The policies and practices we discuss in our final chapter do not emerge spontaneously: new political interests need to develop that make fighting corruption a policy priority. And these interests need to devote resources to creating viable organizations that expose and take on existing corrupt practices.

3.5 Is there less corruption than there was twenty years ago—or more?

Anticorruption crusades have been in and out of the headlines for years. Investigations of U.S. companies doing business abroad have been on the rise since 2000. China launched a major anticorruption crackdown in December 2012 that led to hundreds of arrests and cut luxury imports in half (the crackdown meant there was less demand for the Rolex watches or Dom Perignon champagne used to bribe public officials).[15] In 2013, the Aam Aadmi (Common Man) Party in India formed a minority government for the city of Delhi, the country's capital and the world's second-largest city. In 2016 alone, massive anticorruption protests—often in the millions—rocked the capital cities of Brazil, Guatemala, Malaysia, Iraq, Lebanon, and Moldova.[16] But the explosion of anticorruption protests does not necessarily mean that there was more corruption to protest in 2016 than there was back in 1996—maybe there are better-organized groups driving the demonstrations, or a protest contagion spreading across regions or countries.

Unfortunately, we cannot turn to Transparency International's CPI or other annually announced measures of corruption to examine changes in corruption over time. We cannot infer that corruption in Estonia is worse just because the country's CPI ranking deteriorated between 2012 and 2015. The survey data that are used to generate the CPI change each year. Thus, comparing corruption rankings between 2012 and 2015 is like comparing the heights of individuals in one year and their weights in the next, and concluding that since Johnny weighed more in the second year, he must also have been taller in the first.

Nor can we just recalculate the CPI, keeping the survey components and weighting of them constant: perceptions are a slippery thing, prone to readjustment to a "new normal" reference level of corruption. If countries worldwide became less corrupt, there would probably still be the same chest-thumping pride in the world's least corrupt countries and the same despairing concerns for the most corrupt, even if those in the bottom rungs had made substantial improvements. Because there is no objective benchmark to TI's Corruption Perceptions Index, or to any similar measure, we simply cannot use them to assess whether corruption has changed at all over the last 20 or 30 years.

One answer might have been Transparency International's Bribe Payer's Index, which asks businesspeople around the world about their experiences with paying bribes. But this "experiential" measure—which in theory is based on respondents' actual experiences with corruption rather than only their perceptions of it—has been shown to exhibit substantial inaccuracies.[17] For this very reason, data collection for the Bribe Payer's Index ceased after 2011.[18] TI's Corruption Perceptions Index gives us a reasonable—albeit imperfect—measure of corruption across countries at any point in time, but at the present we don't have a reliable, broad-based measure of the extent to which corruption is changing over time.

3.6 Do government scandals mean that corruption is getting worse?

In December 2008, in an example we have already mentioned in chapter 1, Illinois governor Rod Blagojevich was arrested by federal agents under charges of corruption. Blagojevich had allegedly been trying to sell off the U.S. Senate seat vacated by Barack Obama when the latter won the U.S. presidency. (In the United States, when a senator or congressperson leaves office before his or her term is up, the replacement is at the discretion of the governor of the state he or she represented.) The governor had been caught saying as much in phone conversations taped by the FBI (using language that cannot be reprinted here) in a recording that was endlessly replayed over the airwaves in the weeks that followed.

Unsurprisingly, the revelations were accompanied by collective hand-wringing over the lack of integrity in the U.S. government. Similar consternation had followed revelations that law enforcement agents found US$90,000 in foil-wrapped cash stuffed in Louisiana representative William J. Jefferson's Washington home in 2005, as well as when a corruption sweep of New Jersey officials rolled up nearly four dozen arrests of politicians and bureaucrats in July 2009.

We are often quick to interpret corruption headlines as a symptom of government's growing need for reform. But a more charitable (and we would argue more plausible) interpretation is that it reflects a government's commitment to putting its house in order.

Our argument is built on the insight that there are many steps that make a scandal, only the first of which involves corruption. After a bribe is offered or the funds stolen, this fact needs to be uncovered by law enforcement, enterprising investigative journalists, or nongovernmental organizations (NGOs). The story then needs to circulate via newspaper exposure or—in more recent days—social media. An absence of scandal could indicate that there's no corruption, that there is no policing of corruption, or that widespread exposure of corruption is suppressed. So a scandal itself provides at best a very noisy indication of how frequent or widespread corruption is. In fact, where corruption is rare, evidence of it may generate a *huge* scandal just because the press knows how shocked the public will be.

The absence of scandal might thus indicate that we're living in a society of near-perfect virtue, like Denmark (recall that it's Transparency International's pick for least corrupt country on earth) or Kerala (the least corrupt state in India). Or it might indicate that we're in a society of near-total corruption, where bribes are paid and received without fear of punishment or censure, as was the case in Indonesia under President Suharto. (Transparency International only started publishing its corruption index near the end of Suharto's 32-year reign, but in its first ranking Indonesia came dead last.) Despite its reputation for corruption, there was no public discussion of Indonesia's First Family's ill-gotten gains, hardly surprising given the fate of those who spoke out against the regime.[19]

On the other hand, when corruption hits the headlines, we argue that it's likely an indication that its frequency is actually falling.[20] Scandal occurs, by definition, when government malfeasance is publicly exposed after years in which it was successfully kept secret. This exposure occurs because the judiciary or the press—or both—is finally successful in uncovering and publicizing corruption, an indication of increased oversight and prosecution.

In short, although public revelations of corruption fascinate voters and sell newspapers, a rash of articles on government corruption may mislead us into thinking that the problem is getting worse, when the opposite is likely to be the case. If reading newspaper accounts of politicians' misdeeds encourages you to think more about corruption and mobilizes the public to become politically more engaged citizens, that's wonderful. But as social scientists—and others interested in gauging the true level of corruption—we need to treat media reports as just one of many sources of information on corruption, and a highly partial and incomplete one at that.

Case Study: The Peruvian Vladivideos

Governments wishing to suppress unpleasant or unfavorable news need not use a heavy hand. There's the carrot or the stick (in the poetical expression favored by Mexican drug cartels, the choice of "plata o plomo"—silver or lead). The suitcase of cash or a bullet to the head? I'll take the suitcase, please.

Peruvians got a sense of how much it cost to buy off the media—as well as judges and opposition politicians—as the result of a scandal that began to unfold on September 14, 2000. That's the date when a videotape was broadcast on national television showing the country's director of intelligence services, Vladimiro Montesinos, offering US$15,000 per month to opposition congressman Alberto Kouri in exchange for his support for the ruling Peru 2000 Party. It turned out that Montesinos had made a habit of filming the many illicit exchanges he made on behalf of his boss, President Alberto Fujimori. Opinions varied on how many tapes were made, with estimates ranging as high as 2,000. It wasn't quite as foolish as it might initially appear for Montesinos to have amassed what amounted to a library of incriminating evidence, since each transaction implicated not only Montesinos himself but also the hundreds who accepted his favors.[21]

It's not clear who leaked the Montesinos tapes—the *Vladivideos*, as they were later called—to Canal N, the one television channel not co-opted by the ruling government. But in the weeks and months that followed, the station aired a surreal sort of political reality TV based on select tapes from the Montesinos collection, implicating members of Peru's legislature, the judiciary, and business elite, while providing a direct view into how the Fujimori-Montesinos political machine exercised such tight control over the country. One tape showed Montesinos paying off Ernesto Gamarra, a member of a congressional committee tasked with investigating Montesinos's mysterious sources of wealth, ensuring that the investigation hit a dead end. The biggest payouts were reserved for the media—a major stockholder in the national paper of record, *Expreso*, received a payoff of a million dollars, while the owner of the tabloid paper *El Tío* received US$1.5 million through an incentive contract that rewarded favorable coverage of Fujimori.[22] Other tabloids received similar pay-for-coverage arrangements. When combined with the government's own media operations, which spanned print, radio, and television, this gave Montesinos near-complete control over the flow of information to Peruvian citizens. Had it not been for the upstart Canal N—launched just one year earlier—the *Vladivideos* might have remained locked away in Montesinos's file cabinets.

The Peruvian example illustrates the importance of a free press in exposing corruption—and the value that corrupt politicians put on the press, revealed by the extraordinary amounts of money used to bribe the media, far in excess of the bribes paid to silence Peruvian judges, for instance. It also shows why *not* reading about corruption in the newspapers may be highly misleading about the state of the nation. It's possible there are no revelations because there is nothing to reveal—but also possible that the press has been bought off, if not suppressed outright.

3.7 Are anticorruption campaigns smoke screens for political vendettas?

The rise of a global anticorruption political agenda, and the increasing attention paid by large international organizations such as the World Bank to issues of corruption, also give governments perverse incentives to create the appearance of cracking down. If international aid is tied to making progress in cleaning up government, then making a show of fighting corruption becomes all the more important. So across Africa and other aid-receiving nations, governments that are deeply enmeshed in corruption have learned to pay lip service to the global agenda of good governance, while often diverting large chunks of the international aid they receive.

Even worse, an anticorruption agenda may be used by politicians looking to dispense with their political opponents. The 2012 anticorruption campaign launched by China's leader Xi Jinping led to the arrests of the country's security chief, members of the government's planning commission, and numerous high-ranking members of the military. Few doubt that those arrested were guilty as charged. (Evan Osnos of *The New Yorker* reported that "when police searched homes belonging to the family of Lieutenant General Gu Junshan, a senior logistics chief, they removed four truckloads of wine, art, cash, and other luxuries."[23]) But at the time of this writing, it remains unclear even to Chinese government insiders whether the main purpose of the crackdown was to get rid of corruption, or instead to get rid of political opponents of Xi Jinping, who seemed disproportionately targeted for arrest.[24] Similarly, the *Christian Science Monitor*'s correspondent, Ryan Lenora Brown, asked, "Is Nigeria's Corruption Crusade Aimed at Clean-Up or Political Opponents?"[25] Because anticorruption campaigns are politically popular, it makes sense for self-interested politicians to wrap partisan endeavors in the banner of fighting corruption.

Politicians in the United States or other developed nations are not above using anticorruption campaigns for partisan purposes. A study of corruption cases brought by the U.S. attorney general during the presidential administrations of Democrat Bill Clinton and Republican George W. Bush found that, during the Clinton administration, relatively more Republicans were charged with corruption just before elections took place. The pattern reversed when Bush took office.[26]

Because politicians are strategic in their adoption of political slogans, we would do well to be wary of anticorruption campaigns launched from on high. They may be genuine. But ruthless leaders have always had ways to dispose of their political enemies.

3.8 Have developed countries merely legalized corruption with money in politics?

In the United States and other wealthy nations, the debate around overly cozy relations between business and government tends to focus on legal forms of favor-seeking rather than bald-faced bribery and corruption. Legalized influence would appear to suit those involved. If you can bend the will of legislators or judges to pass laws and judgments to suit your fancy (or pay lawyers to uncover loopholes to get around them), it's easier and less risky than a secret handoff of cash.

Whenever we mention the greater prevalence of corruption in poor countries, someone in the audience will raise the point that rich countries have simply "legalized it." What they have in mind is the kind of influence peddling—legal but often against public opinion and/or public interest—that we discussed in chapter 2.

While we're sympathetic to some aspects of this argument, it's also worth highlighting that there are important differences between bribery, on the one hand, and influence peddling via lobbying or campaign finance, on the other. The fact that we're able to document the comings and goings of lobbyists and the passage of individuals through both sides of the revolving door is itself revealing of differences between the two. Lobbyists register, and their activities are public. Many public officials' appointment books can be accessed under freedom of information laws. Campaign donations are a matter of public record. In other words, lobbying is legal and public, whereas corruption is illegal and secret.

Precisely because it's legal and public, if citizens don't like influence peddling, they can express their displeasure at the voting booth or by marching in the streets. We can, as voters, lobby the government to change laws around political access. We don't pretend that these changes are easy to make—despite the fact that voters seem to dislike influence peddling and object to money in politics, there have been surprisingly few reforms of the system.[27] However, recognizing influence peddling as a problem that is tough to change in developed countries—a point we agree with—does not put it on an equal footing with bribe paying, vote buying, and electoral fraud that are pervasive in many developing economies.

3.9 Why aren't there just two levels of corruption in the world—high and low?

Before concluding, we need to address a concern that may have been nagging at some readers throughout this chapter. In chapter 1, we proposed an equilibrium framework for thinking about corruption. The framework proposes that countries will converge on either ubiquitous corruption or no corruption at all. But according to the cross-country measures we've used here, corruption runs the full gamut from Denmark (almost nonexistent) to Afghanistan (ever-present), and everything in between. It's not merely an artifact of using perceptual measures of corruption—reported bribe frequencies also vary widely. That is, there's corruption in Italy, the Ukraine, and Indonesia, but nowhere near as much as in Haiti, the Democratic Republic of the Congo, or Afghanistan. And while corruption is a modest problem in France, the United States, and Chile, these governments aren't as squeaky clean as those in Denmark or Singapore. How do we reconcile corruption realities with our equilibrium framework?

We can begin to see how to resolve this apparent tension by observing "league tables" like the CPI, which attempt to summarize the highly varied corruption experiences that characterize interactions in any given country. But as we've seen already in section 3.2, Indians in, say, Bihar, confront much more corruption than Indians in Gujarat. India's CPI ranking of 85th least corrupt is a composite of these very different corruption experiences. The same is true in every country—by any measure, Minnesota is less corrupt than Louisiana, both of which feed into the United States' CPI ranking of 17th least corrupt. Similarly, government branches within a country differ in their probity. For example, in a Transparency International India survey in 2008, 48 percent of respondents reported paying a bribe to a police office in the previous year, while only 3 percent had paid a bribe to an education official.

Since governments are involved in a great many activities in many locales, country-level measures are composites of corruption across potentially hundreds of activities in thousands of localities. We'd conjecture that, if you look at any particular function in a specific place, you'd find that our equilibrium model fits quite well. There are instances of corrupt equilibria prevailing in otherwise low-corruption countries. In 2008, for example, New Yorkers were shocked to learn of abuse of disability benefits by Long Island Rail Road (LIRR) employees. For the preceding decade, virtually every LIRR worker claimed disability benefits after retirement, defrauding taxpayers of millions. In low-corruption settings, norms of corruption need to be highly localized if they're to persist, because persistent corruption depends on everyone covering up for one another (and even when a localized culture of corruption becomes entrenched, participants are still far more likely to get caught—as did LIRR retirees—by uncorrupted enforcement authorities).

When we say that a whole country is stuck in a high-corruption equilibrium, we mean that lots of these distinct corrupt equilibria exist, often reinforcing one another (if the New York office of the FBI had been corrupt, the LIRR disability scam might have persisted). We do not mean to suggest that corruption is necessarily ubiquitous even in such places—the Election Commission of India, for instance, is widely regarded as incorruptible, despite the general prevalence of corruption in India.

In summary, when we talk about high- and low-corruption equilibrium, we have in mind a set of norms that prevail in particular places or organizations—silos of corrupt cultures, if you like. Where there are many of these in a single nation, outside experts will be more apt to view the country as corrupt overall. Where there are few, experts will have a more favorable view of a country's corruption.

3.10 What did we learn in chapter 3?

- According to widely used corruption perception surveys, wealthy countries are much less corrupt than poor countries.
- Among poor countries at comparable levels of income, there is much variation in the extent of perceived corruption.
- Interpreting the corruption-income relationship is impossible on the basis of cross-country data alone—very likely corruption causes poverty, poverty causes corruption, and other factors plausibly contribute to both problems.
- We may think of the corruption-causing-poverty-causing-corruption cycle as a "poverty trap" that is difficult for countries to escape.

- It is challenging to evaluate the extent to which corruption is changing over time, for two reasons: (1) standard cross-country measures cannot be reliably compared across years; and (2) the greater visibility of corruption could indicate that governments are more earnest in confronting the problem.
- While legal business-government relations in many developed countries may be overly cozy, there are substantive differences between influence peddling and bribery in their visibility and their consequences. The two also differ in how citizens need to confront the problems.

4

WHAT ARE THE CONSEQUENCES OF CORRUPTION?

In the previous chapter, we took an agnostic view of whether corruption causes poverty, poverty causes corruption, or if some other factor—call it general dysfunction or poor governance—causes a society to be both corrupt and impoverished. On the basis of cross-country data alone, it's hard to make stronger claims than these. In this chapter, we delve more deeply into the theory that links corruption to economic development. To do so, we will explore the microeconomic interactions—such as the particulars of the relationship between briber and public official—that shed light on the channels through which corruption tends to undermine prosperity. As we pointed out in chapter 1, corruption's effects ripple through the economy, causing multiple levels of distortion to political and market institutions, so that the price of corruption is larger than the direct cost of bribes, embezzlement, and misuse of government property. We will also discover that, when it comes to economic growth, all corruption is not created equal: some circumstances and types of corruption prove much more damaging than others.

4.1 Does corruption reduce economic growth?

Given the moral undertones to the debate around corruption, many take it as an article of faith that its effects are always harmful. However, only a half-century ago, leading scholars espoused an "efficient corruption" view, which encouraged organizations like the World Bank to largely turn a blind eye to the issue. The argument can be traced back to a 1964 essay by economist Nathaniel Leff called "Economic Development through Bureaucratic Corruption."[1]

Leff was, like many economists of his (and our) era, a believer in the market's Invisible Hand as a force for social good. The term "Invisible Hand" first appeared in Book IV of Adam Smith's *Wealth of Nations*, published in 1776, and has since taken on an outsized role in economists' and others' conception of the market. As Smith wrote:

> Every individual necessarily labours to render the annual revenue of the society as great as he can. He generally indeed neither intends to promote the public interest, nor knows how much he is promoting it. ... He intends only his own gain, and he is in this, as in many other cases, led by an **invisible hand** to promote an end which was no part of his intention.[2]

Market prices reflect how much consumers value bread or peanut butter or jelly. If tastes shift so that there's more demand for peanut butter and less for jelly, the price of peanut butter will go up, attracting more peanut-butter–producing entrepreneurs, while jelly-producing ones go bankrupt (or move into the nut butter business instead). Soon, the market returns to its efficient equilibrium.

What might interfere with this gloriously efficient state of affairs? The meddling hand of government. Leff suggested that in the presence of misguided antimarket policies—common, in his view, in many countries—bribery of public officials would help the market keep working its magic. He cites examples like Argentina's ill-conceived import quotas that, without the option for importers to bribe customs agents to keep critical machine parts and other goods coming in, would have destroyed the country's economy. In response to runaway inflation (also the result of misguided government policies), Brazil's government froze food prices. Had these price controls not been sabotaged by bribe-taking bureaucrats, the nation's farmers would have cut back on production, leading to a flourishing black market driven by increasingly scarce food.

In the best of all possible worlds, we wouldn't have crushing government bureaucracy and red tape, and we wouldn't need corruption. But according to Leff's arguments, given the existence of pointless (or misguided) regulations, bribery makes us better off. Observe that this *wouldn't* be true if government rules were properly conceived. Leff's framework illustrates what social scientists call the "theory of the second best"—an institutional failure along one dimension (red tape) may require what might appear as an additional failure (corruption) to correct it.[3] From the perspective of the second best, you can be grateful that corruption exists.

Leff goes even further, suggesting that the Invisible Hand will allow the market for bribery itself to function efficiently. To understand his argument, think about a government that is selling off rights to the wireless spectrum. Who will offer the highest bribe to secure the spectrum rights? By definition, the wireless operator that expects to generate the highest profits from their use. Leff argues that the highest briber will thus surely be the firm that will use the spectrum most efficiently—that's why it places such a premium on winning. We shouldn't expect as efficient an outcome if bureaucrats are left to pick who gets government contracts and assets based on other (nonbribe) considerations.

In the decades since Leff's much-referenced essay (whose arguments were expanded upon by political scientist Samuel Huntington in his influential 1968 book *Political Order in Changing Societies*),[4] scholars have provided counterarguments to each of Leff's claims. The assumption of "free entry" into paying bribes seems a poor fit with the reality that corrupt leaders tend to favor their own (often highly inefficient) kin or clan; and corruption may allow firms to skirt both bad *and* good regulations.[5] Such reasoning suggests that corruption is very plausibly inefficient and can be exploited to undermine rules that are socially beneficial.

These counterarguments eventually led the World Bank, among others, in the mid-1990s to do a complete about-face on the question of corruption. In 2013, the organization's president, Jim Yong Kim, labeled corruption as, "public enemy number one" for developing countries.

Critics of the efficient corruption view can also point to strong circumstantial evidence in a much-cited 1995 study by International Monetary Fund (IMF) economist Paolo Mauro. His analysis showed that, after accounting for their initial levels of prosperity, corrupt countries' economies grew significantly slower during the period 1960–1990.[6] Consider, for example, Venezuela and Norway, two countries that started with similar per capita income levels in 1960 and comparable oil reserves that might have been used to help their economies grow, but with very different levels of corruption. By 2015, Norwegian per capita incomes were around eight times those of Venezuela (a gap that's surely widened further with Venezuela's political and economic collapse in 2016), as the placement of the two countries in Figure 3.2 shows.

In the remainder of this chapter, we turn to more focused case study and microeconomic evidence to explore what might explain the macro-level relationship between corruption and economic prosperity. By the end, we'll see that neither recent history nor scholarly research has been kind to the efficient corruption view.

4.2 How does corruption affect the regulation of business (and vice versa)?

In its purest form, the efficient corruption hypothesis asserts that bribery can allow an economy to grow in the presence of "bad" laws or regulations that put sand in the gears of market functioning. But this argument ignores where the bad laws come from in the first place. Government regulations are the way they are for a reason. They don't fall out of the sky or appear at random—they're the result of conscious and deliberate choices by the politicians and bureaucrats who write them. As we'll see, consideration of where laws come from will drastically affect the logic and conclusions of Leff's arguments.

Leff's pro-corruption stance is based in large part on the presumption that corruption serves as a convenient way for the market to override the inertial or misguided policies of stupid, lazy, overbearing, risk-averse bureaucrats. There's an enormous body of evidence for Leff to marshal in his favor, in the form of the regulations that burden companies and private citizens. Efficient corruption proponents will cite examples like the "license Raj," the rules that governed business in India until 1990. The regulations prescribed how much a company could produce, as well as the minutest details of what it could make, detailing, for example, the precise physical dimensions of an engine that could be put in an automobile.

In the late 1990s, a team of social scientists collaborated with the World Bank to document the extent of bureaucratic encumbrances around the world through a massive data collection effort to determine how long it took to execute various undertakings that require government approvals or oversight. Working with experts in each of nearly a hundred countries, they determined the number of steps required to open a new business. There were only two steps required in Canada, for example, versus twenty in Bolivia. They also calculated the number of days the process took from beginning to end: the two steps took only two days in Canada (per capita GDP in 2014 of more than US$50,000), versus 82 days for the 20 steps in Bolivia (per capita GDP of US$3,250); for Mozambique (GDP per capita of just US$600 in 2014), despite having "only" 17 steps, the estimated time was 174 days, the highest of any nation. The research team went through a similar data-collection process for labor regulation a few years later (least onerous: Zambia; most onerous: Sweden).[7]

For business entry regulation, the researchers find that the Canada-versus-Bolivia/Mozambique comparison holds more broadly across countries: richer, more developed countries tend to have fewer regulations, and the regulations they do have can be dealt with relatively quickly. So, according to Leff's reasoning, it's a good thing that entrepreneurs in Bolivia and Mozambique (CPI rankings of 103rd and 119th in 2014, respectively) are able to bribe their way around business incorporation laws, or no one would ever be able to start a company in those countries. (In fact, when the World Bank ran a Business Climate Survey in Mozambique, it found that the time that most entrepreneurs took to start a business was much less than the formal figure. And yes, entrepreneurs reported paying bribes to get their businesses up and running.[8])

The problem with this logic, though, is that Mozambique and Bolivia might have such onerous regulations precisely *because* corrupt bureaucrats foresee the extra bribes they can extract by wrapping every business activity in excessive red tape. That is, corruption doesn't just provide businesses a way around pointless regulation—corruption is the reason some rules exist in the first place.[9]

The notion that bad regulations are created (or at least maintained) for the purpose of extracting bribes also finds support in an analysis of firm-level survey data from around the world conducted by Daniel Kaufmann and Shang-Jin Wei.[10] Kaufmann and Wei observe that businessmen who report paying a higher fraction of their revenues to public officials in the form of "irregular payments" (i.e., bribes) spend *more* time dealing with bureaucrats, not less. Instead of greasing the wheels and allowing businesses to operate more efficiently, corruption actually increases the friction in businesses' interactions with regulators. If this is a more accurate depiction of the relationship between regulators and businesses, we need to pressure countries like Mozambique and Bolivia to remove excessive regulations, rather than allowing corruption to flourish as a way around them.

Note, however, that we aren't advocating the wholesale scrapping of regulations. Seat belts are good. Speed limits are good. Many workplace safety and employment laws are good. There are many regulations that businesses would be happy to get rid of because they harm profits even though they're good for workers and for consumers. (Automobile manufacturers didn't support seat belts initially, despite the many analyses showing that the benefit-to-cost ratio is far greater than one.) It would be a shame to use anticorruption reforms as a smoke screen for doing away with regulations that businesses previously bribed their way around because they didn't like them. We may end up with weaker consumer and worker protections and higher corporate profits, without much of a reduction in corruption.

4.3 How does corruption affect worker welfare?

On April 24, 2013, Rana Plaza, an eight-story building in a suburb of Dhaka that housed a number of textile factories, crumpled into a heap of rubble. The building's collapse was amazingly rapid—as one survivor put it the following day, "suddenly, the floor wasn't there."[11] By the time Bangladesh's government called off the search for survivors three weeks later, more than 1,130 corpses had been pulled from the ruins, making it the deadliest accident at a manufacturing site in modern history by a wide margin. (The runner-up was a fire at a toy factory in Thailand that killed 188 workers in 1993.)

As information trickled out about the accident, it was learned that the structure and the activities that went on inside Rana Plaza violated all sorts of laws and regulations. The building was zoned for commercial rather than industrial use, yet it housed five garment factories stacked one on top of another (the vibration of sewing machines helped to bring down the building). It was built—without authorization—on top of a pond. Its height extended three stories above what was specified in the original (nonindustrial) permit. The builders used substandard construction materials. Rana Plaza had been evacuated just the day before when inspectors discovered cracks in the pillars, walls, and floors—and then workers were ordered back inside to continue churning out clothing for companies that included JCPenney, Joe Fresh, Walmart, and Mango.

Many wondered how on earth the building could operate in such flagrant violation of the law. They didn't have to search very hard for an answer. The press quickly discovered that the owner, Sahel Rana, was a local political boss whose power and influence allowed him to operate above the law. (He was having yet another floor added at the time of the collapse, again without regulatory approval.)

The Rana Plaza tragedy provides a particularly poignant illustration of the necessity of regulations, and the very tangible human costs when businesses use bribery or connections to get around them. It also emphasizes that corruption to circumvent regulations is distinct from—and possibly far worse than—corruption with the goal of obtaining standard government services like seeing a doctor or renewing a driver's license. Both types of corruption can lead to inefficiency. The former can have far more dire consequences.

There are many, many other examples that illustrate the social costs of companies paying bribes or exploiting political connections to skirt regulations. A chemical plant in Shangdong, China, was built without appropriate reviews of its operations, and captured headlines worldwide when it exploded in August 2015. It later came out that an owner of the plant was the son of the local police chief. A coal mine in Zhonglou, China, operating without any of the requisite licenses, caught fire in 2009, trapping and killing thirty-five miners inside. The owner had nearly two dozen local bureaucrats on his payroll.

To move beyond a few compelling anecdotes, one of us (together with collaborator Yongxiang Wang) set out to examine whether corruption generally makes for more dangerous workplaces or whether—as implied by efficient corruption arguments—it serves primarily to allow companies to get around outdated and pointless regulatory constraints.[12] We focused on companies in China, a nation with a dismal record of workplace safety, where employee death rates are more than twenty times that of the United Kingdom. Bribery is often implicated in cases of poor safety compliance, leading the Chinese national ministry charged with production safety to state publicly that "corruption [is] behind many major deadly accidents."[13]

Our hunch was that more politically connected executives might be able to get away with lower compliance with safety regulations by exploiting their personal ties or through out-right bribery. To see if this was true, we collected data on 276 publicly traded companies in industries in which workplace safety is a major issue: construction, mining, and chemical manufacturing. We then compared the rates of workplace fatal-ities at politically connected companies—where at least one top executive had held a government rank of vice mayor or higher prior to joining the firm—to companies without high-level connections. We found a surprisingly large difference in the safety records of the two groups: even our most conservative estimates indicate that workplace death rates were more than twice as high at politically connected companies.

It would be bad enough to discover that well-connected business leaders were sloppy, lax on safety, or incompetent. But another set of findings suggests that more insidious forces were also at work: despite their poor safety records, we also found that politically connected companies are less likely to be targeted with safety audits. In fact, in the absence of a fatal workplace accident (which itself triggers an investigation), we do not observe a single instance of a major safety audit at a well-connected company. (For unconnected companies, the audit rate is about 5 percent.) Together, these results show that well-connected Chinese companies are both more dangerous and less likely to be inspected for safety problems, a pair of findings that points strongly toward these companies exploiting their ties to circumvent safety-enhancing regulations.

Our findings are a useful reminder that some rules and regulations are there for a reason—to protect the interests of workers, consumers, and others vulnerable to exploitation. And that implies that corruption doesn't simply grease the wheels of commerce by allowing firms to circumvent pointless regulations—it also allows them to grease regulators' palms at the expense of others.

4.4 What are the consequences of corruption in public construction?

As long as government has been involved in construction, there has been corruption in it. Some of the most outrageous acts of history's most infamously corrupt figures involved building construction of one sort or another. William "Boss" Tweed, a notorious character in nineteenth-century New York politics, oversaw the construction of the New York County Courthouse on Chambers Street, at a cost of $13 million, more than twice what the United States paid for Alaska in 1867. Why so much? As Dan Barry recounted in the *New York Times* in 2000:

> A carpenter was paid $360,751 (roughly $4.9 million today) for one month's labor in a building with very little woodwork. A furniture contractor received $179,729 ($2.5 million) for three tables and 40 chairs. And the plasterer ... Andrew J. Garvey, got $133,187 ($1.82 million) for two days' work; his business acumen earned him the sobriquet "The Prince of Plasterers." Tweed personally profited from a financial interest in a Massachusetts quarry that provided the courthouse's marble. When a committee was assigned to determine why construction was taking so long, it spent $7,718 (roughly $105,000 today) on printing its lightning-quick findings

that everything was above-board; the printing company, of course, was owned by Tweed.[14]

Ultimately, the details of corruption and profiteering at the "Tweed courthouse" and other construction projects around the city were exposed in a series of *New York Times* articles in 1871. By then, Tweed and his cronies had already enjoyed a remarkably profitable run in municipal politics.

Public construction has a number of characteristics that make it particularly vulnerable to corruption today, just as in Boss Tweed's era. Day to day, the public doesn't observe or directly suffer from the kickbacks, misdirected contracts, and other misuses of their taxpayer dollars. It's obvious when there's no teacher in the classroom, but not apparent if the school was constructed using cheap materials and overpaid, underqualified workers (at least not until an earthquake hits), rather than following higher, more costly standards. Furthermore, because each courthouse, highway, or airport is complicated in its own particular way, politicians and bureaucrats are necessarily given some discretion in who gets the contract and at what price. Later, they get to decide if the deal should be renegotiated in the contractor's favor owing to unforeseen circumstances like higher material costs or less-stable-than-anticipated subsoil conditions. Even after the fact, it's tough for voters to assess how much these projects *should* have cost to build, how long construction should have taken, and whether the projects were built to standard. Once construction is completed, voters are forced to rely on the very same government to audit its own work. That may be fine if the construction project is in Denmark, but not if it's overseen by the modern-day equivalents of Boss Tweed—of which there are many.[15]

We find ourselves in this position because governments the world over build a lot of things—things that are important to economic development, which wouldn't magically appear if left to the whims of market forces. These are "public goods"—roads, schools, electricity grids—that involve a scale and level of coordination that require the guiding hand of government if they are to be built at all.

So public construction is both necessary—on an epic scale that makes it even easier to bury graft in the balance sheet—and out of the public eye, two conditions that make it perennially vulnerable to corruption.

One ambitious attempt at getting a sense of the scale of corruption in public construction comes from Benjamin Olken, still a graduate student when he undertook the research we describe here.[16] The study was conducted in collaboration with the World Bank, which helped to finance road building projects in each of 600 Indonesian villages. Olken wanted to know how much money was stolen due to corruption in each case, and used a "leakage study" of the type we discussed in section 2.3 to figure it out. He knew the amount that was disbursed to fund each project—an average of about US$9,000—so if he could determine how much the roads actually cost to build, he could estimate how much had "leaked" into the pockets of unscrupulous contractors and public officials by subtracting the road's actual cost from the funds that were provided. To do so, Olken sent teams of experienced engineers to assess the quality of each road (for example, by digging up road core samples to calculate whether the builders skimped on the amount of gravel they used) and to estimate its likely cost, taking into account local prices of inputs like gravel and labor.

Olken found that villages given US$9,000 to build a road ended up constructing something that should only have cost US$6,800, suggesting that nearly a quarter of the funds disappeared as a result of theft or incompetence. It doesn't quite match the astonishing rate of theft in Boss Tweed's New York, but if it's reflective of the broader rate of corruption in public construction today (even in the subset of high-corruption countries alone), it suggests that theft in this arena could easily run into the trillions.[17]

It's not just the *quantity* of infrastructure that's affected. If construction firms—where they can get away with it—use less expensive building methods and cheaper materials, we'd expect building safety to suffer. You can save hundreds of thousands of dollars in a building's cost by spacing the rebars six feet apart rather than three. But doing so makes the building more vulnerable to collapse.

This issue typically finds its way into the spotlight in the wake of natural disasters that put buildings' structural soundness to the test. In a 2008 earthquake in Sichuan, China, thousands of inadequately reinforced schoolrooms collapsed, leading to an outcry over their shoddy construction resulting from, among other things, corrupt contractors selling off designated building materials for personal gain. Three years later, near-identical allegations were replayed in Turkey after the collapse of thousands of buildings following an earthquake in that country. These aren't mere curiosities: a study in the scientific journal *Nature* published in 2011 calculated that 83 percent of all deaths from building collapse in earthquakes over the prior thirty years took place in countries that were "anomalously" corrupt, meaning, more corrupt than their incomes alone would predict.[18] While this sort of cross-country calculation is subject to all of the caveats and shortcomings that we described in earlier chapters, it nonetheless gives a provocative indication of the potentially high human cost of corruption in public construction.

Thus, the consequences of corruption in public construction can be measured both in terms of financial cost and human tragedy. It likely results in wasted public funds running into the trillions, and lives unnecessarily lost when earthquakes or hurricanes strike the unfortunate residents of corrupt nations.

4.5 Does corruption increase economic inequality?

It's useful to start with the sort of aggregate country-level analyses of corruption and income that we presented in chapter 3 to depict the relationship between corruption and inequality. (Because of the difficulties in assembling data on inequality, there are far fewer countries included here relative to the figures shown in chapter 3 that show national income and corruption.) The measure of inequality that we use is called the Gini coefficient, which ranges in value from 0 to 1. A country where every individual has the same income gets a Gini of zero (i.e., no income inequality at all). If a single individual earns 100 percent of a country's income (an obviously fictitious case), the country's Gini is one. High-inequality countries include South Africa—with the world's most extreme income inequality—and a flock of Latin American and Caribbean countries, including Haiti, Guatemala, Brazil, and Chile. The United States, which we have also labeled on the figure, is the rich world's most unequal nation.

Like corruption and national income, we find a strong relationship between corruption and inequality: more corrupt societies tend to have more inequitable income distributions, as illustrated in Figure 4.1. A 2002 study suggests a few channels through which this relationship may occur: corrupt countries are less likely to tax the rich, and also less likely to spend on social programs. Because public education is frequently undermined by corruption, access to schooling is often only available to those who can afford to pay bribes or opt out of the public system entirely, leading to inequities in human capital and ultimately to wider rich-poor income disparities.[19]

Even the incidence of bribery can fall disproportionately on the poor. First, even if the bribe rate extracted by cops and bureaucrats is the same for rich and poor, it will be more onerous for a poor person. The reason is that, if the corruption "tax" requires a fixed bribe (as, for example, economist Jennifer Hunt finds in her work on healthcare in Uganda), the poor have to fork over a relatively larger share of their assets than someone with more wealth.[20]

Worse still, the poor may get shaken down for bribes more often than the middle class because, while officials recognize

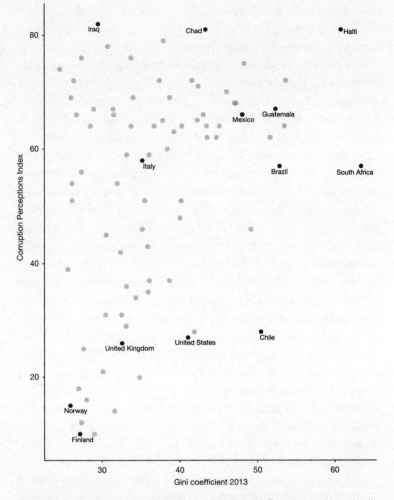

Figure 4.1 Scatterplot of Index of Economic Inequality and Transparency International's Corruption Perceptions Index for 83 Countries (2012)

Note: Data on the Gini coefficient from 2013; where that is unavailable, we use 2012 or 2011. No data available for India or China, which are omitted from the figure. Data on inequality from the World Bank.

that pressuring members of the rich or middle class might lead to repercussions, the impoverished are powerless to complain. An ingenious study examines this possibility among traffic cops in Mexico City. The authors of the study—political science Ph.D. students at the time—hired confederates to make brazenly illegal left turns at intersections monitored by the police to see if they'd be issued a ticket, asked for a bribe, or given a warning. Some of the confederates drove luxury cars (and dressed the part), whereas others drove older, less expensive vehicles. The researchers found that the police stopped affluent and poor drivers with equal frequency, but were more likely to extort bribes from the poor-looking drivers (not a single driver received a ticket—the affluent-looking drivers were just issued warnings rather than extorted). When the researchers talked to the police afterward about what they'd found, they were told that the cops feared that more affluent drivers might complain if they were asked for bribes, leading to possible consequences for the officers involved.

A 2013 study suggests that this problem may be widespread.[21] Using survey data from the World Justice Project, the study shows that, worldwide, more educated respondents are more likely to report public officials for misconduct. We can easily imagine why. The educated are less easily intimidated by authority, more capable in dealing with the bureaucracy, and more able to file written complaints.

Thus, corruption isn't just bad for everyone—it's worst for those who are least well off, and who have the fewest political and economic resources to begin with.

4.6 Does corruption reduce trust in government?

As we will see in chapter 8, the link from corruption to democracy may be illusory, but the connection to citizens' faith in the government is unmistakable. Persistent, widespread, and well-known political corruption erodes the legitimacy of the regime, causing citizens to lose faith in political institutions and in extreme cases in democracy itself. In Figure 4.2, we depict this relationship for Latin American countries in 2012–2013 using data from the Latinobarometer survey, which asked respondents about perceptions of corruption and also about support for democracy. The figure shows a strong negative relationship between the two sets of responses: in countries where perceptions of corruption are higher, support for democracy is eroded. Of course, the relationship likely goes in both directions—if citizens have little faith in democracy, they may unthinkingly continue to vote for even notoriously corrupt candidates, thereby allowing malfeasance to flourish unchecked. This creates a vicious cycle of political disappointment and cynicism-enabling corruption, which leaves voters feeling ever more disillusioned.

The cross-country relationship that we observe in Figure 4.2 holds more generally across the democratic world: as citizens believe that there is more political corruption among officials, their trust in government and their belief in the legitimacy of government decline.[22]

One might hope that corruption and the discontent that it breeds would mobilize citizenry to overthrow—or at least reform—government. Sadly, the effect may be the opposite, particularly when corruption is the norm, and voters thus operate with the expectation that corruption is common among politicians. Consider the finding of a recent experiment conducted by a group of political scientists and economists working in Mexico, a country where many politicians are believed to be corrupt.[23] The researchers provided voters in a randomly selected set of precincts with flyers that detailed the percentage of municipal funds that had been diverted illegally. In other precincts, voters received flyers that provided the municipal government's expenditures on "social infrastructure." In the precincts that received information on mayoral corruption, fewer voters turned out to cast their ballots in the elections, and votes were reduced for both incumbents and challengers alike. Knowing that politicians are corrupt does not mobilize voters

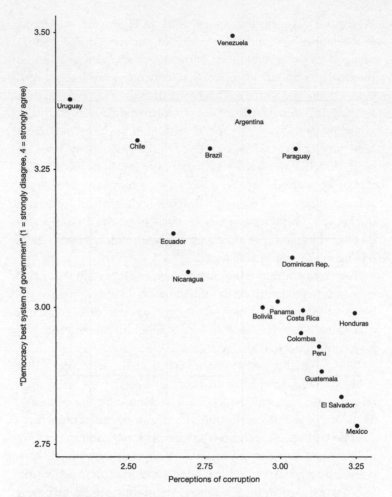

Figure 4.2 Scatterplot of Latinobarometer Perceptions of Corruption by Support for Democracy for 18 Countries (2013)

Note: Country averages in responses to 2012–2013 Latinobarometer survey, Q43A, "Democracy may have problems but it is the best system of government" and Q65 "How widespread do you think corruption and bribe taking are in the national government? Would you say hardly anyone is involved? (1); Not a lot of officials are corrupt (2); Most officials are corrupt (3); Almost everyone is corrupt (4)."

against dishonest officials: instead, the study suggests that it may discourage them from taking part in politics entirely. The reduced trust that comes with extensive corruption may thus serve to dampen democratic participation, leaving politicians even less accountable to their citizens.

4.7 Are some types of corruption more damaging than others? Part I: Centralized versus decentralized corruption

Suppose you'd like to open a business in Mozambique. You're willing to pay a little extra to get it up and running in a timely manner. Would you prefer that the business licensing process be controlled by a single bureaucrat, or dispersed among seventeen independent offices that each require separate approval?

It's not immediately obvious that it makes a difference one way or the other: one might imagine that seventeen independent extortionists would each collect no more and no less than they would if the process were overseen by one all-powerful bureaucrat. This is, in a way, how we think of the market's Invisible Hand, applied to bribery—market forces will somehow lead each office to set profit-maximizing bribe "prices" without knowing what others are doing.

It turns out that in this case, that reasoning would be misapplied. If you get to pick your type of extortionist, choose the centralized shakedown. The fact that centralized corruption is good for an individual entrepreneur also makes it better for the economy overall—centralized corruption kills fewer aspiring businesses that might have provided jobs and greater prosperity.

To understand why, let's start with the centralized case, in which an all-powerful director of business licensing can dictate to each of his permit-granting offices—environmental, workplace safety, and so on—what their individual bribes will be. In effect, there is only a single bribe price, decided upon by the director, which is then distributed among lower-level officials.

How should the business permit director set the bribe for each entrepreneur? A higher price brings in more cash per business, but as the price rises, more and more aspiring entrepreneurs will throw up their hands in frustration and set up shop elsewhere, or give up on starting a business entirely. If the director is setting bribe prices right, he'll pick an intermediate level that doesn't scare off too many would-be bribe payers.

Now consider what happens instead if a reform gives greater autonomy to each license-granting official, including greater discretion in setting the bribe prices that had previously been under the director's tight control. The environmental permit official will still demand payment for approval and, free to pick his own price, he will think about the trade-off between a higher bribe and the loss of income if the applicant chooses not to start a business. But, in contrast to the centralized case, what he fails to consider is that if he sets his price higher, he'll also be taking away bribe payments for the many other permit-granting officials, who lose out because the exorbitant bribe that needs to be paid to get an environmental permit scares off so many entrepreneurs. (In fact, if officials *don't* ratchet up their prices after they're given greater autonomy, each independent official might think himself a chump for leaving too much money on the table for others.) The workplace safety official (just like every other permit granter) goes through the same reasoning, and as a result, the uncoordinated shakedown ends up setting overall bribe prices higher and killing off more businesses relative to the case where bribery is dictated and coordinated from above.

This insight into the evils of decentralized corruption was first made by Andrei Shleifer and Robert Vishny, who noted that after the fall of the Soviet Union, the Russian government splintered into an assortment of separate bureaucracies.[24] Starting a business required bribing the local legislature, the central ministry, the local executive branch, the fire authorities, the water authorities, and myriad others, none of whom seemed to communicate with one another. This bribery free-for-all was, in their view, part of what dampened the benefits of economic reforms in a liberalized Russia. (Shleifer surely drew from his own experiences as an advisor to Anatoly Chubais during the privatization of Russia's state-owned enterprises.)

There's solid evidence, beyond Shleifer and Vishny's casual observations, that corruption is in fact more taxing when it's decentralized than when it's run from a central office. Support comes from a 2009 study by economist Benjamin Olken (who was responsible for the Indonesian road building study we described earlier in the chapter) and political scientist Patrick Barron.[25] The pair hired surveyors to accompany truck drivers on their delivery routes on the Indonesian Island of Sumatra.

When the researchers conducted their study in 2005–2006, a peace accord had just been signed between the Indonesian government and the Free Aceh Movement, which had fought a thirty-year war for independence in Sumatra's northern most province of Aceh. As a result of the protracted conflict, travel on Aceh's roads was interrupted by frequent police checkpoints. For example, truckers driving the 637 kilometers from Medan, the capital of North Sumatra, to the Acehan city of Meulaboh, faced more than sixty checkpoints en route. To get through each stop, the driver handed over a small wad of bills or a pack or two of cigarettes. These petty bribes added up to about 13 percent of the value of a shipment, more than what the trucker earned from his thirty-five hours of driving.

With the signing of the peace accord in August 2005, police checkpoints started disappearing along Aceh's roads. On the Medan-Meulaboh highway, the number fell from fifty in November 2005 to close to zero just six months later. Over the same period, the number of checkpoints across the border in North Sumatra held steady at around fifteen.

The partial disappearance of checkpoints afforded Olken and Barron a rare opportunity to test whether centralized bribery is less taxing on business. Think of each checkpoint as being like a permit office in our discussion above. Shleifer and Vishny's theory predicts a reduction in total bribes paid by truck drivers as they traverse a route with fewer grabbing hands, even as each individual checkpoint raises its prices as they grow to monopolize a larger and larger share of the extortion market.

Olken and Barron's analysis provides resounding support for the benefits of centralized (relative to decentralized) extortion—with fewer checkpoints, total bribes paid by each truck driver went down. Bribe prices at each checkpoint did go up: at police checkpoints in both North Sumatra (where there was no change in police presence at all) as well as Aceh, soldiers upped their bribe requirements as the number of checkpoints declined. But bribe prices didn't go up nearly so much as to compensate for the reduced number of checkpoints faced by truckers (and hence the number of bribes paid). That is, the soldiers understood that by keeping their bribe increases modest, they would encourage more truck drivers to use the Medan-Meulaboh road, thus increasing the number of bribes they would collect. (Things would have been even better for both truckers and soldiers if the checkpoints could have put their bribe demands under the control of a single, centralized authority.) [26]

Thus, while corruption is taxing on businesses in general, it's at least less taxing if it's controlled by fewer extorting officials who can better coordinate their shakedowns.

Case Study: Extortion in San Pedro Sula

As of this writing, San Pedro Sula, Honduras, is the most violent city in the most violent country in the world. In 2013, one out of every 1,000 Hondurans was murdered, a rate that was more than 50 percent higher than its neighbor El Salvador, the world's second most violent country, in the same year. San Pedro Sula had two murders for every 1,000 residents, which works out to three killings *per day*. That makes for a precarious existence for the city's residents, who regularly encounter assassination attempts and gun battles while going about their daily lives. The life of a San Pedro Sula bus driver is particularly fraught with danger.

While the source of this danger is organized crime rather than corruption, the story of San Pedro's bus drivers provides a compelling illustration of why decentralized shakedowns (whether perpetrated by Central American gangs or corrupt bureaucrats) are so much worse than centralized ones. One reason that driving a bus in San Pedro Sula is among the most dangerous jobs in the world is that the gangs that control the city's streets fail to coordinate their protection rackets.

The two rival gangs that dominate the lives of San Pedro Sula's residents, the Barrio 18th Street and Mara Salvatrucha (or MS-13), are descendants of groups formed in Los Angeles and subsequently exported to Central America as its members were deported from American prisons. The Mexican cartels have also fomented municipal conflict in Honduras by sometimes supporting smaller gangs to weaken or destabilize their Honduran competitors.

Each gang has its turf. Everyone pays what residents call the *impuesto de guerra*, or "war tax," to whichever gang controls the neighborhood. As long as your payments are up-to-date, no one will burglarize your home or vandalize your market food stall. Fall behind, and bad things start to happen. Just how bad? As the *Los Angeles Times* reported in 2013: "In San Pedro Sula, people are mowed down on soccer fields, in shoe factories and at the airport. In [the neighborhood of] Chamelecon a few weeks ago, three women selling food were shot to death in the streets; six members of one family were slain at a kindergarten."[27] In short, the war tax is protection money that feels a lot like a bribe you need to pay to stay alive.[28]

In 2014, a National Public Radio (NPR) reporter interviewed "Francisco," a former member of the MS-13 gang who had been involved in setting up the war tax for bus drivers back in the early 2000s.[29] Francisco describes the bus extortion business as exactly that—a business. Before opening shop, he and his fellow gang members did their market research, examining bus companies' routes, estimating their buses' capacities, and calculating their likely revenues. This information helped the MS-13s figure out how much they could collect without driving bus owners out of business. As the sole extortionist, they set efficient, revenue-maximizing prices for protection payments.

The MS-13 enjoyed six gloriously profitable years: under its control, the bus companies flourished and bus owners reliably paid their weekly tributes. But profits attract entry, and soon the bus protection racket in Honduras became a competitive business. First, the Barrio 18 gang decided to diversify from contract assassinations into extortion; smaller gangs soon followed. As a result, a bus driver who used to pay only the MS-13 now had perhaps five independently negotiated protection payments to make. As with the case of uncoordinated bribe-takers at Russia's regulatory agencies, each gang set its prices too high, and ended up killing off more businesses (and nonpaying bus drivers) relative to the earlier era when MS-13 ran the show alone. The gangs now make less money, fewer buses remain in business, and the ones that do spend more on protection money than they did in the "good old days."

As NPR reported, the same problem afflicted many other industries in Honduras, from taxi drivers to fruit vendors to plastic surgeons, all of whom found that the pressure to pay off multiple competing gangs was such that it was no longer worth it to stay in business.

4.8 Are some types of corruption more damaging than others? Part II: Uncertainty

In 2008, the Moscow news magazine *Kompromat* published an unusual price list, which provided the going rates for anything you might want from a corrupt bureaucrat, politician, or judge. Looking for a guilty verdict in a criminal case? That'll cost you US$50,000 to US$100,000, depending on the nature of the accusation. Want to get your competitor in trouble with the tax authorities? US$50,000. Initiating a piece of legislation in the national parliament? US$500,000, and for another US$500,000 you could apparently guarantee that it'd pass.

Whether you think this a happy or depressing state of affairs depends on your point of reference. Compared to the honorable conduct of parliamentarians and judges in, say, Sweden or Denmark, it's pretty awful—better that courts provide judgments on the basis of evidence and politicians make laws to serve the public good. But if you're going to have corruption, it may be preferable that all sides have an understanding of both prices and the "goods" that will be delivered in return.

To understand why, think of the situation from the perspective of a company. For a business owner, in some ways bribery looks like a tax—it's a cost of doing business. If the government raises taxes, perhaps fewer entrepreneurs will open businesses, and employees will work a little less hard—why bother to put together a business plan or work overtime if 90 cents on the dollar goes to the government?[30] If you have to pay a fraction of profits or earnings to bribes, some might argue, it's not that different from a tax.

We (and others) beg to differ. Ask yourself: would you rather have $10 with certainty, or a 50-50 shot at $20? Most people will take the sure thing. If there's risk, investors need a higher return to compensate for it. (That is, you need to drop the amount you would have to pay for the gamble below $10 to compensate for its risk. But there's surely some number between $0 and $10 where you become willing to part with your money in exchange for the "investment" in a 50-50 gamble for $20.) Taxes reduce profits, while leaving risk unchanged. Bribes reduce profits but also increase risk: what if, after taking your money, the labor inspector decides nonetheless to report you for workplace safety violations? You can't report him to the police for failing to honor the bribe you paid. And what if your friend in the bureaucracy were to be transferred, arrested, or to die in a car accident? His replacement might not be so accommodating, or might demand payment as well to turn a blind eye. Almost by definition, you have no legal recourse. By both reducing profits *and* making these profits riskier, bribery is doubly taxing to the sort of business creation and investment that drives economic growth.[31]

Economist Shang-Jin Wei has documented the outsized drag that corruption has on investment, and has also shown that this is likely in part because corruption introduces uncertainty that scares off investors. In a 2000 study, Wei showed that investment by multinational companies—firms like Siemens, Toyota, and Coca-Cola that own operations in many different countries—is lower in countries with higher tax rates.[32] His analysis also shows that corruption has a much greater negative impact on investment than taxes.

In an accompanying study, Wei considered the extent to which uncertainty can explain why corruption discourages investment so much more than taxation.[33] To measure how much uncertainty investors face from bribe-demanding officials, Wei used responses to the Global Competitiveness Report (GCR), a survey conducted by the World Economic Forum since 1996 to rank countries on economic competitiveness. GCR respondents are leading businesspeople who are asked, among other things, whether they are required to make "irregular, additional payments connected with imports and exports permits, business licenses, exchange controls, tax assessments, police protection or loan applications." To illustrate, Wei contrasts two high-corruption countries—Indonesia and Ukraine—both of which had very high average corruption in the 1990s, but very different levels of corruption uncertainty. (Their placement in Figure 3.2 shows that even in 2014, both countries still had relatively high corruption.) In Indonesia, all respondents agreed that bribes were at least sometimes required to get things done. In Ukraine, experiences were much more mixed—some respondents reported very high levels of corruption, while others said that it was virtually nonexistent. That is, Indonesia's corruption "tax" was high yet certain; Ukraine's was just as high on average, but with much greater variability. Simply focusing on the average level of corruption obscures the very different experiences that businesses reported in their interactions with the government. In Suharto's Indonesia, businesses knew they were in for a shakedown; in Ukraine, businesses really didn't know *what* they were getting into.

Wei found that this uncertainty had a big effect on multinationals' investment decisions: holding the average level of corruption constant, increasing bribe uncertainty can reduce foreign investment by as much as a third. If you don't know whether you're suddenly in for the surprise expense of a large bribe you failed to plan for, better keep your money in the bank.

4.9 Are some types of corruption more damaging than others? Part III: Holding up businesses via corruption

In 1989, a consortium led by the Japanese construction company Kumagai Gumi signed a contract to build and operate a 20-kilometer (12-mile) elevated toll road through the city of Bangkok. This was to be the second stage of an expressway that was the centerpiece of the Thai government's ambitious plans to reduce the gridlock that gripped the city daily. The contract spelled out in excruciating detail exactly what each party to the agreement was responsible for and when, as well as the date of completion, the toll increases that would be permitted, and what would be done in case disagreements arose (because no contract, however detailed, foresees every possible contingency). Essentially, Kumagai Gumi and its bankers were going to cover the billion-dollar cost of constructing the road, funds the Thai government didn't have, which would then be recovered through a 60 percent share of tolls collected from drivers.

Other companies took the agreement as a sign that the Thai government had become a reliable business partner, thus launching a series of further infrastructure contracts for half a dozen other projects that promised to fill Bangkok with intracity railroads and modern highways. But only a few years and one billion dollars later, all was not well in the Kingdom of Thailand. With the second-stage expressway all but complete, the government informed Kumagai Gumi that the toll would be 20 baht (about 80 U.S. cents at the time) rather than 30 baht, as had been clearly specified in the contract. Great for Bangkok voters; devastating to Kumagai Gumi's profits.

This put Kumagai Gumi and its investors in a very uncomfortable position—and more or less guaranteed that no foreign company would be investing in Thai infrastructure anytime soon after. Recall that the road was already completed and could be operated without much help from the builder. All that kept the Thai government from seizing the project outright was the need to maintain at least a facade of contractual compliance.

In the end, the two parties negotiated the sale of the expressway to a group of Thai investors at a price that allowed Kumagai Gumi to recoup its costs but left the company, after four years of work, with no profits whatsoever.

Kumagai Gumi's misadventures in Bangkok are a classic illustration of what economists call the "hold-up problem"—one party to an agreement makes an irretrievable investment and, once committed, the counterparty goes back on the original terms and tries to renegotiate new, more favorable ones.

Since there's no such thing as a perfect contract, a great many relationships have at least a bit of a threat of hold-up—there's always *something* that's ambiguous, left out of the fine print, or impossible to enforce.[34] However, the nature of corruption makes a bribe "contract" that much more vulnerable to the hold-up problem. A bribe is an investment that's made with the expectation of later benefits. In other words, it's a transaction that takes place over time. In that sense, it's no different from Kumagai Gumi's toll road construction costs. But if parties to bribery know what they're doing, they'll leave no paper trail for prosecutors or journalists to uncover down the road. As a result, what's a bribe-paying construction manager to do if, having paid for a building permit, his contact stops returning his phone calls or claims that additional payments are needed? Even if there *were* a written agreement to point to, there is no court of law to enforce it. Kumagai Gumi was at least able to use the court of global public opinion to get their money back, hardly an option for making sure a bribe agreement is followed.

The hold-up problem can explain, at least in part, why so many investments in corrupt countries seem focused on making a quick buck rather than generating a potentially higher profit over the long term. Why invest if the value may get captured by corrupt and grasping officials? As a result of hold-up concerns, Bangkok kept its traffic jams and, more generally, developing countries face shortages in precisely the types of infrastructure requiring upfront investments. How else can one explain the floating power barges, ready to be towed off at a moment's notice, that supply power to cities in Nigeria, Pakistan, and elsewhere in the developing world? The alternative is breaking ground on an immovable land-based power plant that leaves investors vulnerable to escalating demands from local government officials.

The attempted rewrite of the Bangkok expressway contract proved very costly to the government, at least in reputational terms. As one observer noted in the venerated *Financial Times*, as a result of various attempts at renegotiating infrastructure contracts, "[t]he government of Thailand is considered less and less a reliable partner and that makes it difficult to get money."[35] These funds were desperately needed to finance a rapidly growing economy. A government taking the long view might have chosen not to stick it to foreign companies even if it could have gotten away with it, since that scares off other potential investors. Similarly, a forward-looking bureaucrat or politician might do well to honor bribe agreements, knowing that if word gets out that he doesn't, it will endanger his lucrative side business.

The "good" type of corrupt bureaucrat—the kind that Nathaniel Leff had in mind in singing the praises of corruption half a century ago—is one who, while taking his share of the road or power construction contract, at least ensures that it gets built on time and without any surprises.

That the effect of corruption can vary so vastly depending on its particular characteristics is an insight that would-be reformers would do well to keep in mind. A corrupt leader ousted through upheaval or reform may leave behind a power vacuum that is quickly filled by disparate forces jostling for control. Even if, in this new era, there are greater checks against corruption, the combined effects of less-coordinated bribery, greater uncertainty over who's in charge, and increased bureaucratic and political turnover could make the corruption that remains more economically damaging than what it replaced. As one longtime insurance executive observed shortly after Indonesia's Suharto was driven from office, under the old regime, "there was a price for everything and everyone knew the price and knew what he was getting for what he paid." By contrast, the same executive lamented that in post-Suharto Indonesia, "you see chaos instead."[36]

4.10 How do natural resources affect corruption—and how does corruption affect the environment?

Are natural resources a blessing—or a curse? You might think that a country flush with oil, gold, diamonds, or other natural endowments would enjoy a huge economic advantage, allowing the population to dig or drill its way to prosperity. If the wealth thus created is in turn deployed in the fight against corruption, resource-rich countries should also have more honest governments (recall the very strong positive relationship between income and corruption). This logic, however, fails to line up with the experiences of countries like Nigeria, Sierra Leone, and Venezuela, which, although blessed with abundant natural resources, have been cursed with anemic or even nonexistent economic growth, and governments whose officials are known to be regularly and deeply involved in corruption. The British economist Richard Auty coined the term "resource curse" in 1993 to describe this unfortunate reality, but the problem (and recognition of it) is far older, perhaps as old as the problem of corruption itself. (The attribution of the term might fairly go to Zambia's first president, Kenneth Kaunda, who used to say that he and his compatriots had the "curse of being born with a copper spoon in our mouths.")

Why have oil and diamonds brought these (and other richly endowed nations) so much misfortune? And what distinguishes these economic basket cases from places like Norway (rich with oil) and Botswana (rich with diamonds), which have succeeded in turning their natural wealth into economic prosperity?

Corruption has a prominent role in explanations of the resource curse. Natural resources create "rents," which, as you may recall from chapter 1, represent wealth that is created essentially without effort. If the government can extract revenues from easily controlled resources (as is the case for mines or oil fields), it can finance state functions without levying taxes. And when citizens are recipients of government benefits and services without having to pay for them, they are less motivated to hold officials accountable and more tolerant of corruption (or at least the story goes).[37] The funds can also be deployed to limit dissent by buying off voters through patronage and other clientelistic practices. Finally, in a society flush with government-controlled resources, the most profitable opportunities for aspiring moguls may be through government rather than commerce: if there is so much money sloshing around in poorly monitored government ministries, it may be easy to skim a bit off the top, or to demand kickbacks from companies vying for extraction rights.[38]

In an influential 1995 study, economists Jeffrey Sachs and Andrew Warner documented a negative correlation between natural resource exports and economic growth at the country level over the period 1970–1990.[39] This launched a small cottage industry of scholars running variants of the Sachs-Warner

analysis—with decidedly mixed results. These follow-on studies compare the resource-growth relationship for democracies
versus nondemocracies (the pattern only holds for nondemocracies); use different measures of natural resource dependence
(the pattern is there for some measures, not for others); deal
with missing data in various ways (it turns out that how you
do so matters a lot for the results); look at growth over much
longer time periods rather than just a few decades (longer-run
growth measures turn up no evidence of a relationship); and
take different views on what other country attributes need
to be accounted for in the analysis (whether you control for
initial income matters a lot). One study concluded that natural
resources historically nurtured economic growth—think of the
United States—but in the closing quarter of the twentieth
century, the blessing curdled into a curse, corrupting political
regimes and undermining economic development.[40]

Given its often contradictory, confusing, and inconclusive
findings, this cross-country research agenda has hit a bit of
a dead end. Perhaps this isn't surprising given the many
factors that determine whether a country becomes rich or
poor: natural resources (like corruption) are far from the sole
determinants of a nation's destiny. And, as we have repeatedly
stressed, cross-national relationships reflect so many different
underlying phenomena at work that it's inevitably difficult to
make any decisive claims about causation.

Paralleling (and even preceding) these efforts at uncovering a country-level link between resource endowments and
economic and political success, scholars have undertaken case
studies and microeconomic analyses that document the resource curse at work within many countries, both rich and
poor—although it's mainly the poor countries that suffer. This
evidence, more than cross-country comparisons, can help us
understand when and how natural resources foster corruption
and ultimately hamper growth.

Let's go back to basic resource curse principles, to provide
one example of the type of microeconomic analysis we have in

mind. When the government controls or otherwise regulates something of value—as is the case with natural resources—it will have rents to hand out, creating profitable opportunities for regulators and bureaucrats. Take timber. Even in the poorest of nations, cutting down trees is strictly regulated (most tropical forests, for instance, are government-owned). This is in part to satisfy the international community, which is understandably alarmed at the disappearance of rainforests. But it means that the government must employ someone to oversee these many rules and regulations. By all accounts, in countries that are already plagued with corruption, overseers use their power to extract bribes rather than protect trees.[41] The problem is not merely that regulators wield their bureaucratic authority to extort loggers who have been awarded legitimate logging concessions. Much worse, regulators take bribes to turn the other way while trees are felled and exported without permits. One study of illegal logging in Cameroon found that government officials earned about as much from taking bribes from illegal timber harvesting as they did from their official salaries.[42]

In this version of the resource curse, not only do natural resources nurture corruption—corruption, in turn, encourages the even more rapid destruction of the environment. The problem is global. Interpol estimates that illegal logging—logging in violation of laws or regulations in the country of origin—contributes nearly a third of the wood on the global market, and somewhere between 50 and 90 percent of the volume of wood leaving the world's main producer countries in the Amazon basin, central Africa, and Southeast Asia. The value of illegal timber exports is comparable to the production value of the global drug trade. Across the tropics, corruption links members of local governments, forest officials, police and military, and local residents in highly profitable collusive networks, which use, by one count, at least thirty different documented ways of selling illegally harvested timber. Falsification of logging permits; bribes; hacking government websites; tax fraud; mislabeling wood products; falsification of eco-certification; log laundering ... the list goes on.[43]

There are situations in which natural resources are protected rather than over-exploited. Nobel Prize–winner Elinor Ostrom devoted her career to studying the many small communities that successfully protect their natural resources. Ostrom found that some Alpine villages in Switzerland had arrangements dating back nearly a thousand years that regulated use of common grazing land; in Turkey, fishers established and main-tained rules that prevent overfishing; in the Philippines, hun-dreds of irrigation societies that have been in place for centuries manage water resources for the good of their communities. But Ostrom also found that even small-scale societies sometimes fail to maintain arrangements that protect natural resources. Although some Turkish communities successfully developed rules to manage their fishing waters, others did not.[44] And these small-scale, decentralized community arrangements are easily disrupted when the resources become more valuable on domestic or international markets: where once villagers had sustained their own arrangements for gathering firewood or hunting wildlife, if the economic value of those resources increases, national governments and corporations swoop in to scoop up the rents. Once that happens, we are back in the situation of formal rules and regulations, which are highly profitable to break.[45] If those responsible for enforcing the rules that are meant to protect natural resources instead find it too lucrative to break them, corruption may prevail, and ordinary citizens grow more tolerant of participating in these collusive arrangements.[46]

What can we take away from the resource curse literature overall? If a country is lucky enough to find oil or diamonds when its economy is already thriving and political institutions are functional and well established, that's great. But for the poor, dysfunctional nations we're most interested in here, it would be better, to paraphrase a Saudi oil minister, to discover water rather than oil. And in settings where natural resources are readily available, if corruption is already the norm, public officials do not hesitate to strip their own lands of timber, wildlife, and groundwater. Not only do natural resources foment corruption—corruption, in turn, accelerates the destruction of our collective natural heritage.

4.11 Does corruption have any benefits?

Nathaniel Leff's argument that corruption helps business get things done in over-regulated countries—so influential when he first presented it half a century ago—has largely fallen out of favor. The main reason lies with the accumulation of evidence that corruption carries costs that overshadow any benefits.

There may be some types of corruption that are more harmful than others, and the effects of corruption differ according to the type of actors involved. The consequences of corruption for entrepreneurship and inequality are different when firms have to pay bribes to get government contracts compared with situations where families have to pay bribes to enroll their children in school. (Leff's argument was centered on the former, where the possible economic benefits of corruption are clearer.) Corruption is worse when it's decentralized and uncertain, so if you can pick your type of corruption, better that it's organized and orderly. Once corruption becomes common practice, reducing it may be hard, expensive, and carry unintended consequences.

However, we shouldn't let all this obscure the fact that we'd prefer not to have corruption in the first place, and that reducing corruption has generally put countries on track to greater prosperity. We don't know of anyone these days who has given the topic much thought who actually thinks that corruption is a good thing overall.

This brings us back to a point we first made in chapter 1: corruption may have immediate benefits for some of those directly involved, but it is detrimental to society as a whole. Even bribe payers "benefit" in only limited ways: paying may be preferable to the direct alternative of not having a phone line, or a business license, or an X-ray. But if bribe payers could be magically transported to a world where bribes were not the norm, they'd almost surely be happier and richer.

So, does corruption have any benefits? Yes, it has limited immediate benefits to firms that pay bribes to be awarded contracts or to speed up onerous regulations that were devised precisely to slow down businesses and extort them in the first place. Do these benefits, on balance, provide justifications for corruption? If they once did, they do no longer. If once ordinary people might have excused corruption on various grounds, they have become less and less tolerant of it even in the world's poorest nations. And if once firms could justify to themselves and their employees the necessity of paying bribes, the rising intolerance for corruption worldwide—perhaps best embodied in the U.S. Foreign Corrupt Practices Act of 1977, which makes it illegal for American firms to pay bribes abroad—has pulled the rug out from under such self-serving rhetoric.

4.12 What did we learn in chapter 4?

- Until relatively recently, corruption was seen as harmless or even beneficial to economic development, on the basis of the "efficient corruption" view, which contended most notably that corruption allows businesses to circumvent costly and unnecessary regulations. The efficient corruption hypothesis has largely fallen out of favor in recent years.
- One important counterargument to the efficient corruption view is that, if businesses are able to bribe their way around unnecessary regulations, this will in turn motivate government officials to devise red tape for the purpose of extracting bribes.
- If businesses can bribe their way around regulations, they will also be able to avoid rules that reduce profits but are otherwise socially beneficial, such as worker and

consumer protection laws and regulations designed to prevent overexploitation of natural resources.

- In addition to its negative impact on economic growth overall, corruption tends to increase economic inequality and to undermine trust in government.
- Not all corruption is created equal. It tends to be less damaging to economic growth when:

  - bribery is coordinated by a centralized authority;
  - there is less uncertainty about whether bribes will be demanded;
  - there is less uncertainty about whether officials will deliver on their promises in exchange for bribes.

5

WHO IS INVOLVED IN CORRUPTION, AND WHY?

In laying out the corruption-as-equilibrium concept that serves as our book's primary framework, we emphasize that citizens, companies, and public officials take bribes because they are better off individually by doing so, even if their actions are collectively harmful to society. In this chapter, we delve more deeply into what these costs and benefits are at an individual level, as a way of starting to think about what we might do to change these individual incentives. As rational-minded social scientists, our focus will primarily be on economic incentives, though we would be remiss if we did not also discuss the role of ethics and conscience in governing an individual's choice to engage in corruption.

5.1 Why do civil servants take bribes?

Social scientists tend to model an individual's choices as those that maximize some objective or set of objectives. We usually take the overall objective to be lifetime happiness. There are myriad inputs into an individual's happiness. For example, human companionship improves the odds a respondent will tell a surveyor that, all things considered, she's happy. Divorce makes people less happy than if they'd never been married at all. The single best predictor of long-term misery in the United States is a long commute to work. And, yes, money too buys happiness.[1]

If you're trying to understand why civil servants take bribes, a good starting point is that taking bribes increases their incomes, which in turn increases their happiness. What limits the ability of civil servants to grow richer (and thus happier) through bribe taking?

Everything in life involves trade-offs. For most bribe-taking officials, the main cost of corruption is the possibility of getting caught and punished. In thinking about corruption as a cost-benefit trade-off, researchers are operating in the broader tradition first pioneered by Nobel laureate Gary Becker, who applied economic analysis to many aspects of daily life: marriage, addiction, and—most notable for our purposes—crime. In his own telling, Becker started thinking about the trade-offs would-be criminals faced when he found himself in search of a parking spot near Columbia University, where he taught early in his career. As he reminisced to a newspaper reporter shortly before his death in 2014, "The question [I asked myself] was, 'Should I park closer in a spot that was illegal, or should I park in a lot which was somewhat further away?' So I had to make a calculation: what was the likelihood that I'd be caught if I parked it down the street versus the time, the money, that would be lost by parking further away?"[2] We all make these kinds of trade-offs in breaking rules—whether to cross against a traffic light or drive a bit above the speed limit, for example. Civil servants confront them in deciding whether and how much to break the law to benefit from bribery.

This somewhat obvious division of a choice into its distinct cost and benefit components can be helpful for examining the set of conditions that lead civil servants to accept (or demand) bribes. On the benefits side, willing bribers need to be lined up to pay. Suppose, for example, that whatever the civil servant has for sale—driver's licenses, oil concessions, military contracts—drops in value. Then voilà—less benefit from bribery and fewer bribes on offer. For some government functions it may be easier (or more desirable) to drive down bribe prices than for others. A well-meaning government could, with relative ease, clean up procurement for standard-issue items like copy paper and pencils by forcing schools, hospitals, and municipal offices to buy from a catalog with a standard price list. This was done to great effect by the Italian government when it created a centralized procurement agency, Consip, in 2002. Italian researchers estimated that, prior to Consip's establishment, some government agencies were paying over 50 percent more than others for routine items like gasoline, printers, paper, and phones.[3] This ended once Consip provided a price list, partly because dishonest bureaucrats could no longer get kickbacks in exchange for directing business to high-priced vendors, and partly because lazy bureaucrats didn't need to do any legwork to find the lowest-cost provider.[4] (Of course, if Consip officials themselves were corrupt, and took bribes from suppliers to get onto the national price list, offering centralizing procurement wouldn't have helped much.) Alternatively, anticorruption reformers can focus on increasing bribery's costs; for example, creating independent anticorruption enforcement authorities to increase the chances that corrupt officials get caught and stiffening punishments for those who do. This raises the point, which we treat in chapter 9, that for monitoring to be effective in reducing corruption, we need to find a way to get the monitors themselves to do their jobs effectively and honestly.

Changing the cost-benefit trade-offs faced by government officials is a fraught and uncertain process, however. One might be tempted to argue, for example, that standardizing decisions—as in the Italian procurement example given above—could keep officials honest. However, as we pointed out in section 4.4, many functions performed by government are idiosyncratic, with each military contract or road to be built differing slightly from the next. This inevitably leaves discretion in the hands of officials who award the missile or highway contract.[5]

These nuances should not obscure the fact that considering the trade-offs that officials confront in deciding whether to take bribes is an essential step in understanding why government employees take bribes. Put simply, they take bribes first and foremost to increase their incomes and when their fear of being caught and punished is low.

5.2 Why do politicians extort bribes?

Like the civil servants they deploy, elected politicians and political appointees take bribes to increase their private incomes. But they also divert some of the money for distinctly political purposes, using the proceeds to get themselves reelected.

There are two distinct reelection "technologies" that relate to bribe taking and embezzlement. The first aims at the deliberate conspicuous display of wealth to signal to voters access to resources. This is all too common in poor countries: the legislator who shows up in a remote rural village to campaign for reelection in a Mercedes SUV and sporting a Rolex. The candidate himself may enjoy the perks of a luxury car and fancy watch. But they are also aimed at appealing to voters as a demonstration that the candidate controls economic resources that—if reelected—he might share with voters. That the car and watch are obviously ill-gotten reinforces the notion that the community is stuck in a corrupt equilibrium where, given prevailing circumstances, the best way to better one's situation is to reelect—and then benefit from—corrupt politicians. Conversely, these conspicuous displays of assets obtained through dubious means can also serve as a subtle form of intimidation for those who might denounce corruption, given who is in power. (Unfortunately, these lavish displays may motivate others to follow a corrupt path, as they demonstrate that corruption pays.)

The second political purpose of bribe taking is to pay for political campaigns, either of individual candidates or for a political party more broadly. In many countries, candidates have to self-fund their campaigns. This is largely true in India and sub-Saharan Africa. It's also the case for European countries that use what is called "open-list proportional representation," an electoral system in which multiple legislators are elected from each parliamentary constituency. This allows voters to designate which individuals on a party's list of candidates they most favor. (This system put candidates from within the same party into competition with each other.) Self-funded electoral campaigns also occur in single-member district electoral systems that use primaries, such as the United States, where candidates seeking nomination need to cover the costs of primary races that take place within each political party. Finally, in closed-list proportional representation systems, parties compete against each other for votes, but may find that government-provided funds are inadequate.

Bribe taking is one way of raising the necessary campaign funds, especially where there are limits (legal or economic) on how much individual candidates or parties can raise. The most prominent example in recent years comes from the still-unfolding scandal at Brazil's state-owned oil company, Petrobras. The scandal revolves around nearly US$3 billion in bribes that contractors paid to Petrobras officials to secure construction and service contracts. Hundreds of millions of these dollars were diverted to the ruling Workers' Party, which used the money to finance its political campaigns.

Such practices have occurred even in countries that normally perform well in cross-country corruption rankings. In 1999, Helmut Kohl, the former German chancellor, admitted to accepting over two million Deutschmarks (well over a million U.S. dollars) in improper campaign donations—half of it from an arms dealer—on behalf of the Christian Democratic Union (CDU). The scandal uncovered a long-standing system of illegal contributions to the CDU, used by the party to fund political campaigns. The German case is, as we noted in chapter 2, hardly unique: illegal fund-raising linked to bribes in exchange for public contracts appears to be common across Europe, with scandals exposing illegal party financing in Hungary, Spain, Portugal, France, Italy, and Belgium. In the

Canadian province of Quebec, a massive bribe-for-contracts scandal—again with the proceeds deployed to run political campaigns—was uncovered by a long-running investigation that wrapped up in 2015. The resulting 1,600-page report described a web of corruption implicating local politicians, contractors, and organized crime groups.[6]

Turning to the cost side, many of the factors that limit bureaucrats' bribe taking apply equally to politicians—they sometimes get caught and punished. Even for the highest-level politicians, who are difficult to sanction, there is a cost to excessive corruption, since unrestrained bribe taking will destroy businesses that won't be around in the future to pay more bribes. It's the difference between grab-all-now and grab-over-time. Consider a rape-and-pillage kleptocrat like Mobutu Sese Seko of Zaire (now the Democratic Republic of the Congo), who spent public funds on, among other indulgences, flying a private Concorde to Paris for shopping sprees while Zaire's infrastructure and economy were left to decay. Contrast Mobutu with Indonesia's Suharto, who took the long view. Suharto amassed a family fortune that is said to have run into the billions, but nonetheless nurtured the economic growth of his country. The results are apparent if you examine the placement of the two countries in Figure 3.2: the average Indonesian is about 100 times wealthier than the average inhabitant of the Democratic Republic of the Congo.

It's more patience than selflessness that differentiates Suharto from Mobutu, as a wealthier Indonesian economy created a far bigger pie to tax and steal from. The eminent economist Mancur Olson distinguished roving bandits—who follow a scorched-earth policy of all-out theft—from stationary bandits who nurture growth so they can "harvest" greater tributes in years to come. If you get to pick your dictator, far better to go with the stationary sort.[7]

Case Study: Profiting from political office in India

Up to this point in the book, we've provided specific instances of politicians profiting from public office: the embezzled hospital or road funds, and the bribes extracted in exchange for wireless spectrum rights, construction licenses, or military contracts.[8] Most of what we know about politician wealth comes from these sorts of anecdotes—usually extreme ones, involving high-level politicians. And often as not, they're based on no more than hearsay and incomplete evidence: the rumors of billions accumulated by Vladimir Putin in Russia, the Suhartos in Indonesia, and the Qaddafis in Libya. Even the revelations from large-scale leaks such as the Panama Papers, which detailed the offshore holdings of politicians worldwide, provide only piecemeal evidence on how much politicians own, and where they keep it.

It used to be nearly impossible to measure the wealth of politicians, or the rate at which they grew their fortunes. Now, however, in the name of increased transparency, many governments require elected officials—as well as candidates running for office—to publicly declare their financial assets. Researchers are analyzing these data to gain a clearer picture of the degree to which politicians profit from public office.

One of us (Ray, in collaboration with Florian Schulz and Vikrant Vig) has used disclosure laws to study politician wealth in India, where it's been possible to keep tabs on what politicians have stashed away since 2003.[9] Our analysis was made possible by the efforts of the Association for Democratic Reforms (ADR), a nonprofit group that successfully petitioned the country's Supreme Court to require all candidates for state or federal office to provide detailed financial disclosures when filing their candidate papers. Disclosure requirements include a list of bank deposits and loans outstanding; stock portfolios; and the value of cars, jewelry, buildings, land, and other potentially valuable holdings. (Candidates are also required to list their educational credentials and any criminal history or indictments. A surprising fraction of Indian politicians—nearly a third—have criminal backgrounds to report.)

The study used a decade's worth of disclosure data, which meant that there had been at least two elections to every state legislative assembly in the country. This made it possible to calculate how fast the wealth of an elected Member of the Legislative Assembly (MLA) had grown during each term in office, at least for the state assembly members who sought reelection. Critically, there were also many candidates who lost in earlier elections who chose to run again. In fact, in many assembly constituencies—about 500 of those we studied—the winner faced off against exactly the same runner-up the next time around. This allowed us to benchmark the wealth accumulation of an MLA against that of an otherwise similar yet unsuccessful would-be politician who had made a living in the private sector between elections.

The Indian disclosure law generated some jaw-dropping figures. Most astonishing of all were the asset disclosures filed in 2004 and 2008 by Mayawati Kumari. In 2004, Kumari (known to the public by her first name, Mayawati) declared assets of US$400,000. For the next four years, she served as chief minister (a rank equivalent to state governor in the United States) of India's most populous (and reputedly very corrupt) state, Uttar Pradesh. When she came up for reelection in 2008, she declared US$13 million in assets. This represents a rate of asset growth of over 100 percent per year, all while earning an official annual salary of just US$30,000. (Mayawati was put under investigation for what are called "disproportionate assets"—wealth that exceeded what she could plausibly have afforded on her official salary—although the case was eventually dropped.)

When we look at the wealth accumulation for the full set of MLAs, most of whom are of the backbencher variety, the benefits of public office look decidedly more modest. The wealth of an elected MLA grows, on average, 3–5 percentage points faster relative to his runner-up. You might think that the candidate who prevails in the election is a smarter, better campaigner—that's why he won—and his bigger brain may also mean that he is better able to pick stocks and otherwise earn money more quickly than his opponent. But we found that the winner's premium for MLAs was even larger when we looked only at cases where the election had been decided by a margin of just a few percentage points—close enough that the outcome was essentially a matter of random chance.[10] The attributes of winners and losers in these very close elections were very similar, with roughly comparable initial wealth, education, and criminal histories.

For anyone familiar with the magic of compound interest, just 5 percent a year can add up pretty quickly—at the end of five years in office, winners end up with assets worth nearly 60 percent more than those of their unelected counterparts, or about US$50,000 in extra wealth. This is more than can be accounted for by the meager official salaries of state parliamentarians, earnings that were generally no more than a few thousand dollars a year during this period. (Mayawati, as chief minister of India's most populous state, had a much higher official salary than most of the MLAs in our dataset.)

But that 3–5 percent difference between winners and losers obscures some important details. First, in high-corruption Indian states, the benefit to holding office is far, far higher—10 percent per year versus near zero in low-corruption states. Second, there is a much bigger divergence between winner and runner-up asset growth when it comes to members of state cabinets. (Keep in mind that Indian states all operate as parliamentary systems, where government ministers are typically selected from elected legislators—those are the state-level cabinet positions we are discussing here.) MLAs who are appointed to cabinet-level posts in the state's Council of Ministers see their wealth grow at a rate that is 15 percent faster than the rate of runners-up. By the time they finish a five-year term in office, they've got more than double the wealth of lower-level MLAs. Once you take MLAs who become ministers out of the picture and compare winners to losers, the MLAs who are left behind don't do any better financially than election losers. The fortunes made by state ministers aren't a smoking gun—cabinet posts aren't handed out randomly, so someone with the smarts to be appointed minister may also be a better investor than a backbencher. But this result still suggests that watchdog organizations like the ADR should take an especially careful look at the land deals and bank transactions of state ministers and their families.[11]

This approach is by no means without its problems: we only account for the wealth that MLAs themselves report in their disclosure documents. Funds or jewelry may be hidden in foreign accounts, secreted away in bank vaults, or "loaned" to cousins—though given these holes in the disclosure laws, it is all the more surprising that the data reveal the rich returns of state ministers they do. To the extent that disclosure requirements are comparable across countries, one advantage of this approach is that we can accumulate evidence for a wider set of nations to compare the degree to which officeholders in different political environments or economic conditions benefit from getting elected. We know of studies exploiting asset disclosures to analyze politician wealth in several Scandinavian countries, the United Kingdom, and the United States during the nineteenth century, for instance, and more are surely on the way.[12]

Asset disclosure studies cannot tell us where the extra money comes from. Though we cannot provide direct evidence, we infer that some substantial fraction of it likely comes from bribe taking and embezzlement. Nor do we know what the politicians with these excess assets do with them. Mayawati Kumari, for instance, is well known for her conspicuous displays of personal wealth—and also for her lavish campaign spending, vote buying, and gift giving. Thus, while asset disclosures do not yield definitive proof of corruption, they provide useful information to voters, researchers, and enforcement authorities on which politicians in their midst may require further scrutiny.

5.3 How do we incorporate morality into our model of bribe giving and taking?

If you think this chapter's discussion up to this point takes a hyperrational view of human decision-making, you're not

alone. People sometimes make choices based on principle rather than payoff, or they act on the basis of
emotion—impetuously and rashly, in the heat of the moment.
But the existence of moral commitments and human emotion
doesn't preclude the sort of rational-minded cost-benefit
calculations we've invoked above: if the price of gasoline
doubles tomorrow, you'll drive less—that is an economic, not
emotional, response. Similarly, if the punishment for bribery
is made twice as harsh or the chances of getting caught are
doubled, there's good reason to expect less corruption. This is
all the more true for full-time politicians whose energies are
focused on calculations of how best to further their political
goals, first and foremost on how to gain reelection. They're
as hyperrational a group as any we can imagine. This isn't
to diminish the role of ethics, but rather to emphasize that
the rational terms in which social scientists have traditionally
framed decision-making can get us quite far in understanding
the decision to behave corruptly.

One way to incorporate the ethics, morals, and emotions of
individuals into this framework is to view feelings as a part of
the larger set of preferences that people operate with (rather
than as a fixed barrier to giving or receiving bribes). Inevitably,
we end up making trade-offs in satisfying some preferences
at the expense of others. You may have a moral sense that
says that extorting bribes is wrong, while also responding to
other pressures and incentives. You may not like paying bribes,
but you don't want to lose your job either, and you need to
provide for your family. Also, you want to fit in with what
others around you are doing. Every individual has a different
balance between the prosaic demands of society and the claims
of conscience. The more demanding one's local environment,
the stronger one's moral fiber has to be to resist the calls of
corruption. At some point, many succumb.

If we don't consider, say, the costs of going against one's
conscience or acting contrary to social pressure, our framework for thinking about corruption can be misleading in
important ways. A reasonable approach to understanding

corruption takes into account human nature's mix of both rational calculation and emotion. This tension was well recognized by, among others, James Madison, the "Father of America's Constitution," who observed in 1788 that voters would need to have "virtue and intelligence to select men of virtue and wisdom." He went on to argue that if there was no virtue among legislators, "we are in a wretched situation. No theoretical checks—no form of government can render us secure."[13]

Below (and elsewhere in the book), we'll take up some aspects of corruption that don't fit neatly into the standard rational choice framework—the pangs of conscience; the social pressures to do the right (or the wrong) thing. But just as virtue is necessary for honest government, some checks and oversight are surely necessary to limit the rational-minded temptations that officials will inevitably face. In the world's least corrupt countries, politicians have so internalized these checks that they have become a form of common morality.

5.4 How do politicians foster corruption among bureaucrats?

Thus far in this chapter, we have discussed civil servants and elected political leaders as if they each independently decided whether to engage in corruption. If it were that simple, reducing bureaucratic corruption would be pretty easy: politicians could just appoint some independent auditor or monitor to watch the bureaucrats. But the world doesn't work that way. It's more apt to be the opposite, with politicians deliberately using their powers of appointment to hire bureaucrats who will abuse their positions in part to help secure reelection for their patrons.

Where they can, elected officials often use their control over jobs in the public sector to grow and fortify their political support. Patronage appointments, which we discussed in chapter 2, provide elected officials opportunities to offer jobs to loyal followers. Those supporters, in turn, know to whom they owe their livelihoods, and are happy enough to do their patrons' bidding in order to keep them in office. The appointed bureaucrat's job—and his family's well-being—may depend on it.

When a government position can be filled without consideration of merit or qualifications, the job is usually considered a patronage appointment. As we discussed in chapter 2, a patronage appointment is not itself necessarily illegal (although evading civil service regulations to make patronage appointments often is), but what happens after the appointment occurs may well be. Persons appointed to government jobs who owe their positions to a political superior are easily pressured to use the resources at their disposal to help their patron gain reelection—after all, if he fails to be reelected, the appointee may find himself out of a job, demoted, or transferred to a less opportune location. In nineteenth-century America, for instance, every congressman was able to appoint hundreds of postmasters to the post offices located in his district. The postmasters, in turn, regularly inserted election campaign materials for their congressman into the mail they distributed in their communities. Their appointments were perfectly legal, but using their offices for partisan political purposes was not.[14]

Patronage politics is alive and well today. Budget crises from Brazil to South Africa are blamed on bloated government payrolls that serve primarily as vote-buying patronage networks for ruling politicians.[15] These networks, in turn, help ensure that the politicians who are ultimately responsible for the chronic misuse of public office remain in power.

An interesting example of how patronage appointments intersect with and exacerbate electoral fraud—and thus, reelection success—comes from a study that economist Michael Callen and political scientist James Long conducted in Afghanistan in 2010.[16] Callen and Long studied fraud in the process of aggregating vote totals across polling places. How did they know vote fraud was taking place given that, like corruption, it is something that perpetrators do their best to hide? The researchers were helped by the fact that the corruption of Afghan elections was of a particularly observable and straightforward kind. Votes in the elections were counted locally, then the ballots were passed up to a regional authority to be added to countrywide totals. Callen and Long simply went to polling stations and took photos of the sheets of paper that showed the vote tallies on the day of the election and compared these results to the totals reported at a higher level of aggregation. There were often discrepancies between the two figures: nearly 80 percent of polling place results differed from the aggregated totals. At least some of the fraud could be tied more directly to the system of patronage that political leaders in this notoriously corrupt country had put in place. Callen and Long report that legislative candidates with personal connections to the election officer in charge of the aggregation process received an average of 3.5 fraudulent additional votes per polling station (about 13.7 percent of their polling station average). Callen and Long interpret this as evidence that election officials, who are supposed to be politically neutral and nonpartisan government employees, were helping "their" candidates win by committing vote fraud—a form of patronage payback to friends in high places.

What Callen and Long observe is far from unique to the political dysfunction of Afghanistan. Where public officials owe their jobs to a specific politician, they're well motivated to see that person remain in office. A study conducted in the 1970s in India by Robert Wade uncovered an extraordinary pattern to the hierarchies of corruption there.[17] Wade describes a system that worked as follows: the engineers who opened and closed the sluices in the canals in one south Indian state demanded bribes from the farmers who needed water to irrigate their crops. So far, that's a pretty simple (if ugly) exchange. But the engineers kept their posts by the grace and goodwill of politicians above them. The engineers couldn't be fired, but politicians had regular opportunities to transfer uncooperative ones to other, less lucrative locales. So part of the money raised through bribes from farmers was passed up to politicians, lest they act on the threat of sending canal operators to less desirable postings.

The case of Indian canal irrigation illustrates aspects of corrupt hierarchies that makes them so resistant to external control. Politicians and government bureaucrats collude in corruption, so it is near-impossible to get one group to report on or monitor the other. You can't ask politicians to limit the bribe taking of civil servants if the very same politicians are benefiting from the bribes that are collected. These durable connections between politicians and civil servants thereby form systems of corruption that are particularly difficult to expose and untangle, as we have already noted in chapter 2. In settings where corruption takes root, individuals who do not wish to participate in the system—and who thus represent a threat to its secrecy and security—are not hired in the first place, pressured or manipulated into colluding, or transferred out. The "collectivization of corruption," as it has been called, makes for robust collusive networks that are very effective in neutralizing potential threats. One China expert recounts the story of the hapless customs official sent to Zhanjiang—a port city notorious for smuggling—to curb corruption who succumbed to the wiles of a female smuggler. Once lured into the smuggling racket, the would-be exposer worked with the hundreds of other customs officials, ranging all the way up to the city's vice mayor, to conceal and perpetuate a massive operation that ultimately implicated more than a hundred officials, and resulted in death sentences for six major offenders in 1999.[18] The value of goods involved was estimated by *The Economist* to have been more than US$7 billion.[19]

This section describes what is an essential component to a corrupt equilibrium: in exploiting their positions, there is a mutual dependence among officials in various positions up the hierarchy of government. Bureaucrats' bribe taking depends on the corruption of politicians, and vice versa. If it is difficult to disrupt a corrupt equilibrium, this mutual dependence is an important reason why.

5.5 Why do individual companies pay bribes?

Much corruption would end today if companies refused to pay bribes to government officials. It would seem that bribes are an additional cost of doing business, so why don't companies just stop paying?

To think about this, we'll take the same rational-minded perspective we've used earlier in this chapter, with the difference that we'll model companies as maximizing profits rather than happiness. The desire for profits isn't evil: it can motivate companies to develop better products, treat their customers well, and maybe even pay their workers more (if they believe a happy worker is a more productive one).[20] But pursuit of profits also leads companies to peddle subprime mortgages, pollute lakes and rivers, and pay bribes.

All too often, discussions about business and bribery focus on trading off profitability in the short- versus long-run. Certainly there are long-term risks from bribery—the possibility of punishment, or the worry that a bribe-taking official will fail to make good on awarding a contract or providing a license (though a corrupt bureaucrat who doesn't deliver won't be long in business). We *wish* that it were possible to make the case against corruption on this basis alone, since it would imply that we could end bribery by appealing to the enlightened long-term self-interest of shareholders and executives.[21]

But the reality is that, for many businesses today, paying bribes has been highly profitable—even over the long-run. Sure, there are companies that get busted. Siemens management, for example, might regret paying off procurement officials worldwide to secure contracts for, among other things, hospital equipment supplies in Russia, power generation in Malaysia, and subway signaling devices in China. That's because they got caught, and paid US$1.6 billion in fines in 2008.

By definition, it's hard to say how many companies have done the same and gotten away with it, but we'd conjecture more than a few. (It's even possible that, despite being caught, the bribes were nonetheless worth it for Siemens, given the profits they made from the many contracts they won as a result.) In some industries and in some locations, it may simply be impossible to get contracts without offering a bribe to sweeten the deal.

Businesses are not always victims of corrupt officials; they sometimes actively instigate the transactions. In Nigeria, for instance, where 41 percent of firms expect to make regular "informal payments" to government officials in order to "get things done," a set of semistructured interviews with entrepreneurs found them to be active perpetrators of bribery rather than victims of extortion.[22] That said, these actions are embedded in a culture of corruption, where expectations and norms for bribe paying are clearly understood by all involved. In such cases, it thus becomes difficult to distinguish perpetrator from victim.

Does that mean that all firms in high-corruption environments succumb to the culture around them and pay bribes? Not at all. Even in Nigeria, for instance, interviews revealed a handful of companies that refused to pay bribes outright.[23] The firms suffered, as they were frozen out of doing business with the government as a result. Thus, while it's possible to resist paying bribes even in places where it's the norm, it's costly to do so.

Case Study: The value of political connections in Indonesia and in the United States

What's it worth to be the president's son?[24] Ask the average Indonesian in 1990, and he would almost surely have told you that it's worth a whole lot. How else could then-President Suharto's son, Mandala Putra Suharto, have afforded his multimillion-dollar vacation homes and fleet of luxury automobiles? The exploits of Tommy, as he's still known, were a window into the privileged lives of the Indonesian First Family. Tommy driving around Jakarta in his Rolls-Royce; Tommy attending a celebrity-studded black tie dinner; Tommy with his latest supermodel girlfriend—so that's what being the president's son is worth!

How did he afford it? Suharto family firms—those run by Tommy and two of his siblings, Bambang and Tutut—did remarkably well securing government contracts: Tommy was selected to spearhead government-subsidized efforts to develop a "made-in-Indonesia" national car, and one of Tutut's companies won the bid to build toll roads through the nation's capital, Jakarta. From electric power projects to roads to timber, someone in the president's family saw a piece of the action.

But to his dying days, Suharto denied that his children's successes in business were the result of anything other than shrewd investment acumen and management talent. So, was the Suharto family reputation for corruption well-deserved? Or were his children found guilty by association?

In a 2001 study, one of us attempted to resolve the question of what connections to the Indonesian First Family were worth, by examining the real-stakes bets that investors made on the value of companies traded on the Jakarta Stock Exchange.[25] Economists frequently make use of stock market data to figure out how different circumstances and company attributes affect its long-term profits. A stock, or share, in a company is essentially a tiny ownership stake that gives its owner a claim over future profits. Apple, for example, has about six billion shares, so each one gives the owner a claim on 1/6,000,000,000th of the profits the company earns. At the time of writing, the company's share price was about US$110 dollars. If investors believed that this was less than you'd get by taking a six-billionth of Apple's yearly profits, they would drive up the price by trying to buy more shares. If they believed the price was too high, it'd be driven down by investors trying to unload their shares.

There's a constant flow of information that affects a company's profits, and hence what investors are willing to pay for ownership stakes in the form of shares. For example, a medical breakthrough will send a biotech company's price through the roof—future profits with the blockbuster drug will be higher than without it. When Volkswagen's share price fell by over a third on September 18, 2015, in reaction to revelations that it had illegally manipulated emissions tests, it tells us something about what investors believe the scandal will cost the company in terms of fines, vehicle recalls, and reputation. More generally, by analyzing the ups and downs of companies' share prices we can learn a lot about what drives corporate profits (or at least investors' perceptions of them).

We apply this approach to examine how much of the Suharto family firms' profits were the result of connections to the president, by analyzing how investors responded to news that led to worries that these ties were at risk of disappearing.

The shocks to connections we consider relate to the president's health. By the mid-1990s, Suharto was already well into his seventies. Every few months, there were rumors that he had fallen ill. Each time, the stock market went down. There were concerns about the leadership vacuum he would leave behind and the chaos that might ensue. That's bad for everyone's business. But if political connections matter for company profits, we'd expect that well-connected companies' stock prices would suffer more. By comparing the share price changes of well-connected companies to those of firms built more on product quality and management expertise, we can put a market value on connections.[26]

We illustrate our approach in Figure 5.1, which shows stock price movements around July 4, 1996, when the government announced that President Suharto would fly to Germany for a health checkup. That may not sound like a medical emergency, but no one travels ten time zones for a routine physical. Investors at the stock exchange were inundated with rumors that Suharto had already suffered a stroke, or might be headed to Frankfurt for emergency heart surgery. The Jakarta Composite Index (JCI), an indicator of Indonesian stocks' overall performance, much like New York's Dow Jones Index, fell by 2.3 percent on the day of the news.

Things were far, far worse for Bimantara Citra and its boss, Bambang Suharto (one of the Suharto children). In the weeks leading up to the July 4 announcement, Figure 5.1 shows both the JCI and the price of Bimantara Citra bounced around a bit, not gaining or losing very much. Then, with the market awash with rumors on July 4 and 5, Bimantara's stock price took a nosedive: the prospect of a connectionless Bimantara led shareholders to dump their shares, driving its price down by more than 10 percent in just two days.

The following week, Suharto's German doctors gave him a clean bill of health. The reports of imminent bypass surgery turned out to be pure rumormongering, and all of Suharto's test results looked good. In fact, he lived another decade, until 2008. With its connections now more secure, for the moment at least, Bimantara shares all of a sudden looked like a relative bargain. Investors snapped up Bimantara shares and its price jumped back up—although not quite back to its pre-checkup levels. The trip to Germany had clearly reminded investors that Suharto and his regime couldn't last forever, making them that much more cautious about the long-term prospects for Bimantara Citra's political ties and profits.

How much were political connections worth overall? By examining the stock price movements of Bimantara Citra and dozens of other companies with varying degrees of connections over six separate episodes that led investors to worry about Suharto's health, we come up with a figure of about 25 percent as the fraction of well-connected companies' value that can be attributed to their presidential ties. That's comparable to the fraction of Volkswagen's value that was destroyed when its emissions fabrication came to light, tarnishing its brand, ruining its relationships with regulators and customers, and leading to the recall of more than ten million vehicles.

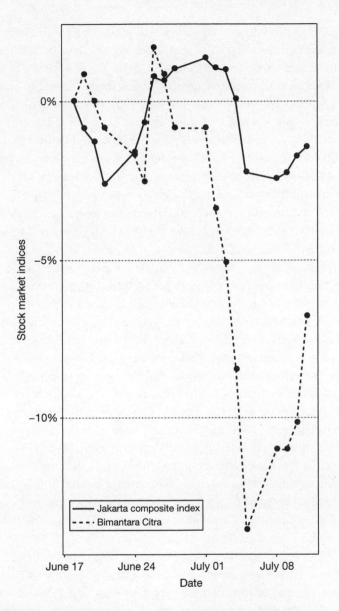

Figure 5.1 Line Graphs of Daily Stock Price Movements for the Indonesia Stock Exchange and for PT Bimantara Citra (June 18–July 12, 1996)

When Apple released the iPhone to much fanfare in 2006, its share price went up by about 8 percent. By any benchmark, connections in Suharto's Indonesia were worth a lot.[27]

We can take the same approach used for Indonesia to study corruption in other countries where there's an active stock market, again using investors' bets to back out a measure of how they value political ties. This includes the United States. Consider the case of Vice President Dick Cheney, who arrived in Washington in 2000 after a stint as CEO of energy services giant Halliburton. During the election campaign, concerns of corporate favoritism emerged, which only intensified with the lucrative no-bid contracts awarded to Halliburton and others during the Iraq War.

If the U.S. vice president had been instrumental in generating government contracts for Halliburton, the company's stock price should have suffered each time Cheney got his heart checked, and his heart attacks (November 2000 and March 2001) and blood clots (September 2005 and March 2007) should have made investors *very* anxious. Yet each time Cheney's health was in the news, Halliburton's stock price barely budged; the share prices of other companies with personal ties to Cheney failed to respond to his health problems as well. These nonresults indicate the limits of political favors in Washington. A number of factors could account for this: as vice president, Cheney's every decision was intensely scrutinized by numerous watchdog organizations and media outlets spanning the ideological spectrum, and their frequent warnings of potential conflicts of interest may have helped to limit his favor giving, rather than reveal it.

This isn't to say that connections in the United States don't matter. If that were true, we'd have a hard time explaining the scramble to hire members of Congress and their staffers as lobbyists and corporate executives when they leave government.[28] But these connections are at least more visible and, in theory, reined in by the regulations and laws that govern them. This sets them apart from the illicit favor-trading that defined business in Suharto's Indonesia, and continues to play a role in commerce in much of the world.

The cases of Suharto and Cheney fit with the more general findings of economist Mara Faccio, who has applied the stock market event study method to measuring the value of connections between members of corporate boards and politicians across the globe. To create a comprehensive political connectedness index, she's followed the political careers of business tycoons as well as the business careers of politicians, traced bloodlines to detect family ties, and read the society columns of local newspapers to find out who dines with whom. One particularly striking observation from Faccio's study is the preponderance of close political-corporate ties in most countries. In Russia in the 1990s, she estimates that fully 87 percent of the Moscow Stock Exchange's value was held by companies with close Kremlin ties. Maybe this isn't such a shock in the Wild West capitalism of post-Soviet Russia. More surprisingly, nearly 40 percent of the London Stock Exchange was politically connected at that time. And as Faccio observes, her approach misses some political ties, so these are underestimates.[29]

Faccio then estimates the value of these connections by taking advantage of close election outcomes—outcomes that produce unexpected governments with (therefore) unexpected corporate connections.[30] She finds that even in countries where political ties are common, there are large differences in how the markets value them. At one extreme, there's the United Kingdom. While business-politics connections are very common there, Faccio finds that when these ties are unexpectedly strengthened, stock prices of affected companies don't budge. By contrast, in Faccio's native Italy—true to the Hollywood stereotype—insider connections do matter. For example, as we observed in chapter 2, the Italian Senate appointment of leading Fiat shareholder Giovanni Agnelli boosted his company's stock price by 3.4 percent, which translates into billions of dollars in additional value.

This line of research gives us a clearer sense of how commonplace political connections are, and how much those in businesses with connections to political elites profit from them. Much of what this research has found won't shock or surprise anyone on the streets of Jakarta or Rome. But the findings are useful in getting past cheap talk on the topic by those who, like the Suhartos, have every incentive to underestimate the value of connections, and those who may be motivated to overestimate them (like political opponents of Suharto). And it can also help in those cases, like Cheney and Halliburton, where popular perceptions about the value of connections may be out of line with the underlying realities.

We've provided these insights without ever having had to ask investors or other experts about how important political ties are to a business's profits: the market itself provides the answer.

5.6 Why don't companies band together to refuse to pay bribes?

The preceding section takes the perspective of a single company, which often finds it to be profitable to pay bribes given its particular circumstances. But that doesn't mean that companies are made better off as a group when they *all* pay bribes rather than collectively refusing to engage in corruption. Available evidence—which we cover in chapter 4—indicates that corruption is harmful to business growth and investment, so the corruption-free scenario should be preferable to business generally. Why, then, don't business owners band together to repudiate corruption?

To appreciate why it's so hard for a group of companies to pull this off, it's useful to think of the situation facing them as a *prisoners' dilemma*, which, in its classic formulation, presents the following quandary to a pair of criminals. Both have been arrested, and the cops are trying to elicit a confession from each suspect separately, offering the same deal: if the suspect confesses while his partner remains silent, the confessor goes free and the silent one suffers the full force of the law—say, ten years in jail. If both remain silent, the police don't have enough evidence to push for a harsh sentence, so each one gets only a few months of jail time. Finally, if each betrays the other, the cops will have their charges, but also go easier on the prisoners for cooperating; both receive a year-long sentence.[31]

Do you betray your partner or remain silent, even though he won't know your choice when he makes his decision?

If each prisoner cares only about serving the least amount of jail time, the "rational" choice leads both to confession and betrayal, because you get less prison time that way regardless of what your partner chooses to do. If your partner confesses, you get one year in jail instead of ten by confessing; if he stays silent, you can still get a few months less prison time (and screw your partner over) by confessing and going free. No matter what the other does, each prisoner is best off confessing. The dilemma is that both could be better off if only they'd both stay quiet. The cruel genius of the prisoners' dilemma is that selfish motivations undermine the common good.

Companies in a corrupt environment face, in effect, a prisoners' dilemma: the rational, profit-maximizing choice is to pay bribes, *regardless* of what other companies choose to do. If others offer bribes, you need to follow suit to compete on an even footing, or else go bankrupt. If other businesses stay honest (the equivalent of remaining silent in the classic prisoners' dilemma), by paying bribes you'll get rich by winning every contract that's put up for bid. This leads to an ever-present temptation to deviate from a no-bribe agreement, making such pacts inherently unstable.

We cannot, therefore, expect that businesses will end corruption through collective self-interest and action. We might be able to nudge them along, though, by altering the cost-benefit trade-off they face. If we are successful in increasing enforcement or sanctions such that some companies see bribery as more cost than benefit, we might be able to set off a virtuous cycle of stronger enforcement and ever-fewer bribe-paying firms. The reason is that companies that decide to stop paying bribes turn from adversaries into allies in fighting corruption, since they will see themselves as disadvantaged relative to those firms that continue to pay bribes.

This reasoning can help to explain why U.S. companies lobbied for years to have other nations adopt more stringent laws against paying bribes abroad. American firms have been barred from paying bribes to public officials in other countries since 1977, with the passage of the Foreign Corrupt Practices Act (FCPA). The FCPA, U.S. firms argued, put them at a disadvantage in competing with businesses from other countries, like Germany, the Netherlands, and Switzerland, where no such law existed.[32] The efforts of U.S. firms finally bore fruit in 1997, when the Anti-Bribery Convention was signed by members of the Organization for Economic Cooperation and Development (OECD), which includes all of the world's richest nations. The convention committed all OECD countries to put in place legislation akin to the FCPA, thereby criminalizing bribery of foreign officials for most companies worldwide.

Are there still OECD companies that pay bribes abroad? Of course.[33] Enforcement of anticorruption laws has been lax in many member nations. And despite increased enforcement in the United States and elsewhere, there will always be businesses that are tempted to get a leg up through whatever means and whatever the risk. If we can't end bribery—and we don't take this as a realistic goal—at least we can get more companies to see corruption as more cost than benefit, and enlist them as allies in the larger fight against corruption.

5.7 What do ordinary people think about corruption?

Most people say they don't like corruption, but they deal with it because they have little choice. Take one recent example from the Eurobarometer, a representative opinion survey of European citizens that has been run since 1973. In a study published in 2014, the Eurobarometer reported that the vast majority of Greeks and Italians—who live in countries perennially plagued by corruption—said that it was *never* acceptable to give gifts or money to public officials in exchange for a favor. When asked about the prevalence of corruption, nearly every respondent in both countries (99 percent in Greece; 97 percent in Italy) said that corruption was widespread.[34] A Pew Research Center Global Attitudes Survey from 2014 interviewed people in thirty-four countries in five regions across the world (the Middle East, Asia, Latin America, Africa, and Eastern Europe) about the problems facing their country. Corruption was ranked the second-biggest concern, after crime. On average, 76 percent of respondents reported that corruption is a "very big problem" facing their country. This ranges from a low of 23 percent in Jordan to a high of 90 percent in Tanzania. This percentage has increased over time. Pew had previously run a similar survey in 2007, at which point 63 percent of respondents reported corruption was a "very big problem" facing their nation; 73 percent of respondents from countries included in the earlier survey gave this response in 2014.[35]

We expect that most of the respondents to these surveys do not habitually pay bribes themselves (recall that a study on bribe experiences that we describe in chapter 2 indicates that, even in highly corrupt west African nations, less than a fifth of ordinary citizens reported having paid a bribe in the prior year). We thus interpret the high rate of condemnation of corruption as disapproval of bribe paying by others—for instance, bribe paying by businesses to boost profits—rather than condemnation of grandma's right to see a doctor.

5.8 If they don't like corruption, why do individual citizens pay bribes?

Where corruption is the norm—that is, in societies that have settled into a high-corruption equilibrium—citizens pay bribes to officials because it is expected and necessary in order to obtain government services, often of the most routine kind. Healthcare, for example, typically appears atop survey respondents' lists of sectors where bribery is most common.[36] Imagine arriving at the hospital with a desperately sick family member and being asked to pay a bribe before you can see the triage nurse—few would have the "virtue" to resist. Similar pressures may exist to obtain exam grades from a school registrar, to get water service, and to have a court case heard—all government entitlements that citizens in less corrupt countries take for granted. It's a simple cost-benefit calculus, one that heavily favors just paying the bribe, especially if it's a relatively small one.

If there's a temptation to jump the queue or otherwise get ahead, odds are others are already doing it. And "everyone is doing it" is the all-powerful rationalization that we all use to do something that we know we shouldn't do that we do anyway. It's just one example of what social psychologists call *self-serving bias*, a powerful idea for understanding how individuals distort their perception of reality to maintain their self-esteem and belief in their own virtue. A large majority of citizens in just about every country believes that paying bribes is inexcusable. In a culture where bribe paying is a part of daily life, it's only human nature to search for justifications of what is so often necessary just to get by. Auditors at Enron may have glossed over the company's accounting shenanigans deliberately, knowing that its finances were a complete fraud. Or they may have misled *themselves* into believing corporate executives' explanations of off-balance-sheet transactions because, if they couldn't convince themselves of it, they would surely risk losing a valuable client.

An intriguing experimental study suggests a direct role for self-serving bias in dishonest behavior.[37] The subjects in the experiment were students from a large university in Argentina who were brought to a computer lab to play a game in which they were given the chance to "steal" from one another. Many subjects chose to take money from each other, and they justified it with the belief (or excuse) that the other subject would also engage in stealing. In fact, subjects consistently overestimated the chances of being paired with a thief—you need to believe that's so in order to justify your own stealing—and did so despite being paid for accuracy in predicting whether their partner would steal.

Thus begins the slippery slope, however. Once you've justified paying a bribe to obtain a grade, will you pay something extra to have a C turned into a B? Or an A? If you'll pay to have a case heard, would you spend a little more to have the ruling go your way? There are powerful forces that can impel citizens of already-corrupt countries to worsen the never-ending cycle of bribe payments and bribe demands.

So although on the whole we view the bribe paying of ordinary citizens as evidence that they are victims of more powerfully placed individuals in their societies, it's important also to observe that when an average person pays a bribe, she becomes complicit in the system and an accessory to illegal behavior. Paying a bribe, even under duress, changes one's tolerance for corruption, creating a greater likelihood that the payer will justify persistent corruption as necessary and tolerable. It thus contributes to a culture of corruption.

5.9 What did we learn in chapter 5?

- Conceiving of corruption as an economic cost-benefit trade-off is a useful starting point for understanding why public officials embezzle or take bribes. We can think of ethical concerns as constituting an additional "cost" to an individual's willingness to behave corruptly.
- Politicians additionally engage in corruption to fund their reelection bids. The proceeds may be used to fund political campaigns and to finance vote-buying efforts.
- Corruption among politicians and bureaucrats is often linked: bureaucrats depend on politicians for their bribe-taking positions, and must in turn pass on a portion of the proceeds to politicians to finance their reelection efforts.
- Companies pay bribes to avoid regulations or to beat out competitors with the ultimate objective of increasing profits. For an individual firm, bribery pays.

- For companies as a group, profits might increase if they could band together and refuse to pay bribes. But no-corruption agreements are hard to maintain because of each company's individual bribe-paying incentives. The situation facing firms is an illustration of the prisoners' dilemma.
- Survey evidence indicates that private citizens overwhelmingly believe that corruption is wrong. But to some extent they are victims of their circumstance—when bribe paying is the norm, it is very costly not to follow along.

6

WHAT ARE THE CULTURAL BASES OF CORRUPTION?

For social scientists, the term "culture" evokes a particular meaning: it's a combination of values and norms that defines how individuals in a society behave and interact. We'll see that the "norms" part of this definition of culture aligns nicely with the idea of equilibrium that we have emphasized throughout the book, and our discussion of norms will emphasize culture-as-equilibrium. But we'll also explore whether thinking about culture as particular sets of values is useful for understanding corruption. That is, maybe some groups or even entire societies simply have values that are more tolerant of corruption. We can't discuss culture, and cultures of corruption, without allowing for that possibility. So in the latter part of this chapter, we'll examine whether some groups—based on ethnicity, religion, or historical identity—tend to be more permissive of corruption than others.

6.1 What is meant by a culture of corruption?

Let's start with the more general question: "What is culture?" It is tempting to put the term in that vast category of phenomena defined by examples, that is, "I know it when I see it"—the fact that a greeting comes in the form of a bow in Japan but a kiss in Italy; that no one wears a jacket or, God forbid, a tie to work in Silicon Valley, whereas at law firms in midtown Manhattan, you see nothing but suits. We'll also include, as components of culture, the little angel and devil perched on our shoulders telling us what's good and bad, right and wrong. Help an old lady cross the street; don't steal; don't kill.

Whether angel or devil, we can think about culture as an inner voice that provides guidance on how to act in the absence of law, or a rule book telling us what to do. It's part conscience. You give up your seat to an elderly stranger on the bus to avoid pangs of guilt or dirty looks from fellow riders, not fear of arrest. But it's also coordinating your actions with those of people around you. There's nothing inherently better about kissing or bowing, but it makes for more efficient and less awkward introductions if both sides know the norm.

What we mean by a culture of corruption follows straightforwardly from this general definition. First, it may be that some societies have fewer moral qualms about bribe giving and taking. (Later in the chapter, we will turn to the question of whether "cultural" traits affect attitudes toward corruption.) Second, we can think about a culture of corruption as a mutually consistent and reinforcing set of norms about bribery. This notion of a culture of corruption dovetails with our framing of corruption as a social equilibrium, which, as we've emphasized from the outset, can help us understand how two communities with comparable ethics and similar levels of anticorruption enforcement can nonetheless end up with very different rates of corruption.

We suspect that the "coordination" view of a culture of corruption is less likely to be familiar to the reader, so to illustrate, we begin with a simple example, which reprises and expands upon our equilibrium discussion from chapter 1. Consider a driver who's pulled over for speeding. To focus on the coordination aspect, put aside the ethics of the situation for the moment. Would you recommend that the driver offer a bribe in lieu of paying a fine? Your answer probably depends on whether you believe the driver is dealing with a policeman who's open to taking bribes, or a cop of the law-and-order variety who will reward bribers with a night in jail. In other words, your answer hinges on whether you think the interaction is taking place in a high-corruption society, where bribe taking is common, or a low-corruption society, where bribe taking is unusual.

Again, putting ethics aside, what advice would you give to the cop? Should he try to extract a bribe from the driver or issue a ticket that will allow the local government to collect a fine? It again depends on what he expects from the driver: if the motorist is happy to pay $5 directly to the policeman in order to avoid paying a $10 fine, then demanding a bribe is the cop's income-maximizing option; if the driver will refuse to comply with a bribe request, a bribe-demanding cop may find himself under investigation or out of a job.

It's important that bribe exchanges be routine, because the interaction only works when both parties have mutually consistent expectations for how a traffic stop works: demand and offer a bribe or issue a ticket and pay the fine. Mismatched expectations lead to trouble for one or both of them: the driver spends a night in jail, the cop loses his job, or the two parties spend hours locked in a stalemate and misunderstanding on the side of the road. Offering a bribe in Denmark or refusing to pay one in Benin is the equivalent of bear-hugging a business acquaintance in Japan, or offering only a bow in Italy.

A friend of ours, political scientist Jasper Cooper, experienced the utter routineness of traffic bribery of exactly the sort we just described during a series of long drives—totaling some 1,500 kilometers—accompanying truckers through West Africa.[1] Cooper wanted to observe firsthand the nature of bribe paying to officials manning the many checkpoints that dot the highways of Africa. In a single ride, a trucker might be stopped dozens of times by police, customs officers, gendarmerie, and various other types of government officials. As might be expected, Cooper found that the process of paying bribes conformed to a standard script that was followed by both sides.

Even when the security officials observed a young white man (thus possibly a foreigner) in the front seat with the driver, they demanded bribes of about the same size and at about the same rate as when the driver appeared alone. (Cooper knows this because sometimes he hid in the backseat, out of sight of security officials.) In his experience, bribe paying clearly consisted of stable and mutual expectations of what to do at a highway checkpoint: pay the bribe. It's what we'd call a culture of corruption.

The stakes are relatively small for a traffic stop, but a similar model governs favor-trading of greater consequence. Imagine that you're looking to get the contract to build a billion-dollar toll road through Bangkok. Just like a driver who is pulled over for an illegal left turn, you need to assess whether the city's mayor is the "type" who will take a bribe, and he needs to determine whether you're really offering a bribe or are instead part of a media sting operation aiming to take down the government. It's useful if everyone has the same stable and rehearsed expectations about how business and government work together, and if there are no surprises about what's in play.

Sometimes outsiders have the wrong set of expectations about how to behave. Finance professor Andres Liberman (also Ray's former Ph.D. student) offers the following illustration: every so often, Liberman recalls, a story would appear in his hometown Santiago newspaper describing the plight of a hapless American or European backpacker who presumed that everything south of Texas was one amorphous mass of South American corruption. The ill-informed traveler discovered, on trying to pay off a cop or customs official, that he'd arrived in the law-abiding and orderly nation of Chile (ranked 21 in the world, just behind the United States and Ireland in Transparency International's corruption rankings in 2014).[2] His night in jail hopefully provided a valuable lesson in the perils of making such cultural generalizations.

6.2 Can we change individual attitudes toward corruption?

The preceding anecdote suggests quite a bit of ethical mal-leability on matters of corruption: when in Rome, you try to do as Romans do. We've both heard plenty of colleagues and acquaintances tell of encounters with police or other officials in Asia or Africa or South America that ended in bribe payments to get out of whatever trouble they'd gotten themselves into. We'd conjecture that the same individuals would never think to try bribing their way out of a speeding ticket in America or Northern Europe. The fact that these stories of corruption are told so freely indicates not only a willingness to operate according to local circumstance but also the belief that friends back home will understand that it is reasonable—or at least necessary—to operate according to different standards in high-corruption environments. This isn't purely a matter of personal anecdote: thanks to anticorruption enforcement actions and the information they collect, we now know that expatriate employees of Western companies are often implicated in bribery schemes when working in corrupt locales. Presumably such individuals would not have been paying bribes in their home countries, but feel pressured to do so in the places where they have relocated.

At the same time, there are limits to personal adaptability. This is because culture isn't only a matter of coordination but, as we noted at the outset to this chapter, also of values. If you spend your formative years in a law-abiding culture or in a bribe-taking one, your values develop accordingly. People come to feel that certain behaviors are right or wrong, regardless of what those around them are doing. By the time they're adults, Japanese are uncomfortable with a greeting that comes with a kiss (how physically intrusive!), whereas Italians are uncomfortable without one (how unfriendly!).

One evocative illustration of the persistent effects of living amid corruption comes from a 2006 study that Ray coau-thored with economist Edward Miguel.[3] To focus on the role of culture—what individuals do in the absence of legal enforcement—we studied the behavior of diplomats at the United Nations in New York. Or, rather, we studied diplomats' willingness to rack up parking tickets for which, courtesy of diplomatic immunity, they went unpunished.

Diplomats' immunity to arrest and prosecution abroad is something of an anachronism. As recently as the Cold War, it might have served a useful purpose, protecting emissaries of both the East and West from harassment or arrest based on fabricated charges. (The practice goes back much earlier, dating at least to the thirteenth-century builder of the Mongol Empire, Genghis Khan, who insisted on safe passage for his ambassadors.) Mostly, though, modern diplomats have abused the privilege—in 1997, a drunken Russian official invoked diplomatic immunity to evade arrest after a scuffle with a New York policeman. And what was the cause of the scuffle? A parking ticket.

Immunity doesn't protect diplomats from receiving parking tickets but, back in 1997–2002 when we collected our data, it meant that officials never actually had to pay them. (In 2002, Mayor Michael Bloomberg convinced the U.S. State Department to allow the New York City Police Department to remove the license plates of vehicles with three or more unpaid tickets.) The unpaid tickets leave a paper trail revealing which country's diplomats were most willing to exploit their protection from the law for personal gain—countries with the most unpaid tickets per diplomat abused their diplomatic privileges the most.

Many of the worst offenders also fare poorly in Transparency International's Corruption Perceptions Index (CPI) rankings: Egypt, Chad, Sudan, Bulgaria, Mozambique, Angola, Senegal, and Pakistan fill out the bottom rankings for unpaid tickets. At the other extreme, many missions with spotless records were from low-corruption nations like Canada, Norway, and Sweden. While there are noteworthy exceptions (Kuwait, for example, has only moderate corruption but its diplomats had lots of unpaid tickets, and several high-corruption countries had no violations committed by their officials posted to New York), overall there is a very strong positive relationship between the extent of home-country corruption and willingness to abuse one's office to park illegally in New York.

This is by no means the only evidence that, as the saying goes, "you can take a boy out of ol' Dixieland, but you'll never take ol' Dixie from a boy." A much-noted study by Andrea Ichino and Giovanni Maggi examined how employees at an Italian bank performed when they were moved from postings in the country's less developed (and less industrious) South to offices in the North and vice versa.[4] While not exactly focused on corruption, the study looks at the closely related question of whether shirking and inefficiency by bank workers are better predicted by place of origin or by current environment. Ichino and Maggi find that southern workers who get transferred to the North are less apt to miss work or be charged with misconduct even before they move—that is, it's the more diligent southern workers who choose to relocate to the more industrious Italian North in the first place. They also find that their behavior further improves after they move, suggesting positive peer pressure from their new northern Italian coworkers. Yet they never quite catch up—southerners who transfer to the North are still more apt to shirk than their northern-raised colleagues.[5]

The message from the Italian study may be that people carry the values and behaviors they were raised with, but they also seek to assimilate when they encounter other norms and other cultures. So, perhaps unsurprisingly, a culture of corruption is a combination of things. For any given individual, some behaviors are easily changed depending on the situation—that's the part that undergoes chameleon-like alteration based on what neighbors and coworkers are doing. Other aspects are more immutable and might take generations to shift.

6.3 How do cultures of corruption propagate themselves?

In September 1959, Frank Serpico graduated from the New York City Police Academy, thus realizing his lifelong ambition of becoming a cop. Within days, the young recruit's idealistic view of the New York City Police Department (NYPD) as the good guys upholding the law was crushed by the endemic corruption he observed all around. His fellow officers were engaged in many of the same activities as the criminals he thought he'd signed up to fight. According to Peter Maas's 1973 bestselling biography, *Serpico*, most of his classmates from the academy quickly adapted to department norms, running protection rackets and collecting bribes just like older members of the force. "Everybody's doing it"—that timeless rationale — was surely part of how they justified their behavior.

Serpico didn't jump on the renegade cop bandwagon. He tried to do his job by the book, refusing his share of the weekly collection that others in his precinct extorted from neighborhood criminals. His bribe-taking colleagues were understandably suspicious of Serpico the honest cop. What angle was he working? Was he going to blackmail them? Rat them out? As his old friend and fellow patrolman, Tom Keough, told him, "Who can trust a cop who don't take money?"[6]

Keough, part of the extortion ring himself, tells Serpico to take at least a token share of the bribe money to prove he's part of the club. Serpico refuses, instead reporting his colleagues' misdeeds up the chain of command. Frustrated by the lack of response, Serpico eventually takes his case to the mayor's office, enraging his fellow cops—even the few honest ones—for airing the department's dirty laundry in public. It doesn't end well for Frank Serpico. In a botched drug raid in 1970, he's shot in the face, possibly by another officer looking to silence him. Once a culture of corruption takes hold, the path of least resistance *by far* is to just quietly go along (or at a minimum just keep quiet).

The fact is that most of the cops in Serpico's precinct weren't just quietly going with the flow—they liked the power and extra income that police corruption afforded them. Some, no doubt, became cops precisely because of the bribe-taking opportunities.

That's a further reason why organizational cultures can be so tenacious: they serve in part as the basis on which prospective members choose to join. Like attracts like. If the young idealist Serpico had known that the NYPD was rotten to the core, he might never have enrolled in the police academy in the first place. Who would have been attracted to the life of a New York cop at the time? Someone who had no ethical qualms about the daily shakedowns, and didn't mind (or possibly took pleasure from) the occasional cracking of heads when payment wasn't forthcoming. An organization tends to fill its ranks with people who, before even joining, already have values that fit with its culture.

In 2012, economists Rema Hanna and Shing-Yi Wang ran an experiment with university students in Bangalore, India, that provides a compelling illustration of the corruption-attracts-the-corrupt hypothesis.[7] They found that participants who revealed themselves to be dishonest were more inclined to report a desire to enter the notoriously corrupt Indian civil service.

The university students in Hanna and Wang's study were told to roll a six-sided die 42 times, and instructed to record the outcome of each roll. They were further informed that they'd be paid based on the sum of the numbers that came up. Higher values led to higher payments at the end of the experiment.

The outcome of any single roll is a matter of chance, so some participants will end up with more sixes than others. It is therefore impossible to say that any given roll of the die was misrecorded or even that any individual participant necessarily cheated. But we can compare the outcomes across two groups of individuals and, given the many, many rolls that take place, if one group ends up with a notably higher average than the other, we can say that it is very likely that more fudging of the numbers occurred.[8]

Hanna and Wang found that lots of participants cheated—the number six was recorded in nearly a quarter of rolls, while ones appeared only about 10 percent of the time. Overall, we'd expect, if students were reporting honestly, the sum of 42 rolls would exceed 170 only one percent of the time, yet more than a third of the 669 students enrolled in the experiment ended up with point totals higher than this figure (only a few were brazen enough to list their total as 252, or 42 times six). More interesting than the general pattern of cheating, though, the researchers also found that those with higher point totals were much more likely to say that they aspired to join the civil service on graduation.

Researchers in Denmark—one of the world's three least corrupt nations, according to Transparency International—ran a virtually identical experiment with university students in Copenhagen.[9] They obtained the opposite result from Hanna and Wang: cheating rates were *lower* for Danish subjects with civil service aspirations.[10]

The results from these two experiments don't help us with the question of how Denmark's government bureaucracy became honest and India's corrupt in the first place. But they shed some light on why, once established, their cultures are so very hard to change: once government agencies start using their authority to perpetrate corruption, their ranks tend to be filled by individuals who actively embrace such practices. Individuals committed to cleaning things up either don't seek government employment in the first place or are squeezed out if they do.

6.4 Is corruption more common in "gift-giving" cultures?

Any businessman who's gone to China to seek his fortune (and there have been many) can tell you of the challenges in navigating a culture with a reputation for gift exchange.

The catchall term *gaunxi*, often translated as "connections" or "relationships," captures the broad sense in which a personal connection can allow one individual to prevail upon another for a favor. An individual's guanxi network provides a set of contacts that can be drawn upon when needed—if the harvest fails, for help finding a doctor, and so forth. It's also a term that's often equated with bribery or corruption—the requisite lavish dinners, expensive watches, and greased palms that are part of doing business in China.

The conflation of gift exchange and bribery is understandable. Both involve the exchange of favors, and both require a sense of trust that the favor will be repaid. One is a virtue, the other a sin. In the words of legal scholar Daniel Hays Lowenstein, distinguishing the two "means identifying as immoral or criminal a subset of transactions and relationships within a set that, generally speaking, is fundamentally beneficial to mankind, both functionally and intrinsically."[11]

The resemblance between gift giving and bribery leads naturally to the question of whether they tend to appear together: does a culture built on gift exchange extend this sense of reciprocity to favor trading with public officials? And is some of what outsiders call corruption just a part of long-standing cultural practices that require lots of gift giving, as some anthropologists used to contend?[12]

Before examining whether corruption and gift exchange go hand in hand, we need to clarify what we mean by gift exchange, and assess whether some cultures are in fact more gift-oriented than others.

The topic of social exchange is very well-traveled ground among sociologists. It goes back at least to Marcel Mauss's 1925 classic *The Gift*, a book that examines giving as a means of creating a sense of obligation between individuals, and that describes the methods that givers deployed to ensure that the obligation would be returned.[13] Gift exchange of this form looms large in virtually all human (and many nonhuman) societies. Every culture has ways of giving expression to the sentiment of quid pro quo ("something for something"): you scratch my back, I'll scratch yours; one good turn deserves another; and so on. This isn't a bad thing: a norm of mutual back-scratching is essential to cooperation, without which we'd all be back in the Stone Age, each independently figuring out how to invent the wheel.

Does this norm of gift giving and receiving differ across countries? A 2002 study argues that it does: in China, the land of guanxi, there are stronger norms of reciprocity than in Korea, Japan, or the United States.[14]

In each of the four countries, the study's authors brought university students to a computer lab where they were paired up to play a "trust" game. The experiment proceeded as follows: one subject was randomly selected to be the "sender" and the other the "receiver." The sender was given a sum of money—say $10—to divide between himself and the other subject. The sender kept whatever amount he allotted to himself when the experiment ended, while the rest was tripled, then passed to the receiver. The receiver then got to choose how much of this amount to keep and how much to send back to the sender. The experiment captures some of the basic elements of gift-giving relationships: it's efficient for the sender to pass the full $10 to the receiver (to have it tripled to $30), but doing so requires a sense of trust that the receiver will reciprocate by sending something back in return. Conditional on getting the full $30 ($10 that's been tripled), there is nothing to prevent the receiver from keeping the entire amount, beyond a sense of reciprocal obligation.[15]

The researchers found that Chinese subjects were the only ones who, as a group, were both trusting and trustworthy. That is, Chinese senders "invested" a high fraction of their initial funds (trusting), and were also very likely to return the favor, giving back more than the sender's initial investment (trustworthy). (American students may have had a case of wishful expectations: U.S. senders "invested" at rates comparable to their Chinese counterparts, but receivers in America returned the favor less than half as often as in China.)

What, then, distinguishes a gift from a bribe? In *Bribes*, legal scholar John Noonan's monumental history of the topic, the author argues that in the earliest records of human history, there wasn't any distinction between the two.[16] That is, there was no notion of morality beyond holding up one's end of a two-sided transaction, and this extended to the execution of one's duties as a public official. In 1500 B.C., bribery wasn't only permitted, it was moral.

As illustration, Noonan presents "The Poor Man of Nippur," an ancient Mesopotamian tale of an "unhappy man" named Gimil-Ninurta who brings an offering to the mayor of Nippur with the hope of improving his lot in life. Sensing that he cannot approach the ruler empty-handed, the poor man literally sells the clothes off his back to purchase a goat to bring to the mayor's residence. He is not mistaken in thinking he must come bearing a gift. The mayor asks Gimil-Ninurta on arrival, "What is your problem that you bring me an offering?" When, after hearing the poor man's case, the mayor gives him nothing beyond some stale beer and a bone to chew, Gimil-Ninurta plots his revenge. In the end, the gods intercede on the poor man's behalf: the mayor is beaten (perhaps to death) and forced to repay the peasant many times over for the loss of his goat. As Noonan emphasizes, the mayor's sin (and the reason for divine retribution) is not his demand of tribute—the initial offering is presented as the natural state of affairs. His failing is in taking the bribe but then shortchanging the briber.

Sometime not long after the mayor of Nippur got his comeuppance, attitudes toward what we now call bribery started to change. By the time that Old Testament figures like Hosea, Isaiah, and Micah were making their prophesies in the 8th and 7th centuries B.C., it was clear that God wasn't the sort to trade favors with earthly beings, and that He expected a similar level of conduct from human rulers and judges. Noonan quotes Isaiah 1:11–13:

> I have no desire for the blood of bulls, or sheep
> and of he-goats
> Whenever you come into my present—who
> asked you for this?
> No more shall you trample my courts. The offer
> of your gifts is useless.

Of course, that didn't mean that our human sense of reciprocity somehow disappeared, or that public officials were all of a sudden immune to their effects. Instead, for the three thousand years since Isaiah, we've been grappling with the tension between the fundamental role of reciprocity in human relations and the demands that we place on public servants to uphold their offices in an impartial manner, unswayed by gifts or offerings.

Over time, however, there has been an evolution toward a clearer delineation of the roles and responsibilities of public officials—that they fulfill their duties and are paid salaries, with no expectation of individual offerings. That's part of why the legacy of gift giving makes us so uncomfortable in interactions with public officials.

The sociologist Mauss and his disciples were attuned to the distinctions involved, and spent a good deal of time distinguishing what constitutes a "legitimate" gift in different social settings, as opposed to illegitimate exchanges like bribery or extortion. A gift should be appropriate in scale lest the receiver feel uncomfortable about what might be asked or expected in return. Giving your neighbor a cup of sugar is okay. Inviting him for dinner at a Michelin three-star restaurant or offering the use of a Ferrari: not okay. If the neighbor invites you for dinner, the appropriate response is to return the invitation, not to pull out your checkbook to pay back the favor in cash. (And best not to return the favor too quickly— as the seventeenth-century French nobleman François de La

Rochefoucauld observed in number 233 of his exhaustive list of maxims, "excessive eagerness to discharge an obligation is a form of ingratitude.") The form in which a favor or request for help is made also matters—borrowing a cup of sugar is definitely *not* okay if you show up brandishing a baseball bat or a gun.

Beyond that, though, what makes an exchange "extortion" or "bribery" rather than a neighborly good turn is to some extent a matter of degree and interpretation. There are clear cases that we can all agree lie on either side of the divide: a cup of sugar is okay. Buying a cup of coffee for a friend: okay. Half a billion dollars given to Indian Minister of Communications and Information Technology A. Raja by wireless spectrum bidders: not okay. But there is much gray area in between, and as sociologist Mark Granovetter put it in his exploration of the social life of bribes, "identical actions may be interpreted very differently depending on circumstances."[17]

We've experienced some of these cultural differences in what constitutes "legitimate" gift-giving firsthand. One of us has a student who came to the United States from China for graduate school, bringing his norms of guanxi with him. Each year, the student would send generous and thoughtfully considered gifts at Christmastime.[18] From an American student, this may have raised some suspicion of attempts at buying a better grade or letter of recommendation. At a minimum, it would have appeared socially inept and a bit peculiar: too friendly, too personal, too much like a ploy to create an obligation of reciprocity. But put in the context of a society where it's normal (as in, "it's the norm") for students to confer gifts on their teachers in return for knowledge imparted, it's in line with the student's sense of appropriate gift giving.

Does that mean the Chinese student takes a more lenient view toward public officials receiving bribes or, if he had chosen to enter business himself, would be more inclined to pay them? To the extent that we have any data on the matter, the answer is no. We don't have the sort of multicountry "investment game" study that might allow us to correlate measures of reciprocity with the indices that are commonly used to measure corruption around the world. But we *do* have some rough approximation in the form of trust surveys that ask respondents in many nations how much, in general, people can be trusted—and such generalized trust is intimately connected to beliefs that others will behave as expected in an exchange of favors. A high fraction of Chinese respondents do in fact say that people can be trusted; the only nations with higher generalized trust are in Northern Europe.

As political scientist Eric Uslaner has shown, in general corruption tends to be *lower* in countries with higher trust.[19] It's easy to see why this might be the case. If, to a large extent, bribery involves "illegitimate" exchange, its prevalence can come to undermine faith in the legitimate trade of gifts or favors. That is, if there's always a catch, you begin to question the motives behind supposedly innocuous offerings, and perhaps wonder whether reciprocity is such a great system more broadly.[20]

Uslaner's finding on the general relationship between trust and corruption also emphasizes that, while one can point to a handful of high-trust and high-corruption countries like China, there are many, many more where trust and corruption go in opposite directions. China is, on this score, an outlier.

And even in China, there are fears that time-honored traditions like Teachers' Day, when students give presents like flowers or cards to their instructors, are being undermined by corruption. In recent years, those from wealthier families have been known to deliver plane tickets or jewelry to their modestly paid teachers. In a recent survey, 80 percent of respondents said that teacher gifts should be banned altogether. Teachers' Day gifts may have been acceptable in an earlier era, before the practice was subverted by presents of such lavishness that they clearly crossed the line into bribery.

Thus, while some cultures—like China—may have deeper histories of gift exchange, across all societies there is a distinction between giving a gift, which is a virtue, and a bribe, which is a vice.

6.5 Is corruption more prevalent among members of some religious groups than others?

In the aftermath of Egypt's Arab Spring of 2011, the Muslim Brotherhood, a political movement that operated according to strict Islamist principles, came to power largely based on a platform of anticorruption reform. In 2014, Indonesia's Islamic parties doubled their support at the polls, a result that was seen as a reaction to corruption scandals that had plagued the Democratic Party of President Susilo Bambang Yudhoyono. Even the justly vilified Islamic State of Iraq and Syria, or ISIS, has found support thanks to its claims of fighting corruption. These are merely a few recent and prominent examples of religious parties gaining support not because of their leaders' diligence in prayer or adherence to dietary laws, but because of their claims that religion makes them less vulnerable to graft. They want their prospective supporters to believe it's more than just talk—in one grisly illustration, ISIS militants in Syria executed and crucified one of their own men under charges of corruption. They circulated photos of his bloodied corpse with a sign hanging around his neck that read, "Guilty: Abu Adnan al-Anadali. Sentence: execution and three days of crucifixion. Motive: extorting money at checkpoints by accusing drivers of apostasy."[21]

Spiritual leaders across all religions and denominations sermonize on the evils of corruption. Their stance against corruption is a natural extension of the admonition by Isaiah, quoted in the previous section, against accepting rewards in exchange for judgment: God punishes those who exploit their positions of responsibility for personal gain. This is one thing that gives anticorruption movements with religious affiliation extra credibility in the eyes of many: if religion preaches that you'll go to hell if you lie, cheat, or take bribes, perhaps religious politicians will be less likely to engage in these activities.

Whether religious parties really uphold their anticorruption rhetoric is a matter very much open for debate. The Muslim Brotherhood found itself mired in its own corruption and nepotism scandals once in power, and as we write this book, Iranians are up in arms over the fancy sports cars driven by sons and daughters of the country's ayatollahs.

It's tricky to adjudicate, at the country level, whether religiosity is associated with higher or lower corruption. Secular societies tend to be much wealthier than religious ones, for many possible reasons: religious groups may be less open to scientific innovation; they may direct society's resources to spiritual (rather than GDP-maximizing) ends; and religious practices may decline as people become more affluent and less in need of religious consolation for the heartbreaks of life. Given the link between wealth and corruption, it then becomes inevitable that, overall, more religious societies have higher corruption. But that's just because secular equals rich equals low-corruption. (American readers may puzzle over this statement, but the degree of religiosity in the United States makes the country unusual among wealthy countries. Most Americans consider religion important; most Europeans, for instance, do not.)

At the level of the individual, though, religion is associated with less corruption: as economist Roberta Gatti (among others) has shown, comparing two individuals in the same community, the regular church attendee is less likely to report paying bribes than the nonreligious one.[22] Religion, then, does seem to produce or attract those who are less apt to engage in corruption (or at least less likely to tell a survey taker that they do).

Does an anticorruption message resonate to a greater degree with any particular religion or sect? Enterprising researchers have looked for such a relationship and, at least in cross-country correlations, have found one. In his wide-ranging analysis of the causes of corruption worldwide, political scientist Daniel Treisman finds that Protestantism is associated with lower corruption.[23] We can, of course, offer some story that fits with this observation: Protestant denominations tend to be more egalitarian and individualistic, and hence may encourage their adherents to denounce the misdeeds of public officials than more hierarchical and state-aligned religions like Catholicism and Eastern Orthodoxy. Maybe. But really, it's hard to say. Protestantism is associated with all sorts of other societal differences—maybe it's Max Weber's idea of the Protestant work ethic; maybe Protestant countries just had the dumb luck of starting the Industrial Revolution. There's no way, from comparing countries with different religious traditions that also differ vastly on other dimensions, that we can reach any strong conclusions.

The most helpful insight we may be able to take away from our discussion of religion and corruption is to observe that anything that increases the psychic cost of corruption—in this case, through guilt or a belief in heaven and hell—helps individuals resist the urge to take or pay bribes. And it raises the question whether religious leaders like the pope or Aga Khan or ayatollah could play more prominent roles in the fight against corruption. We'd like to hope they will use their considerable power and influence to do so.

6.6 Are some ethnic groups predisposed to corruption?

Research linking ethnicity to corruption has little to say about whether any group is somehow predisposed to honest or dishonest behavior. Researchers have focused instead on the consequences of ethnic diversity and have found that nations with a greater mix of ethnic groups (and, as a result, a more varied mix of group allegiances) may be more vulnerable to corruption.

Ethnicity is, to a large degree, a social construct. It's defined on the basis of some common characteristics—religious, linguistic, racial, tribal—but also varies with social context and sometimes with individual choice. A Dominican-born American with a dark complexion can self-identify as African American or Hispanic. A Canadian Jew from Quebec might think of himself principally as French Canadian or as Ashkenazi (Jewish of Eastern European descent). In some countries, ethnicity is institutionalized by the government and recorded on one's identity document, thereby hardening ethnic boundaries. Regardless of its source, ethnicity provides a sense of social identity—of who we are—based on membership in a group or community.

It doesn't take much to get human beings to latch onto a group identity and, as a result, fall into an us-versus-them mentality: our shirts are red, yours are green; your eyes are brown, mine are blue. Social psychologist Henri Tajfel coined the term "minimal group paradigm" to describe the tiny nudge that's required to get a group to form an identity. In a series of pioneering studies in the 1970s, Tajfel explored exactly how little you needed to generate a sense of us versus them. In one experiment, subjects were shown a series of paintings, then asked which ones they liked.[24] They were then told that they'd be grouped based on their tastes in painting into the Klee Group and the Kandinsky Group (the paintings they'd viewed were by Paul Klee and Wassily Kandinsky). In reality, the subjects were grouped at random. Each subject was informed which team she was on, then escorted to a separate cubicle and told to allocate points to other subjects (knowing only their group membership), which would be translated into payments at the end of the experiment. The Klee subjects handed out rewards to other (supposed) Klee lovers, at the expense of Kandinsky group members.[25]

Ethnicity has often served as a source of this kind of us-versus-them mentality. In the ethnically heterogeneous nations of postcolonial Africa, a continent whose nations were carved up on the basis of colonial European power grabs rather than local histories, national borders often bisected ethnic groups' traditional lands. The Maasai, for example, were split between Kenya and Tanzania; the Anyi were divided between Ghana and the Ivory Coast. Colonizers also drew borders around multiple groups—some with historical animosities—which, after gaining independence, led to ethnic conflicts in newly created nations.[26]

There is now a substantial body of research in economics and political science on the long shadow cast by these arbitrary borders. Researchers often use measures of diversity based on the degree of "fractionalization," which captures the probability that two individuals that randomly run into each other will be from different ethnic groups. If everyone's the same, its value is zero. Japan, an extremely homogeneous nation, comes close to this lower bound. If every person considers himself to hold a unique ethnic identity, the fractionalization index would be one. Of course, no country is that extreme. But lots of African nations, with their arbitrary colonial borders, end up with ethnic fractionalization indexes around 0.8, which is very high.[27]

One widely cited study, which defines ethnicity on the basis of shared race and language, found that incomes of ethnically fragmented nations grew more slowly than those of more homogeneous ones.[28] The study also found that ethnically fragmented countries tend to be more corrupt.[29] Thus, ethnic diversity, rather than the presence of any particular ethnicity, appears to be associated with more corruption.

Why does this appear to be the case? Economists Abhijit Banerjee and Rohini Pande argue that it is in large part because voters end up casting their ballots based on ethnic allegiances, rather than electing officials for their competence or honesty.[30] A study by a team of political scientists suggests that voting along ethnic lines may result from fear of punishment by those in one's own ethnic group if one fails to cooperate, rather than because of any greater concern for the well-being of others from the same group.[31]

A second contributing factor is that political patronage and clientelism along ethnic lines is also a common feature of ethnically fractured states. Take the case of Mwai Kibaki, whose National Rainbow Coalition came to power in Kenya (fractionalization index, 0.86) in 2002. Kibaki immediately proceeded to stack the government with members of his Kikuyu tribe: after years of being shut out of power, he was going to make sure that *his* people could take advantage of the opportunities afforded by public office. Kenya stands in stark contrast to relatively homogeneous Botswana (fractionalization index, 0.41), one of Africa's economic success stories, whose growth is driven, at least in part, by better-functioning and less grasping political institutions.[32]

Kibaki's exploitative policies may have been a perfectly rational response to Kenya's divisive political environment—if the government will be controlled by a different ethnic group in a few years' time, best to take what you can when the opportunity arises. Of course, these policies all but ensure that every other ethnic group will act in exactly the same way when it's their turn to govern. As a result, Kenya (and fractionalized societies more generally) are left without decent schools or paved roads, and its people collectively face a much bleaker future.

6.7 What did we learn in chapter 6?

- Culture governs how individuals behave in the absence of rules. It has aspects of both values and coordination.
- Even if individuals are morally opposed to corruption, pressure to conform to social norms can lead individuals to behave corruptly in high-corruption environments.
- Cultures of corruption can be reinforced by the self-selection of less honest individuals entering government in countries where there are opportunities for corruption.
- There is no compelling evidence that any particular religious or ethnic group is especially susceptible to corruption.
- Ethnically fractionalized societies are often more corrupt than ethnically homogeneous ones.

7

HOW DO POLITICAL INSTITUTIONS AFFECT CORRUPTION?

In chapter 3, we saw that corruption is far more pervasive in poor nations than in rich ones. That is, per capita GDP offers a huge amount of information about corruption: the cross-national data that we studied there suggests that you can explain about 60 percent of a country's corruption level on the basis of per capita GDP alone.[1]

That is certainly not to say that political institutions are irrelevant—countries at similar levels of income still have widely disparate levels of corruption, and political arrangements and processes surely play a role. At least as important, dysfunctional political institutions may be an important cause of both poverty *and* corruption. Overall, as we'll see in this chapter, the relationships among corruption, political systems, and income are complex, with each affecting the other two.

Understanding these relationships—especially at the national level—presents a particularly thorny set of challenges to empirical researchers. We cannot run experiments with countries' institutions. Nor do political institutions change suddenly and out of the blue with any frequency—nations don't devolve greater decision-making to local governments, for example, just to see what will happen. So we have no way to see conclusively how corruption is affected by a change in institutions. Because of these limitations, in this chapter we will rely more heavily than elsewhere in this book on theories, along with examinations of correlations we observe in the data. Some of the patterns we identify will be surprising. The first and largest surprise is that the nature of a country's political regime—whether it's a democracy or a nondemocracy—doesn't seem to matter at all for corruption.

7.1 Are democratic political regimes less corrupt than autocracies?

It is commonly assumed that democracy curbs corruption, and it's easy to understand why. A vibrant democracy is—or should be—an effective means of aligning government policies with the public interest. Candidates must vie for the loyalty and support of voters, who in turn can express their dissatisfaction with the performance of the government (or of specific elected officials) by tossing them out of office. A truly competitive election—one where ballots aren't stuffed or results rigged in other ways—gives the electorate a choice of who governs. Voters (presumably) will support good candidates who will serve the public's interests. Electoral competition also has the effect of introducing uncertainty into the outcome, which generates a number of additional benefits. Uncertainty makes voters pay attention to politicians and to their campaign promises, and encourages voters to actually vote—what's the point of doing any of that if the election outcome is a foregone conclusion? Finally, both the greater scrutiny and the need to curry favor with voters also force politicians to take care in crafting their appeals to the public.

Competitive elections create incentives for politicians to generate policies that voters approve of, and thus lead to greater accountability for politicians once they're in office (lest they be removed the next time an election occurs). We'd expect, therefore, that citizens in reasonably well-functioning democracies ought to eat better, be in better health, live longer, receive better government services, and be more prosperous than they would be in political systems where policy is dictated by the whims of unelected rulers. And in theory, governments ought to be less corrupt.

So goes the conventional wisdom. Unfortunately, none of this turns out to be true. We might wish that democracy solved the world's material ills, but the reality is that autocrats, on average, do just about as good a job.[2]

We can see this pattern in Figure 7.1, where we depict the same countries around the world that we examined in Figure 3.2. This time, we classify and label the countries by whether they are democracies in 2008 (the most recent year for which comprehensive data exist for political regime type). This graph allows us to see, in a single diagram, the relationships between democracy, income, and corruption.

The question of how to place a political system on a spectrum ranging from dictatorship to competitive democracy is a field unto itself. We use a definition developed by political scientist Adam Przeworski and his students.[3] They use an "alternation" rule, which has the following criteria: (a) the chief executive must be chosen by popular election (or by a body that was itself popularly elected), (b) the legislature must be popularly elected, (c) there must be more than one political party contesting elections, and (d) there must have been a change in regime sometime in the past, under the electoral system that brought the present government to power. It's this last criterion that distinguishes competitive democracies from those where—even under nominally fair elections—the same party somehow finds itself in office election after election. The alternation criterion distinguishes Italy, where there were fourteen changes in the party that controlled the national government in the 40 years between 1975 and 2015, from Mexico, where a single political party held the presidency for 71 years, from 1929 to 2000. The latter did not qualify as a democratic regime, using the alternation rule, until the Partido Revolucionario Institucional (PRI) lost the presidency in 2000.

A couple of patterns jump out in the figure: first, a bunch of countries are clustered together in the left portion of the graph. These countries have GDP per capita below US$11,455 per year, the World Bank's cutoff for high-income classification

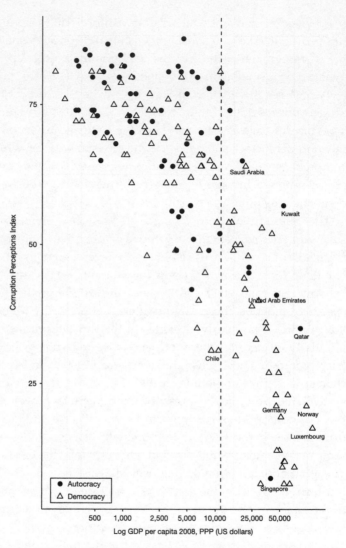

Figure 7.1 Scatterplot of Logged Per Capita GDP by Transparency International's Corruption Perceptions Index for 164 Countries, Indicating Regime Type (2008)

Note: Dashed line at US$11,455 represents World Bank's cutoff for low- and middle-income countries. Corruption Perceptions Index inverted so that lower values indicate lower corruption. Regime type from Cheibub, J. A., Gandhi, J., and Vreeland, J. R. (2010). Democracy and dictatorship revisited. *Public Choice*, 143(1–2), 67–101.

in 2008. (We have marked the cutoff with a dashed line on the figure.) The countries to the left of this line, which constitute a majority of the world's nations, also tend to score poorly on the measure of corruption we use. Second, once we move to the line's right into the richer countries of the world, we find that the latter are virtually all democratic and also have low levels of perceived corruption. (There are a handful of very wealthy autocracies, but these tend to be oil-rich countries on the Arabian Peninsula, such as the United Arab Emirates, Kuwait, and Saudi Arabia, which we have labeled in Figure 7.1.) But it's hard to know what to make of the effect of democracy on income *or* corruption based on this: all three are country-level characteristics that—along with high life expectancy and average education—tend to cluster together. The patterns in the figure show that wealthy countries generally have both low levels of perceived corruption *and* democratic political institutions.

Things get more interesting when we zoom in on the world's poorer nations. In Figure 7.2, we present a close-up from the figure we just discussed, focusing on the 146 low- and middle-income countries with per capita incomes of less than $11,455. (You can see which part of the figure we zoom in on if you refer back to the $11,455 line in Figure 7.1.) Among this group, there's little discernible relationship between democracy and income, nor between democracy and corruption.[4] If democracies were better than nondemocracies at reining in corruption, we'd see the (democratic) triangles mostly below the (autocratic) dots at every level of income, indicating less corruption according to the CPI. But we don't.

What can we take away from this initial look at the data? One reasonable interpretation is that democratic political institutions appear largely redundant in reducing corruption. Wealthy countries aren't corrupt—the collection of factors that causes those countries to be wealthy also reduces corruption, whatever the regime type in place. In poor countries, democratic institutions appear ineffective. Almost all poor

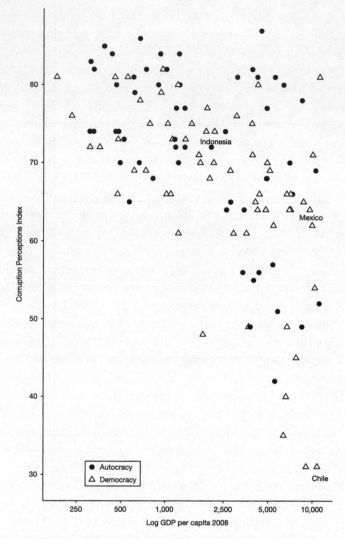

Figure 7.2 Scatterplot of Logged Per Capita GDP by Transparency International's Corruption Perceptions Index for 146 Low- and Middle-Income Countries, Indicating Regime Type (2008)

Note: Low- and middle-income countries defined using World Bank criterion as those with per capita GDP of less than US$11,455. Corruption Perceptions Index inverted so that lower values indicate lower corruption. Regime type from J.A. Cheibub, J. A. J., Gandhi, and J. R. Vreeland, (2010). Democracy and dictatorship revisited. *Public Choice*, 143(1–2), 67–101.

countries have high levels of corruption—relative to wealthy nations—regardless of whether they have a competitive political system or are governed by autocrats.

If you just looked at the raw correlation between democracy and corruption, you might imagine that the two were intimately linked. That is, if you didn't also consider the level of economic development, you'd think that democratic countries were less corrupt than autocratic ones. But the graphical representations in Figures 7.1 and 7.2 indicate that the relationship between democracy and corruption is actually an artifact of economic development—wealth and corruption are also closely connected, and it's not clear, once you know whether a country's rich or poor, that democracy makes any additional difference in predicting corruption.

Why the failure of conventional wisdom—and of the theory that democratic institutions provide political accountability? We'll explore this question from the perspective of an individual voter in chapter 8, where we examine why a voter might support corrupt candidates for public office. In the rest of this chapter, we examine some broad-brush, macro-level explanations for why democratic institutions may not do their job in reducing corruption: the long, hard process of democratic consolidation and the effects of single-party dominance. And we also consider how the particulars of a country's political institutions—such as electoral rules or degree of political centralization—might affect corruption. Before we turn to the question of how corruption can thrive in a democracy, we take a short detour through a discussion of how corruption operates in nondemocracies. This will serve as a natural point of departure for understanding the role of democratic elections in curtailing corruption.

7.2 Are all types of autocracies equally corrupt?

Autocracies are not all created equal.[5] Political scientists distinguish among three, sometimes four, distinct types of autocracy: hereditary regimes, such as monarchies; single-party regimes, such as communist systems; military regimes, such as those instituted by an armed coup; and personalistic regimes, where an individual or small group (rather than a party or the military) comes to hold exclusive power through means other than inheritance (examples include Muammar al-Gaddafi of Libya and Mobutu Sese Seko of Zaire).[6]

Autocracies thus differ according to who exercises power—military men, party leaders, kings or sheiks—and how they got there. Sometimes countries in any of these categories actually hold elections—personalistic regimes are the most likely to do so, but single-party regimes often do as well—but the outcome of such elections is never in doubt.

On an anecdotal level, we'll see that nondemocracies also differ drastically in the extent to which they're afflicted by corruption. It's hard, in fact, to go beyond anecdote. If studying corruption in democratic settings is difficult because corruption is illegal and therefore tends to take place in secret, studying it in autocratic settings is even tougher given the constraints placed on both scholars and the media. So for nondemocracies, we need to rely exclusively on the survey-based measures we examined in chapter 3, despite their many weaknesses.

Before turning to the data, it is worth considering what the concept of corruption even means in the context of a dictatorship. We have contended that corruption involves illegal activities by government officials. In, say, a military dictatorship, where an all-powerful general writes whatever laws he wishes, is legality even useful in distinguishing what we do and don't label as corruption? Perhaps surprisingly, the answer is generally yes: even countries without free and fair elections have rules about how public officials comport themselves. Legally speaking, theft of public property, embezzlement, accepting kickbacks, and other common forms of corruption are equally corrupt in nondemocracies. In fact, one of the most dramatic anticorruption crusades-in-process at the time of writing is taking place in China, a rigidly authoritarian regime. Even autocrats don't want their underlings to steal government property for personal use.

Returning to the scatterplot presented in Figure 7.1, the vast differences in corruption that we observe among nondemocratic regimes is particularly notable. Singapore, a single-party state, is among the world's least corrupt nations, as is clear from its placement on the bottom right of the scatterplot. Equatorial Guinea—a central African nation that is so poor that we don't even know its per capita GDP (so it does not appear in the scatterplot)—is ruled by Teodoro Obiang Nguema Mbasogo, who seized power in a military coup in 1979. The country is also among the world's most corrupt.[7] Dictatorships often make corruption worse: if a leader is inclined to steal, unchecked power helps him do it that much more quickly (recall the story of "Baby Doc" Duvalier's dismantling and sale of Haiti's railway in chapter 3—one would hope such brazen theft could not happen in a democracy). But sometimes dictators double down on fighting corruption instead, as occurred in Singapore under Lee Kuan Yew (and may be happening in China at the present time).

Just as we failed to reach general conclusions about the link from democracy to clean government, there are clearly divergent paths that dictatorships take where corruption is concerned. This is probably because of the different trade-offs that regimes make in their objectives while in office. As with all politicians, nondemocratic leaders aim to stay in power. To the extent that rule is by an all-powerful party organization, one that sees itself governing into the indefinite future, leaders may be more forward-looking in their policies than those in more personalistic regimes, where leaders may be motivated to salt away billions in foreign bank accounts in the event that they lose power.

To explore whether the particular type of autocratic regime is associated with divergent levels of corruption, in Figure 7.3 we present boxplots summarizing the data for Transparency International's Corruption Perceptions Index (CPI) for each of the four types of nondemocratic regime. (A boxplot is a way of showing the distribution of data by depicting the values for the minimum, 25th percentile, median, 75th percentile, and maximum. The box contains the 25th to 75th range, whereas the "whiskers" show the minimum and maximum values. The horizontal line across the middle of each box is the median.) Monarchies—of which there are relatively few in the dataset—are substantially less corrupt than the three other types of autocracies, which are classified as military, single party, and personalistic. We can only speculate about why this might be. Perhaps monarchs look far into the future, through generations of their descendants, and are thus well motivated to maintain a reputation for good government. Or perhaps monarchs are especially adept at keeping a lid on information about corruption. We really cannot be sure.

The data that is displayed in Figure 7.3 also shows that single-party regimes are modestly less corrupt, in general, than military and personalistic regimes. China's anticorruption crackdown, initiated at the end of 2012, is emblematic of the reasons why some nondemocratic regimes choose to limit corruption, and also the advantages they may enjoy in fighting corruption if they choose it as an objective. By most accounts, China's anticorruption crackdown is both very real and a response to popular discontent over the appearance of public officials (and their offspring) wearing diamond-encrusted watches or driving, as well as occasionally crashing, Ferrari sports cars. Given that China has chosen to crack down on corruption in earnest, the regime is unencumbered by such considerations as due process or respect for human rights in making officials fall in line. When you want to get things done fast, democratic constraints can be cumbersome and inefficient.

Whether dictators decide to rein in corruption, or how and with whom they share the spoils of government when they decide to steal instead: these are big questions that, as a result of data limitations, remain largely unanswered. In the remainder

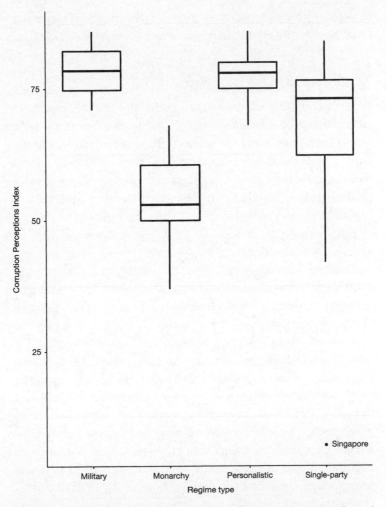

Figure 7.3 Boxplots of Transparency International's Corruption Perceptions Index for Types of Nondemocratic Regimes in 59 Countries (2010)

Note: Corruption Perceptions Index inverted so that lower values indicate lower corruption. Regime types from B. Geddes, J. Wright, and E. Frantz, (2014). Autocratic breakdown and regime transition: A new data set. *Perspectives on Politics,* 12(2), 313–31.

of this chapter, we refocus our attention on democratic political systems. Our discussion begins with the overarching question of whether elections reduce corruption, and gradually narrows to explore how differences in the way democratic systems are organized across countries might affect corruption.

7.3 Do elections reduce corruption?

Today's long-lived democratic political systems generally emerged out of nondemocratic antecedents. This is true the world over, with a few exceptions (the exceptions include the United States and Canada). The preceding political systems were monarchies, single-party dictatorships, or autocracies of one sort or another. The past half-century has seen a further wave of countries emerge out of single-party rule by communist parties or from colonial rule, to become what are at least nominally democratic.

Creating democracy, however, isn't quite as easy as flipping a switch once the monarchy's been overthrown, independence declared, or elections held. Even when genuinely competitive elections are permitted, it takes time for political parties to become established and to operate as intended. Voters in a new democratic regime may initially find themselves choosing among political parties inherited from a predemocratic past, parties with standards, objectives, and machinations that haven't adjusted to the country's newfound commitment to democracy. There are many examples from recent history available to illustrate the sizable lag between the transition in political rules and corresponding shifts in political realities. Mozambique is a case in point. There, the political parties representing the two sides of the country's 16-year-long postindependence civil war became accustomed to operating outside of formal democratic rules. Even well after the war ended in 1992, the parties' leadership continued to negotiate informally (out of the view of voters), at times threatening to settle their differences via armed conflict rather than parliamentary proceedings. More than once, inflammatory political rhetoric between the two led the country to the brink of civil war. Nominally democratic, the country remains politically unstable, and the two major political parties appear only partially committed to democracy, with the ruling party accused of stuffing ballot boxes as recently as the 2014 election. So while Mozambique is classified as a democracy, its institutions are fragile and still ineffective in many ways, including in the fight against corruption. As *The Economist* noted in early 2016, the country is still "floundering amid corruption and conflict."[8]

Another example comes from Brazil, where traditional—and nondemocratic—ways of conducting political business likewise remain in place despite changes in formal political institutions. The parties and politicians who had been in power during the military dictatorship continued to rule for the first decade after democratization in 1985, hindering attempts at post-authoritarian reform. They remained especially influential in the rural and less-developed areas in the northeast of the country, where old-regime politicians continued the use of clientelism and patronage to maintain political control. In these areas of the country, poor voters remained loyal to their traditional parties until preexisting patronage arrangements were replaced in the 2000s by social policies that provided benefits using more objective, formula-based measures of poverty and need. Even so, the northeast remains home to residual vote buying, clientelism, and electoral fraud—and to poor voters who are often surprisingly loyal to traditional political elites.

These examples are telling: when regime change occurs and a new political party assumes power, its first priority is usually not to reduce corruption—even if that is one of its stated objectives. Political parties and elites from the prior regime may continue to exploit their positions even after democratization takes place. Politicians aside, bureaucrats are likely accustomed to doing things in a certain way, which may involve stealing from government coffers or demanding bribes. Getting them to change their behavior requires putting in place new forms of oversight, monitoring, and sanction. These changes cannot be implemented overnight. Cleaning up government takes time; many elections are required for candidates to learn—one hopes—that anticorruption policy commitments attract votes. Too often, researchers have assumed, when analyzing the relationship between institutional political change and corruption, that effects will start to appear within a year or two. This may explain why they tend to find no negative relationship between democracy and corruption: democratic practices take a long time—decades, in reality—to become established.[9]

As a final example, consider Mexico, where voters finally ejected the PRI from the presidency in 2000, after seventy uninterrupted years when the party held executive office. The new party of government, the Partido Acción Nacional, showed no particular interest in reducing the graft and corruption for which the previous regime had been known, and a decade later—despite repeated alternations of executive power—corruption in Mexico remains widespread and organized crime even worse. Even as Mexican voters protest the persistence of these problems, most politicians seem largely oblivious to their concerns. Take a look again at Figure 7.2, where we label the position of Mexico. The country is one of the most corrupt democracies at its level of income—and this despite more than a decade of genuinely democratic rule. No Mexican political party has yet made cleaning up corruption a central programmatic commitment.

But change is coming, we hope, even to Mexico. In 2015, the country's congress approved new anticorruption legislation that authorizes a special prosecutor to tackle the problem and establishes a special court to oversee anticorruption efforts. Since the preceding fifteen years demonstrated that existing political elites were not reliable opponents of corruption, the creation of new institutions, staffed by new personnel, has begun to establish new expectations. A fresh generation of politicians, not implicated in corrupt dealings, is emerging, some of whom are committed to the anticorruption and anticrime priorities of Mexico's restive middle classes. It may take yet more decades for Mexico's new democracy to catch up, but there is now reason to believe that anticorruption policies will begin to succeed.

7.4 Does partisan competition reduce corruption?

As we discussed in the previous section, one reason that democratic political institutions and elections may not eradicate corruption is because they don't automatically or immediately produce parties and politicians able or willing to tackle corruption.

In this section and the next, we examine more carefully the roles of political parties and electoral competition in reducing corruption. Even with time, there is no guarantee that electoral competition will lead to more honest government. That is especially surprising, because a central purpose of competitive elections is precisely to improve government performance.

The intuition for the beneficent effects of competition usually invokes a market analog: more competition should lead to more of what "consumers" want. To understand why this metaphor so often breaks down, it's important to understand how political parties select policy priorities and also how they select their candidates for office. To actually reduce corruption, at least one party needs to make a point of selecting candidates committed to improved governance.[10] Usually that is the party of the opposition, because that's the party that does not have access to the resources of government and so cannot embezzle or misappropriate them. That party needs to make sure that, once elected, its officials toe the party's anticorruption line rather than slipping into the bad behavior of the party they've just thrown out of office. But doing just that is a great temptation: keeping the party together may require allowing lower-level officials to engage in corruption—or risk having them defect to the prior ruling party. In addition, the new governing party may be surrounded by businesses that secure government contracts by paying bribes, and these businesses have an interest in continuing to barricade their industries against competition from firms that do not pay bribes. So business may become a strong force promoting corruption even in a previously clean party—by offering bribes large enough that party agents find it difficult to turn them down. There are many politicians who come to power on anticorruption platforms—but few who are able to make good on their promises over any length of time.

How can a well-meaning party leadership make that happen? By convincing voters that ending corruption serves their interests, thereby breaking up the collusive relationship between citizens and the politicians who buy their votes. As we've discussed in chapter 3, it's hard to accomplish this when voters are very poor, since poverty leaves them more vulnerable to vote buying, patronage, and extortion. If you're living hand-to-mouth, the choice between a bag of rice and a candidate's promise of clean government (and thus, of course, no rice) isn't a hard one to make. It becomes easier to take the bet on a better, less corrupt future when you've got a bit of cash put away. For anticorruption crusades to succeed, incomes must have improved to the point where a large middle class exists, because these are the citizens who can afford to turn down the inducements that capture voters in an ongoing equilibrium of politicians paying voters, who then elect officials who behave corruptly (to finance yet another round of elections).

But there's a caveat. Middle-class voters (like all voters) dislike corruption, but precisely because they are middle class, they have enough money to buy goods and services on the private market if the public sector is too inefficient, patronage-ridden, or corrupt. That gives them independence from corrupt politicians, but ironically, also affords middle-class voters the luxury of opting out of using public resources in the first place. This in turn has the effect of diluting their anticorruption commitments. Middle-class voters prefer to see government fulfill its promises to supply water, healthcare, and education—and to do so without the voter having to exploit personal connections or pay off bureaucrats. But if there is no viable anticorruption party in the offing, middle-class voters can more easily disengage from the public sector than their poorer counterparts, ignoring politics rather than giving voice to discontent. Protest is difficult to organize, and so often ineffective that it's simpler to exit in many situations.[11]

Once a large enough middle class has developed that can afford to sustain anticorruption and antipatronage protest, aspiring politicians *might* run political campaigns that meet this demand, aware that a public anticorruption campaign could potentially propel their candidates in the face of entrenched incumbents. This is the story of the Progressive Movement in the United States at the turn of the century, which we mentioned in chapter 3. And it's also the story of how the Aam Aadmi Party came to govern the city of New Delhi in 2015, when it won 67 out of 70 seats on the city council despite having been founded only two years earlier. The Common Man Party, as Aam Aadmi translates, rose to power on the strength of middle-class disgust with chronic corruption in the city. The party also benefited from an inflow of campaign money from affluent individuals of Indian descent living in the United States, who longed to be able to return to an India free of corruption and inefficiency. Since assuming power, Aam Aadmi has articulated policies aimed at combating corruption in public service delivery in the city and restoring middle-class support for local government.

It's still too early to know where the Aam Aadmi anti-corruption effort will end. But it's a promising beginning. The broader lesson, though, is that partisan competition by itself is often not enough to clean up government. In fact, in high-corruption/low-income settings, political competition can make for even more corruption. Instead of competing on who can govern most effectively, parties might choose to engage in a race to the bottom, trying to outdo one another in vote buying, graft, and bribes. In the Kenyan election of 2002, that brought Mwai Kibaki to power, a survey found that two-thirds of voters had been approached by agents from multiple parties hoping to buy their votes. The *New York Times* quoted a farmer as saying, "A NARC agent stopped me at a bus stop and asked me who I was voting for. When I said KANU, he offered me 500 shillings for my vote." The man turned down the inducement (worth about US$6 at the time), instead holding out for a better offer.[12]

This is a bad equilibrium—one that even candidates for public office would like to escape. It's expensive, and all but necessitates that they engage in corruption once elected in order to restock their campaign chests for the next election. But if some candidates use cash for vote buying, they all have to—or face near-certain defeat. Not even an emerging middle class is enough to ensure that politicians who dream of doing the right thing can act on their principles and escape a corrupt equilibrium. Something—perhaps something external to the political system—has to trigger a shift to move political parties to compete on an anticorruption agenda.

7.5 Does single-party government perpetuate corruption?

A second reason that democratic political institutions may have little effect on corruption is that competitive elections and multiple political parties do not necessarily put an end to single-party dominance, particularly not at the state and local levels. Even when citizens have the choice of electing political representatives from multiple parties, voters may continue to elect representatives from just one. Perhaps the opposition party has no experience with government and is not a credible alternative. After all, no outsider gets a chance to practice governing under single-party rule. Or perhaps the party that comes to power in the early, fragile years of democracy uses its resources to reinforce its hold on power, exploiting the reservoir of goodwill that exists thanks to its early democratic leadership. In doing so, that party's leaders merely mimic their predecessors, exploiting their public offices to ensure that true democracy never takes hold.[13]

Thus, even when they have a choice at the polls, voters may elect and reelect individuals from the same party. If this occurs repeatedly for executive office—such as the president or prime minister—political scientists label what emerges "single-party dominant regimes." An entire country can fall under the control of a single party. It happened in Italy after World War II, when Christian Democracy (known by its Italian acronym, the DC) enjoyed fifty years of political supremacy. It happened in Tanzania, where the Chama Cha Mapinduzi has (as of this writing in early 2016) been consistently reelected since independence in 1961. Sometimes single-party dominance takes hold only in particular regions of a country, as was the case when the Democratic Party held power in the American South in the 1940s, 1950s, and 1960s, on the basis of the disenfranchisement of African Americans. In all these cases, the dominant party used nefarious tactics to become increasingly secure in its hold on power.

Does single-party dominance encourage or perpetuate corruption? As we have stressed in this chapter, the threat of removal from office can play a role in keeping politicians honest. If single-party dominance removes this fear, corruption may flourish. History provides many examples of this, especially among postcolonial African nations, where one-party rule was commonplace in the second half of the twentieth century. Perhaps not surprisingly, so was corruption.

Single-party regimes may choose to deploy the resources of government to enlarge and extend their rule. They may buy off opposition politicians to keep them quiet, pay off potential opponents to keep them out of politics, or use control of the country's election administration to subtly (if not openly) discourage opposition voters from coming to the polls. These corrupt and illegal tactics perpetuate single-party rule.

Ironically, if one-party rule facilitates corruption, when political competition arrives on the scene, corruption becomes an even more compelling option—a way to raise the funds to mount a potentially costly campaign to fight off the opposition. To the extent that politicians need to raise their own funds to finance their campaign expenses, electoral competition tilts their incentives toward corruption. New to the game of democratic competition, aspiring politicians may lack the kinds of established ties to donors that exist in more consolidated democracies; in poor countries, moreover, donors may be scarce. Kickbacks can serve as a convenient means of raising money: a politician takes a bribe from a company awarded a government contract, and the kickback is redistributed to voters in the form of gifts to ensure their support. The overall effect can be to enmesh the party itself in corruption.

In this way, a single party can come to dominate the political landscape without engaging in overt political repression (or at least not very much). "Dictatorship light," some call it. If the party is buying off the right people, there's no need to send tanks into the street, or lock up journalists critical of the government, or prohibit political opponents from competing for elected office: the systematic misuse of government resources to reinforce political control, perhaps in combination with just enough of an atmosphere of fear, means that opponents don't confront the government on an even footing. This creates a vicious cycle: a dominant party uses the financial proceeds from corrupt transactions to buy votes, thereby perpetuating its ability to retain power.

7.6　Are some democratic systems of government better for reducing corruption?

Elections, even competitive ones, are imperfect instruments for curbing corruption. But democratic institutions come in many forms. There are numerous of ways of tinkering with them: for instance, presidentialism versus parliamentarism, single-member versus multimember electoral districts, and centralized versus federal systems. In this and the next section, we examine whether there are particular variants of democratic political institutions that are more effective in reducing corruption.

Democratic nations employ different methods to select their heads of government. There are two main methods in use: the direct election of the executive (the president) by voters; and the indirect election of an executive (the prime minster) when voters elect a governing political party to the legislature and the leader of that party assumes executive office.

Underneath this broad distinction, there's an enormous variety of details that constitution-writers have devised. For example, the number of legislators each voter elects varies. In some electoral systems (known as single-member district systems), voters elect only a single representative from their electoral district or parliamentary constituency. Congressional elections in the United States, for example, follow this model. Other countries are divided into multimember districts, which are exactly what they sound like. In this case, candidates compete for one of any number of seats—at least two, but as many as 150 in the case of the Netherlands—with voters often selecting from the ballot as many candidates as there are seats.

Political scientists have come up with many theories relating these various systems to political accountability and, by extension, to corruption. For example, perhaps increasing the size of electoral districts will reduce corruption, because competition for office will be more intense. But one can just as easily argue the opposite, with smaller districts making politicians more personally held to account.

Data aren't of much help—the evidence is, in the words of political scientist Daniel Treisman, "fragile" at best,[14] and more often contradictory. One set of cross-country studies argues that corruption is lower in parliamentary systems; another set of studies—also using cross-national data—argues precisely the reverse, namely, that presidential regimes are less corrupt.

Research on other aspects of electoral institutions generate similarly unhelpful and divergent sets of findings. And this is all on top of the usual problems of cross-national analyses. For example, Latin American political systems tend to have presidents, whereas European systems have prime ministers, and Latin America is also generally more corrupt than Europe. But does that mean that having a presidential system *causes* the higher levels of corruption observed in Latin America? It's hard to know, because so many other things differ between the two regions, including (but not limited to) their average levels of economic development. But that's as far as we can take the evidence, since national electoral systems only differ across countries, and we'll never be able to experiment with democratic institutions to see what changes in electoral rules decrease (or increase) corruption.[15]

Our view is that unscrupulous politicians emerge in every political system, and there are no formal institutions that decisively do a better job of ensuring corrupt candidates never get into office. That's as likely a reason as any for the lack of clear and definitive patterns in the cross-country data. No set of institutional choices is corruption-proof.

7.7 Does political decentralization reduce corruption?

There's an appealing intuition for moving decisions about government resources out of the hands of politicians in a distant national capital, and giving control to local governments. The basic rationale—at one time supported by the World Bank and other international agencies—is that local control of service delivery will inspire ordinary people to be more active in ensuring that the funds, which can have a direct impact on their lives, are well spent. And these ordinary people—both voters and the everyman amateur politicians they elect—will make better decisions than the arguably corrupt politicians at the national level. Decentralization is thus supposed to help break up a corrupt national equilibrium by inserting the honest voter into local decision-making.

Unfortunately, local politics don't always live up to the ideal that international agencies might have imagined. Experiments in decentralization have found that local political elites often capture disproportionate amounts of resources through theft or deliberately politicized redirection of government funds. Politically and economically powerful groups at the local level, like their national counterparts, may seize what government provides, whether it is electricity, clean water, roads, schools, or health clinics. They shift resources toward the areas where they live, toward their relatives, or toward their core voters, rather than allocating them where they're needed most.[16] These findings surely help to explain why we see no decisive cross-country relationship between decentralization and corruption in either direction.[17]

The nuances and complications that arise in examining the link from decentralization to corruption are highlighted in the work of Pranab Bardhan and Dilip Mookherjee, who meticulously collected data on government programs over two decades for eighty-nine rural villages in the Indian state of West Bengal.[18] The villages were characterized by extensive and extreme poverty, as well as extreme inequality. The authors examined who benefited from various poverty-reduction programs, including, among other things, employment programs, agricultural assistance, and bank credit. They found that within villages, the poor received the goods and services to which they were entitled—perhaps because these were small communities and the delivery of government benefits was highly visible. It would thus have been hard for local politicians to cheat the poor out of their entitlements. But across groups of villages, local political elites directed more benefits to the villages with fewer poor households or other disadvantages. Bardhan and Mookherjee's interpretation is that the allocations *across* villages were carried out by local politicians who operated out of sight of residents, exploiting their positions to direct benefits to their favored villages rather than to the ones with the greatest number of needy households. The two scholars go on to argue that allocating government programs based on simple formulas—as a central government bureaucrat might—would have led to fairer outcomes than handing discretion over to local politicians.[19]

Just like politicians in the capital, local elected officials may perpetuate corruption, employing methods that make it difficult for local voters to discern. It's hard to tell, for example, if a road is built using appropriate materials or if the road builders skim off the top. Likewise, voters cannot easily distinguish a shoddy school building from one that was built using high-quality construction methods—until the school begins to crumble. Allocations that are visible are, as you might expect, more apt to be distributed as intended. If the local government gets a bundle of cash to hand out to the very poorest in the community and everyone knows which families are included in that category, the cash is more likely to reach those recipients. But it's hard for voters to know if their village is receiving its fair share of government benefits or whether other villages in the same electoral constituency—but perhaps those whose voters were more inclined to support the incumbent—are getting more. Sometimes providing voters the information about what they ought to be receiving is enough to correct the problem, especially if voters were previously unaware of their entitlements.[20] Often, however, it is not, because politicians have such a tight lock on public office that they do not fear electoral retaliation.

We're not suggesting that local empowerment is necessarily a bad thing (though it's often turned out that way), but it certainly isn't the panacea for corruption that was once hoped.

7.8 Do term limits limit corruption—or encourage it?

One relatively modest proposal for improving the conduct and performance of politicians is a limit on the number of terms they are allowed to serve in office. Term limits propel new people into office—candidates who have not developed the connections and contacts that facilitate influence-buying and possibly corruption. Much of the justification for term limits lies with the argument that experienced politicians are also experienced in the misuse and abuse of office.

There is a counterargument, however: the problem with term limits is that they free politicians from reelection concerns, which might have otherwise served as a check on corruption and other forms of bad behavior. The desire to continue to hold office may very plausibly encourage politicians to consider the public interest over lining their own pockets. Which effect dominates—the constant infusion of fresh, uncorrupted faces versus the incentives for long-serving politicians to behave responsibly—is ultimately an empirical question.

What little evidence there is on this question is mixed. We know of two credible studies that draw very different conclusions. Both focus on the performance of mayors, one in Brazil and the other in Italy. The first, by economists Claudio Ferraz and Frederico Finan, examines the behavior of Brazilian mayors, who are allowed to spend only two terms in office.[21] Ferraz and Finan utilize the results from an anticorruption program that audits municipalities for their use of federal funds. They find that mayors in their first term misappropriate 27 percent fewer resources than second-term mayors, the ones who are barred from standing for reelection. The scholars argue that this is unlikely to be the result of politicians having gained experience in how to steal during their first term—if that were the case, we'd expect that first-term mayors who come into office with extensive political backgrounds would already be proficient at stealing. But this doesn't seem to be the case— first-term mayors misappropriate less, regardless of their experience prior to taking office.

Italian economists Decio Coviello and Stefano Gagliarducci reach nearly the opposite conclusion—they report that municipalities tend to pay higher and higher prices in procurement auctions as their Italian mayors spend more time in office, and are more apt to award contracts to local companies.[22] They take these findings as evidence that "time in office progressively leads to collusion between government officials and a few favored local bidders." In contrast to the Brazilian findings, Coviello and Gagliarducci find no effect of term limits on whether Italian mayors overpay in auctions.

The two studies highlight a very general point about political reform: very rarely does institutional change have only benefits and no costs. Term limits undoubtedly have benefits because they force the rotation of elected officials. But they also have a cost, since they reduce the discipline imposed by reelection incentives. Why does the "electoral discipline" effect dominate in Brazil, while the "fresh faces" effect is stronger in Italy? To answer that question—and to understand more broadly when we can expect term limits to hurt or help—we need a deeper understanding than currently exists of the complicated interactions among political institutions.

7.9 Do campaign finance regulations reduce corruption— or encourage it?

If political officials are tempted to accept kickbacks and embezzle government funds to pay for their reelection campaigns, perhaps limiting or otherwise regulating campaign expenses will help to curb these illegal practices. This is one oft-mentioned rationale for campaign finance regulations, with activists such as legal scholar Lawrence Lessig arguing that overhauling campaign finance reform is needed to reduce the corrupting influence of money in politics.

The complexities of campaign finance regulation often gets lost in the discussion. Campaign finance covers a wide range of donor types and donation levels. Rules include bans on donations from foreign interests to political parties; bans on donations from trade unions, corporations, corporations with government contracts, and corporations with partial government ownership; caps on personal donations; public funding of candidates or parties; bans on vote buying; limits on donations; and requirements for financial disclosure. Almost every country in the world prohibits vote buying and bans the use of state resources by particular parties or candidates.[23] In highly corrupt countries, these prohibitions are simply ignored. Likewise, political parties have to disclose their finances in most countries, even corrupt ones, but the documentation that parties provide is often incomplete, misleading, or inaccurate. Finally, in most nations, there are provisions for at least some public funding of political parties and free or subsidized access to the media—but often this funding is nowhere near enough. Thus, in many cases, the problem is with enforcement of existing rules rather than a need to reform the rules themselves.

Even in otherwise relatively clean environments, more stringent campaign finance laws can backfire. Consider the German Christian Democratic Union's involvement in illegally raising campaign funds, mentioned in chapter 5. Germany is generally regarded as one of the world's least corrupt nations: its citizens don't pay bribes to see doctors, and police don't try to extract bribes from passing motorists. And although the cost of mounting a political campaign in Germany is modest by global standards, the country's very tough campaign finance regulations apparently led some politicians to conclude that it was worth trying to supplement legal political funding with under-the-table contributions. Similarly, the Italian revelations of massive corruption that occurred in the early 1990s revealed frequent use of illegal campaign donations: in this case, a 1974 law that prohibited political contributions by public corporations tipped the balance for many legislators, encouraging them to accept what were, under the new law, illegal contributions. Corporations that had made donations that were legal under the pre-1974 laws kept making them, presumably in order to retain their influence over and access to politicians. Given their newly illegal status, though, these donations criminalized the politicians who accepted them.

The weakness of campaign finance regulations, then, is that they need to be observed and enforced. Even in relatively law-abiding political systems, this is often difficult given the ease of making illegal donations. In corrupt environments, enforcement is virtually impossible. Our point is not that campaign finance reform is ill-conceived or unneeded—merely that political campaigns are expensive and getting to be more so all the time. Whatever rules we put in place, money has a way of filtering into politics. It's important to consider what (if any) the results of tighter constraints will be for corruption in practice.

Taking stock of this chapter's discussion overall, we favor democratic political institutions, but not because we think they are necessarily very effective in curbing corruption. Over time, with the right kind of competitive political parties and the right kind of politicians, democracy—particularly in wealthy countries—also appears to be effective in combating corruption. But whatever the details of the democratic institutions in place, voters play a central role in making these improvements come about. We turn to examine this role in greater detail in the next chapter.

7.10 What did we learn in chapter 7?

- Despite the compelling argument that electoral accountability should limit government corruption, there is no evidence that, overall, democratic countries are less corrupt than nondemocracies.
- There is wide variation in the extent of corruption in autocratic nations. The unified political authority enjoyed by autocrats makes them both more effective in cracking down on corruption when they choose to do so but also more adept at stealing when they choose to be corrupt.
- Political competition for elective office may, on the one hand, provide incentives for improving the quality of government. But conversely, it may push candidates to

compete based on vote buying or otherwise trying to win
elections through corrupt means.

- We observe no clear link relating institutional differences
  among democracies (for example, presidential versus
  parliamentary systems) to corruption.
- It is often assumed that political or administrative
  decentralization will reduce corruption by bringing
  government decisions into closer contact with the
  electorate. In practice, this does not seem to be the case,
  as local leaders also exploit their positions for private
  gain or to ensure reelection.
- Neither term limits nor campaign finance reform can
  necessarily be expected to generate substantial reduc-
  tions in corruption. In fact, both have the potential to
  backfire: term limits may reduce political accountability,
  and campaign finance reform may push candidates to
  seek illicit forms of financing.

8

HOW DO COUNTRIES SHIFT FROM HIGH TO LOW CORRUPTION?

The world's wealthy democracies all have relatively honest governments. However, that wasn't true a hundred or two hundred years ago, when they looked like governments in today's poor countries. How did they do it? How do countries escape a high-corruption equilibrium?

In this chapter, we look at the three ways that such shifts occur: when voters rise up to demand change; when external actors intervene in the political system and impose change; and when political leaders are motivated to enact change themselves. The three are not mutually exclusive. As we'll see, voters may rise up when the external environment changes to shake up the status quo. But we can tell separate stories about each type of change. (In the next chapter, we turn to specific policies that may help the process along or lead to more incremental improvements. In this chapter, we provide a more descriptive—rather than prescriptive—account of how countries change.)

We focus primarily on the role of voters, beginning with an exploration of the various reasons why they so often reelect corrupt politicians. We then provide details of a rare instance in which voters managed to coordinate their support behind new politicians, thereby ejecting the old and corrupt ones from office. This case study of the extraordinary collapse of Italy's corrupt political parties in the early 1990s provides a more general set of lessons for the role voters can play in fighting corruption in a democracy.

8.1 Why do voters reelect corrupt politicians?

There's a misconception that voters in corrupt countries are happy with the status quo. If they weren't, wouldn't they elect different politicians?

That view is almost surely wrong, as survey evidence that we reported in chapter 5 has already suggested. Around the world, most people think that corruption is a big problem.

Yet politicians implicated in political malfeasance nonetheless get elected and then reelected.[1] In Italy, in a period spanning more than four decades, voters (97 percent of whom, keep in mind, told Eurobarometer surveyors in 2014 that giving and taking bribes is never acceptable) reelected hundreds and hundreds of legislators who were under investigation for illegal dealings. This continued until the party system collapsed under the weight of political corruption in 1994. (We'll have more to say on this later in the chapter.) In India, candidates under indictment for criminal wrongdoing are substantially *more* likely to be elected to state and federal legislative bodies than their unindicted counterparts.

In Japan, a low-corruption country (based on Transparency International's Corruption Perceptions Index [CPI]), legislators convicted of corruption have also been rewarded with additional votes. How else can one explain the fact that 62 percent of legislators convicted of corruption between 1947 and 1993 were reelected?[2] Take the case of Kakuei Tanaka, who eventually rose to the post of prime minister. Early in his career, Tanaka had already been caught taking bribes from coal-mining interests, which landed him in prison in 1947. He nonetheless rose through the ranks of Japan's dominant Liberal Democratic Party, holding several cabinet positions and then assuming the office of prime minister in 1972. He was forced to resign just two years later, when he was implicated in questionable land dealings. In 1976, while a sitting member of parliament, Tanaka was accused of having taken US$1.8 million in bribes during his time as prime minister, in exchange for securing a contract with the country's airline. Following his criminal conviction, Tanaka filed an appeal and was reelected to parliament in 1983 with an unprecedented margin. Then, perhaps just to thumb his nose at those responsible for the bribery revelations, he had himself appointed to the parliament's ethics committee.

Italian, Indian, and Japanese voters are not alone in their willingness to support corrupt candidates. U.S. Congressman William Jefferson— infamous for the brick of US$90,000 in cash that the FBI seized from his freezer in 2005—was similarly reelected just a year later. In fact, Washington lawmakers are regularly reelected amid corruption investigations. And we could go on—politicians involved in malfeasance are more likely than not to be reelected in every country of the world on which data have been collected.

Why, if voters don't like corruption, don't they throw the bums out?

One obvious explanation is that voters may have political priorities other than corruption—they may vote along partisan, caste, or ethnic lines, for instance, or they may elect corrupt officials they think are wiser or more competent than their less corrupt challengers. (Japan's Tanaka came into the prime minister's office in 1972 with the highest popularity rating in that country's history, so presumably voters thought highly of him for reasons other than his experience with corruption.) Or voters may evaluate how well an incumbent performed while in office and decide to tolerate whatever corruption occurred because policy performance was nonetheless good enough. When the economy is doing well, voters may be more tolerant of the malfeasance and misdeeds of individual politicians.[3]

From a voter's perspective, the sense that corrupt politicians are doing a reasonable job is reinforced by their success in directing small bribes (as well as larger chunks of government expenditures) to their constituents. Where clientelism is common, corruption is more apt to flourish. And whatever their illicit dealings, these politicians are experienced in the workings of politics.

Below, we'll focus on two broad classes of additional explanations—let's call them "information" and "coordination"—for why voters might reelect corrupt politicians despite genuinely preferring honest representatives to dishonest ones. These may be less self-evident than the "different priorities" explanation above but, we would argue, are no less important and are potentially of greater relevance for reformers.

8.2 Does lack of information lead voters to reelect corrupt politicians?

Voters might be unaware of corruption when casting their ballots, even when a legislator is charged with or convicted of wrongdoing. Perhaps they don't pay attention to politics because they have other concerns to attend to (which may be compounded by citizens' disillusionment with corrupt politicians). The average American, for example, doesn't know which party controls the Senate or the House of Representatives, suggesting that ignorance of political affairs is all too common. Maybe too many stories of corruption get buried in the back pages of the newspaper. And much of the world doesn't have access to daily news, even if people wanted to know what their political representatives were up to. That's the situation for the hundreds of millions who can't read or who have limited access to electricity—and no television to tune in to the news even if they did. Maybe it's possible to keep up on current events via radio or, today, even by cell phone. But in many poor countries, the government controls the press, so reports of political malfeasance are not broadcast.[4] Even where the government itself doesn't own the media, it's very often controlled by a handful of family-held companies that enjoy cozy relationships with the political regime.

If better information were all that stood between voters' desires and the reality of corruption-free government, then spoon-feeding them facts about legislators' records should go some distance toward solving the problem. The evidence for this is surprisingly mixed, however.

One study, by economists Claudio Ferraz and Frederico Finan, illustrates the potential that information *may* have in shifting voting behavior.[5] Ferraz and Finan focus on a program that aimed to expose municipal corruption in Brazil, implemented in 2003 by the government of Luiz Inácio Lula da Silva (known as Lula to the electorate). The program picked cities at random for audits by the national anticorruption agency, the Controladoria-Geral da União (CGU). The CGU took care to ensure that the selection of cities was not itself corrupted. Selection was done through a nationally televised lottery. If you're picturing a bunch of numbered Ping-Pong balls (with each number corresponding to one of Brazil's 5,570 municipalities) popping around in a clear plastic sphere until one drops out, you've got the right image in mind. Members of the press as well as everyday citizens were on hand to ensure that each municipality's number was entered into the lottery and that no one doctored the balls to protect any municipality from scrutiny.

Once selected, the municipality received a visit from about a dozen CGU investigators charged with examining whether federally transferred funds had been used appropriately by the local government. The auditors looked primarily for fraud or suspicious procurement practices—over-invoicing on hospital or school supplies; awarding of contracts without open bidding; outright embezzlement. Ferraz and Finan highlight a few egregious examples uncovered by investigators: a company with no construction experience that was paid five times the estimated cost to build a 9-kilometer road (it simply subcontracted the job to a construction firm, netting profits of over 150 percent on the deal); expenditures exceeding US$100,000 on medicines that never arrived; and so on.

These reports were then summarized and disseminated via the Internet and through media outlets. In 376 municipalities, the results of these audits were available about a year prior to the local elections that were held across the country in October 2004. In municipalities where the auditors found no improprieties, Ferraz and Finan found that incumbent politicians were elected at higher rates than in places where no audits had been conducted—the investigations had revealed to voters that their leaders were honest. But in places where two or more corruption cases were uncovered, the probability that incumbent mayors were reelected was 17 percent lower than in unaudited municipalities; three or more violations led to a 34 percent lower chance of reelection.

Other evidence indicates that these effects were coming from the audits and the information campaign that followed. First, the effects were stronger in towns that had local radio stations to publicize the audit results. Second, there is a natural "control" group to distinguish the role of dissemination of corruption information from the role of corruption itself. Nearly 300 audits took place in the six months immediately following the 2004 elections. Any corruption revelations coming out of these later audits didn't become available to voters until after they had cast their ballots. For these postelection audit reports, corruption that investigators uncovered had no effect on how incumbent mayors fared at the polls, as one might expect if the audit reports provided useful information for voters.

It's a tantalizing result for would-be reformers: information will set you free! But subsequent research on the impact of information on vote choices has produced mixed results. On one hand, there are the results of a 5,000-person survey administered in India that asked voters to evaluate hypothetical political candidates based on characteristics like party affiliation, ethnicity, and criminal history. Perhaps unsurprisingly, voters say they prefer candidates without criminal backgrounds.[6] These findings line up with those of Ferraz and Finan, but rely on hypothetical choices—they don't necessarily tell us what voters will do in real elections.

A study of a real election in the state of Jalisco in Mexico produced different, and quite discouraging, results (we also discuss the study in chapter 4).[7] There, an information campaign on incumbent corruption led to a large drop in electoral turnout without affecting the incumbent's vote share. That is, telling voters that their elected officials were crooks apparently just confirmed suspicions that politicians were dishonest. This result generates a Catch-22—giving voters information that they need to thoughtfully cast their ballots about corrupt politicians may just make them more distrustful and apathetic, and lead them to stay away from the polls altogether. Without a clearly honest challenger to endorse, reminding voters that politicians are corrupt is simply demotivating and depressing.

We're still a long way from reaching any conclusions based on these (and other) findings about how voters respond to information. Furthermore, much probably depends on the source, some of which are more credible to voters than others. A study of an informational campaign in Brazil found that voters were more skeptical of reports accusing a political candidate of corruption when they appeared to come from another political party than when they were attributed to a nonpartisan federal audit.[8] Such concerns are well founded: given the dirty nature of modern political campaigns, who's to know what's a smear by the opposition and what's an honest report of misdeeds? Perhaps the Brazilian audits studied by Ferraz and Finan were so successful because the information came from a respected and politically impartial auditing body, and because the revealed transgressions could be clearly tied to a single culpable local politician. Such considerations show that resolving voter ignorance isn't the cure-all that advocates of the information view had hoped: who provides the information and how voters evaluate electoral alternatives also matter in subtle ways.

8.3 Why do voters need to coordinate to get rid of corrupt officials?

In a democracy, any single voter is powerless to do much about corruption in casting her ballot. To eject corrupt incumbents from office, voters need to coordinate their electoral behavior around alternative—and noncorrupt—candidates.

What do we mean by coordination in this context? We're using the term in a very specific way, to mean a particular action that an individual decides to make because of her knowledge or beliefs about the actions that others will choose (possibly complementary to her own). We introduced the term *contingent behavior* in the introductory chapter to this volume to describe situations where your decision about what action to take depends on what you think others will do. Here, we go a step further to consider behavior that is contingent on what you know others know. If it seems a confusing or esoteric notion, a concrete example may help. Think back to the Arab Spring of 2011. Put yourself in the shoes of a would-be Egyptian revolutionary deciding whether to go to Tahrir Square to protest against the Mubarak regime. It makes little sense to go if you'll be the only placard-carrying protester facing down the troops. Nor should you go to Tahrir Square if other protesters are headed to Nahda Square. Your choices of whether to protest and where to go depends on what you think others will do, and that in turn depends on what you know that they know (i.e., do they all know everyone else is going to Tahrir Square and hence will they show up there as well). During the Arab Spring, protesters, of course, didn't leave those information flows to chance—they took to the Internet to ensure that everyone knew where and when to show up to take down the government. They used a specific information channel in order to create *common knowledge* to coordinate their protest activities.

In his book-length treatment of the topic,[9] political scientist Michael Chwe argues that the concept of common knowledge explains many otherwise mysterious phenomena. Why, for example, are advertisers willing to pay so much more *per viewer* for ads during the Super Bowl, the championship game of the American football season? It's the most-watched show on U.S. television. So if you're selling a product that's valuable to a customer only if lots of others use it as well, the annual ritual of viewing the Super Bowl—commercials included—is the best way of generating common knowledge that your product may be the next big thing. Chwe gives the example of Apple's 1984 launch of the Macintosh computer, at the time incompatible with other personal computers on the market. Buying a Mac meant forfeiting use of all the software written for other personal computers on the market. Thus, you'd only buy a Mac if you expected you could trade files with your friends and that there'd be enough sales that programmers would produce Mac-compatible games and utilities. Launching the Mac with a Super Bowl ad guaranteed that everyone who was interested knew that everyone else who might be interested also knew about the Mac. If we go to movies partly so we have something to discuss with our friends, a Super Bowl ad for the next installment of *Star Wars* can help us coordinate on all seeing the same film.[10]

Of more direct relevance to our setting, Chwe's arguments can help to make sense of why pure information interventions may fail to change voter behavior. A flyer that arrives in the mail and decries a politician's corruption or ineptitude is seen by only a single voter, who has no idea how many others have received the same information or how they have responded to it. A campaign message on a popular TV show—like the Super Bowl— creates common knowledge. You can be sure that any information you receive during the Super Bowl is also known to a very large community of others.

For a voter hoping to kick out a corrupt political incumbent, this type of common knowledge may be critical. That's because there is probably something a voter needs to give up in order to switch his partisan allegiance. To keep themselves in office, corrupt politicians construct clienteles—groups of voters whose support they buy with payments in gifts or money. Even if the bribe isn't large—a pair of shoes; a toaster; a few dollars—it's at least certain.

The coordination problem confronting voters depends on their country's political institutions. In party list electoral systems, where multiple legislative representatives are elected from each constituency, throwing out one rascal may only serve to punish voters from the localities where most of his supporters had been concentrated. Voters need to somehow coordinate to eject *all* corrupt legislators in a constituency from office at once. Similarly, in single-member districts, throwing out a corrupt but politically experienced representative to replace him with an inexperienced newbie might only generate what is called a "punishment regime" against the constituency as a whole:[11] the denial of government benefits either deliberately or simply because of the inability of the new and inexperienced representative to get anything done in the corridors of power.

How much does coordination matter in practice in shifting voter behavior? One recent study, conducted by researchers Kelly Bidwell, Katherine Casey, and Rachel Glennerster in Sierra Leone, explicitly sought to identify the importance of common knowledge. Their findings suggest that common knowledge may be important both for changing how citizens vote and disciplining politicians once elected. The research team partnered with a civil society organization to provide voters in fourteen constituencies access to candidate debates for the 2012 parliamentary elections.[12] The debates were screened in two different ways: in some communities, viewing was done at large public gatherings; in others, individual voters were given electronic tablets to watch the debates in private. The difference between the two forms of delivery is subtle but meaningful. Learning in a public setting provides more than just the immediate content of the message—it also conveys the fact that everyone else has received the same information. Furthermore, a communal viewing lets each individual see how others react to the debate performances, which may help them to formulate their expectations of how others will respond to the new information.

Candidates who performed well in the debates received more votes in both groups, relative to a control group of communities where no arrangements were made for residents to watch the debates. So voters assessed the information they received in reasonable ways, and incorporated it into their decisions about how to vote. More strikingly, the connection between debate performance and vote share was much stronger in communities where the debate was viewed publicly than in communities where viewing occurred in private. Equally important, the heightened scrutiny affected the behavior of candidates themselves. Where the debates were public, the candidates spent more time and money on their political campaigns. This shows that they became more attentive to their constituents and more concerned with winning their votes, where they knew that voters possessed common knowledge. Even more intriguing was what Bidwell, Casey, and Glennerster found after the election took place. Elected legislators who had been randomly selected to participate in the debates spent more than twice the amount in discretionary development funds in the following year in the communities where the debates had been screened publicly. (Development funds are government monies that are available to legislators to use at their discretion specifically for projects to enhance economic development, such as public infrastructure.) In other words, generating common knowledge about a candidate's promises during the election campaign appears to have led to greater responsiveness to voter welfare once elected.

The study highlights the promise of common knowledge in changing voter behavior—and changing the performance of politicians. Voter knowledge about candidates, it seems, matters a great deal more when it is common knowledge.[13]

We conclude this section with an example that clearly identifies common knowledge as a decisive factor in a major shift in societal norms. While it is unrelated to corruption, it underscores the pivotal role that common knowledge can play in driving a rapid shift in social equilibrium. It is the story of the sudden end to the Chinese custom of foot binding at the turn of the nineteenth century. Despite being a source of pain and deformity, foot binding had been a common practice for centuries, and was essential to a young woman's success in the marriage market. All parents might have preferred not to subject their daughters to such agonizing and dangerous treatment, but none could act alone without endangering their daughters' marriage prospects. (At the time, remaining unmarried was not an option.) Chinese society was in a bad social equilibrium and needed to coordinate its way out of it. In his game theoretic treatment of foot binding and its demise, political scientist Gerry Mackie emphasizes the very public methods of late-nineteenth-century reformers in bringing about rapid change. Reformers advertised the fact that no society other than China engaged in the practice, indicating that coordinating on a different set of norms was possible and, indeed, normal. Reformers created natural-foot societies, where parents could publicly commit to leaving their daughters' feet unbound. (They also ran public education campaigns, in line with a role for information as well.) As is the case for a shift in equilibrium, particularly one where once everyone has made the shift they are all better off, once change began it took place very rapidly. A practice that had persisted for a thousand years ended in a single generation.[14]

In summary, both theory and evidence to date point toward an important role for coordination in bringing about social and political change. Coordinated social change can be rapid and thorough, rather than incremental and piecemeal; it allows an equilibrium to "tip," thereby escaping the pressures that push outcomes back to their initial state, making these forces push instead toward the new norm. If ordinary people are to succeed in substantially changing the status quo, it seems likely that using common knowledge and coordinating their efforts will be part of the solution. We hope that researchers will, in the future, be able to provide reformers with more evidence and better guidance on how best to shift voters' expectations and beliefs that others also care enough about corruption to do something about it when casting their ballots.

Case Study: How Italian voters threw out a corrupt political class

By far the most dramatic contemporary example of voters successfully retaliating against a whole class of corrupt politicians occurred in Italy in 1994. Almost the entire lower house of representatives—known as the Chamber of Deputies—was thrown out of office in the wake of a gripping corruption scandal that implicated almost the entire political elite of the country. The only established political party to survive the turmoil was (under a new name) the Italian Communist Party (its Italian acronym was PCI), which, as Italy's long-standing party of the opposition, remained mostly untainted by corruption. This shift in the political landscape was the result of many contributing factors. We believe that common knowledge among voters of a desire for change was a particularly important one.

In this instance, the press—at the time relatively free and independent of government pressure—played a critical role in coordinating voters' expectations that other voters were also turning against corrupt incumbents.

The voter revolt was set in motion with events that occurred in February 1992, when public prosecutors arrested Mario Chiesa, the head of the Italian Socialist Party (its Italian acronym was PSI) for the province of Milan. Chiesa was charged with accepting a modest bribe of seven million lire (about US$4,000) from the cleaning company that held the contract for a government-run old-age home, where he sat on the board. It might all have stopped there. Except the PSI, hoping to protect its reputation, tried to give Chiesa the cold shoulder. He was not pleased. After seven weeks in jail, Chiesa finally started talking to investigators about corruption among his former colleagues, and within months the judiciary had unraveled a complex hierarchy of bribes and kickbacks that led all the way up to members of the national government. The investigations, known as Mani Pulite, or Clean Hands, implicated—among others—more than a third of the members of the Chamber of Deputies who held seats in the 1992–1994 term as well as six former prime ministers and several thousand local politicians. Within two years, the major political parties that had governed Italy for the preceding forty years had all but vanished, in part because they lacked experienced politicians to run for office who had not been charged with malfeasance and the parties were no longer willing to nominate the same tainted cast of characters.

These were hardly the first corruption accusations to hit Italian politics. The head of the Socialist Party, Bettino Craxi, testified to the Milanese court in 1993 that he had known about bribes and kickbacks to the country's political parties "since I was in short trousers," and that the money was essential to the operation of election campaigns. Nor had these earlier cases escaped the notice of Italian enforcement authorities. You can see this in Figure 8.1, which shows the proportion of deputies for whom the judiciary requested a removal of parliamentary immunity, in order to proceed with criminal investigations, for each legislature since World War II. (At the time, legislators were protected from judicial inquiry unless their fellow lawmakers voted to lift their immunity.) For the ten legislatures leading up to the Chiesa affair, the fraction investigated for serious offenses fluctuated between 10 and 20 percent—hardly insubstantial. While there is a notable increase—to about 35 percent—in the Eleventh Legislature, many investigations had occurred in every postwar session of parliament before then.

It was thus unlikely to have been the direct effect of the increased number of investigations themselves that led to the sea change in attitudes among voters. They'd had the chance to observe hundreds of corruption cases over the preceding decades, and already understood that the political elite was

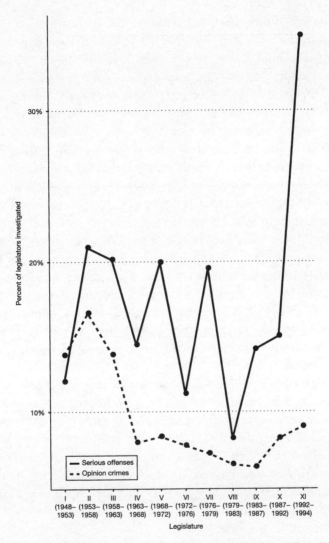

Figure 8.1 Line Graphs of Percentage of Italian Deputies Investigated by the Judiciary by Type of Allegation for Eleven Postwar Legislatures (1948–1994)

Note: Opinion charges are related to libel, slander, and similar; all others are serious. Data from M.A. Golden, Datasets on charges of malfeasance, preference votes, government portfolios, and characteristics of legislators, Chamber of Deputies, Republic of Italy, Legislatures I–XI (1948–92). Available via Dataverse and retrieved from http://dvn.iq.harvard.edu/dvn/dv/golden.

involved in illegal activities. Rather, the high number of immunity requests that occurred in 1992 and 1993 may have served to finally catalyze beliefs in a consensus on the need for change. That, in turn, may explain why politicians could no longer circle the wagons to protect their own. Before 1992, judicial requests to lift immunity were routinely denied by the legislature; between 1992 and 1994, even the continued reluctance of a majority of members of the legislature to permit the judiciary to investigate the accused was insufficient to keep the lid on corruption. The public outcry became overwhelming.

Until 1992, even deputies under investigation for suspected wrongdoing would generally seek reelection rather than voluntarily step away from public office. Likewise, voters tended to reelect them, as shown in Figure 8.2, which provides the fraction of deputies reelected, split by whether or not they'd been under investigation in a prior legislature. Through 1987 (when the electoral system was modified), a deputy had better-than-even odds of being reelected, a rate that was unaffected by whether he had been under investigation for corruption.

All this changed in 1994. In elections that year, not only were more lawmakers investigated, but conditional on investigation, they were far less likely to be reelected—all but 15 percent of charged deputies were thrown out of office. Even deputies unsullied by judicial investigation fared poorly at the polls, probably because the public suspected that if the legislature had not been dissolved for early elections, the judiciary would have gathered sufficient evidence to request the removal of immunity for the latter as well.[15]

Until then, Italian voters had tolerated corrupt politicians for decades. Why did voters suddenly rise up and voice their dissatisfaction with corrupt politicians at the voting booth?

In order to understand the confluence of factors that set these changes in motion, some background on Italian politics circa 1990 is in order. Italian politics at the time were, to a large extent, defined by global geopolitics. The Italian Communist

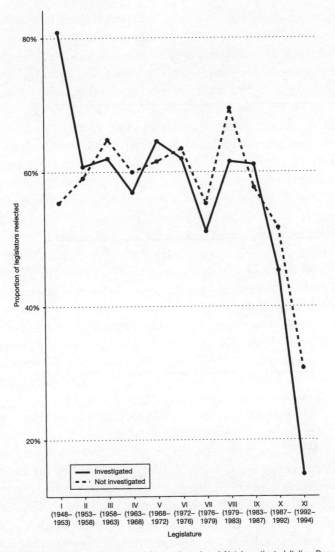

Figure 8.2 Line Graphs of Percentage of Investigated and Not Investigated Italian Deputies Reelected for Eleven Postwar Legislatures (1948–1994)

Note: Serious charges only. Data from M.A. Golden, Datasets on charges of malfeasance, preference votes, government portfolios, and characteristics of legislators, Chamber of Deputies, Republic of Italy, Legislatures I–XI (1948–92). Available via Dataverse and retrieved from http://dvn.iq.harvard.edu/dvn/dv/golden.

Party was Italy's main opposition party. Cold War politics being what they were, this meant that many voters were reluctant to support the opposition, thereby locking themselves into voting for the parties of government. The lack of genuine political options for many voters crippled their ability to hold the governing coalition fully accountable. Fear of losing office, which often helps to discipline political parties, was largely absent in Italy. Politicians from the two parties that dominated postwar legislatures, Christian Democracy (DC) and the Italian Socialist Party, became increasingly embroiled in elaborate schemes for bribes and kickbacks in public works contracting. Initially, a lot of this illegal activity occurred in the Italian South, with the active complicity of criminal organizations such as the Mafia. But by the 1980s, kickbacks in public construction had spread northward, which put the squeeze on small construction companies seeking to win government contracts there as well.

So before we even get to coordination among Italian voters, there was a coordination problem to be confronted by Italian businessmen, whose confessions of bribe payments to politicians were essential to exposing corruption to the electorate.

The first businessmen—including Mario Chiesa himself—who were questioned by the Italian judiciary in 1992 were reluctant to incriminate themselves by ratting out government authorities; some of them sat in jail for months before ultimately cutting deals with the judges. (Italy has no habeas corpus, so businessmen could be held in jail until they agreed to cooperate.) These early deals involved charging businessmen with the lesser crime of having been extorted by politicians (*concussione*, in Italian) rather than the charge of having paid bribes to politicians (*corruzione*, in Italian).

It's understandable why those netted in the first wave of arrests were so reluctant to confess—at that point, everyone still believed that the political status quo would be maintained, and that they'd be protected by the political parties whose members had shaken them down for bribes. Breaking the silence that held together this corrupt equilibrium would shut out the firm from receiving government construction contracts once the businessman got out of jail—resulting in financial ruin.

But as the months passed, belief in the stability of this corrupt equilibrium began to fray. As cases piled up, businessmen began to worry that the hold on political power by the DC and PSI might be less secure than in the past. The April 1992 elections, which occurred just at the start of the Mani Pulite investigations, marked the rise of the Northern League—a federalist, antisouthern party that appeared out of nowhere to capture 55 seats out of 630 in Italy's lower house—and a decline in support for the Christian Democrat and Socialist parties. The election results introduced fear among bribe-paying businesses that their years of political protection might be coming to an end. The concern that surfaced in early 1992 was nothing compared to the panic that ensued among bribe-paying businessmen when, in November 1993, the Christian Democrats saw their vote share cut in half in local elections. In the intervening year and a half, Socialist Party leader Bettino Craxi had his parliamentary immunity stripped so that prosecutors could proceed against him with forty-one separate charges of corruption. No one, it seemed, was safe.

This sequence of events flipped businessmen's incentives upside down. As more of them began spilling the beans to the investigating judges (providing, in turn, more evidence for further investigations), the more likely an equilibrium shift became. Within six months, businessmen in Milan, where the investigations were centered, became so convinced that the old way of doing business had come to an end—and a shift in equilibrium was underway—that, instead of waiting to be subpoenaed, they voluntarily banged on the doors of the courts of justice to confess to the bribes they had paid.

This kind of snowballing is typical in circumstances that require common knowledge to effect change. Consider the situation of a businessman facing the choice between confessing versus staying silent. The very first confessor expects a steep cost to his action, given that a continuation of the corrupt status quo is likely at that point. The next confessor faces a slightly greater chance that the equilibrium will shift, and hence slightly greater incentive to confess. By the time businesses were lining up to sign their confessions, enough had preceded them that the shift had become all but inevitable. A businessman's cost-benefit trade-off was inverted by this point—staying silent only made sense if his connections in government stayed in office, and with the cascade of confessions flooding in (as well as the change in the electoral fortunes of the governing DC), that had become increasingly unlikely. *Failure* to confess now would risk killing a businessman's company, under the increasingly likely scenario that he would get ratted out by another confessor.[16]

The judges understood the importance of securing these early confessions—that's why they offered sweetheart deals to the first businessmen to confess. These confessions gave the judges the information they had long been seeking, which set the stage for formal investigations into suspected corruption by seasoned politicians. This in turn set off a further component of Italy's political transformation. Given their unprecedented scale, the press gave outsized attention to the investigations. Day after day, new confessions and new allegations filled the headlines. In-depth reporting detailed the collusive networks connecting businesses to literally thousands of elected officials. The collapse of the Soviet Union freed voters to switch their loyalties to the communist opposition (by then rechristened the Democratic Party of the Left). Voters could finally see a legitimate opportunity to dump the incumbents. Sensing an opening, new political parties sprang up, taking stronger stands against corruption, the Mafia, and organized crime, and generally against the existing political order. This further served to highlight to voters the shifts and opportunities underway.

There are many elements to this story of transformation: an independent judiciary that was free to pursue leads into political corruption; a free press that publicized the results; the confessions of bribe-paying businesses as the costs of continued collusion rose; and finally the common awareness among voters that others were fed up, making it worthwhile to switch their own partisan allegiances. Italian voters had known for decades that corruption was omnipresent at every level of government. The existence of corruption wasn't new news. The investigations, however, provided a common cause that voters could rally around, leading to an awareness that other voters were equally tired of political corruption and that casting their ballots accordingly could finally result in a change.

In the 1994 elections that followed the Clean Hands revelations, more than 70 percent of the deputies elected had never served in parliament (compared with the previous parliament, in which a third of deputies had already served three or more terms).[17] The two largest parties that emerged were new, and by one estimate more than a third of the voters switched their partisan allegiance.[18] The parties most implicated in corruption—the Socialists and the Christian Democrats—were wiped out. Change was swift, and devastating to the old political order.

Did the Clean Hands revelations cause an equilibrium shift?

The theory we have advanced to interpret the equilibrium shift in Italian politics focuses heavily on voters. We have argued that voters, who had disliked but tolerated political corruption for many decades, were presented new options at the voting booth and became aware that other voters were likely to shift their support to new parties. The press helped voters to coordinate their rejection of the political parties most implicated in long-standing corruption. When the dust settled, was Italy any less corrupt?

There is reason to be at least somewhat skeptical. In 2014, Transparency International (TI) ranked Italy as corrupt as

Senegal, Brazil, and Romania—tied with Greece, and well below the rest of Western Europe. That hardly sounds like much of an improvement. That media tycoon Silvio Berlusconi served four times as prime minister after 1994 compounds the suspicion that corruption may have remained systemic in Italy. Berlusconi was repeatedly tried for various illegal activities and eventually convicted of tax fraud in 2013, confirming both the continued prevalence of corruption and the difficulties in legal prosecution. Most of the hundreds of politicians who were implicated in the Clean Hands investigations avoided prosecution entirely. In 2004, a survey of Italian voters asked whether public corruption had risen, fallen, or remained unchanged since 1992. Forty-six percent of respondents felt it had remained unchanged, whereas only a quarter believed that it had fallen.[19] So was the entire Clean Hands investigation and the voter uprising it generated in vain?

Let's keep in mind that surveys tend to overestimate the extent of corruption (a point we investigated in chapter 3), and for similar reasons may also lead respondents to underestimate declines in corruption. Furthermore, because TI's Corruption Perceptions Index cannot be used to compare corruption in different years (and does not have rankings that predate the Clean Hands investigations in any event), we cannot use it to gauge whether there has been a major shift in the extent of Italian corruption. So the survey data are not very useful for addressing this question.

Other evidence points to a clear reduction in—although by no means the disappearance of—the kind of corruption that the Clean Hands revelations uncovered: the networks that linked politicians, bureaucrats, and businessmen in hierarchies of kickbacks in public procurement and construction. A careful analysis by Italian political scientist Raffaele Asquer found that voters continue to reject politicians who have been exposed by the press for corrupt dealings.[20] According to Asquer's analysis, voters are as skeptical of corrupt candidates in 2013 as they were in 1994: candidates implicated in corruption remain highly unlikely to succeed in getting elected to national office. This supports the view that a fundamental change in expectations has occurred.

Another useful measure consists of reports to the police of crimes committed by civil servants, because these crimes typically involve the misuse of government office for personal gain and are thus direct (if imperfect) measures of bureaucratic corruption. Studies analyzing this data show substantial declines after 1993.[21] Alternate measures show comparable trends: the number of corruption-related crimes investigated by the judiciary as well as the number of civil servants convicted of embezzlement both nosedived after 1994.[22]

One possible reason for the widespread misunderstanding of the extent to which corruption has declined is that the Italian press is now doing a much better job—it continues to provide extensive coverage of politicians charged with corruption, even when the frequency of such cases is tiny. As a result, reading Italian newspapers generates the (mis-)impression that politicians, both left and right, are involved in corruption, when in reality the numbers are small and the ability of voters to keep the corrupt out of national public office is unwavering, as Asquer's analysis shows.

This suggests that voters in Italy have in fact successfully produced a shift in equilibrium and expectations. Despite electing Silvio Berlusconi to serve repeatedly as prime minister, voters no longer reelect standard-issue corrupt politicians. (The fact that Berlusconi is a billionaire inoculated him against the suspicion of using his office for illegal campaign fund-raising—after all, he already had all the funds he needed to run a campaign. The many accusations of illegal activities against Berlusconi generally involved conflicts of interest in how he ran his business operations, whereas the previous political elite had been heavily implicated in bribery and more direct abuse of office.) The country still has many problems—including the continuing role of organized crime, above all in the South—but this shouldn't distract us from the very real progress that Italian voters have made in curtailing corruption.

8.4 How do external forces trigger the fight against corruption?

It is very rare for voters to turn against corrupt politicians. Even when voters individually support change, obstacles to coordinating their anticorruption efforts make it difficult for honest challengers to displace corrupt incumbents.

As a result, anticorruption transformations may be triggered by external pressures rather than emerging out of voter protest and electoral retaliation. Often, this external pressure comes from outside the domestic political system altogether.

Guatemala provides a fascinating example. In 2015, President Otto Perez Molina was forced to resign to face legal charges as part of an anticorruption investigation conducted by the International Commission against Impunity in Guatemala (CICIG), a body created by the United Nations to strengthen the country's rule of law. The CICIG had been deliberately created with the view that only external—and therefore fully independent—investigators would be capable of exposing widespread political corruption. With members of Guatemala's entire political class suspected of corruption and involvement in related criminal activity during the country's earlier civil war, it would have been impossible to clean up politics from the inside. Thus, the establishment of an external investigative body was required to make anticorruption progress possible. The public was aware of widespread corruption—although, of course, ordinary citizens did not have all the details that were revealed in the course of the investigations—but was helpless to do anything until the CICIG began its work. Between 2007 and 2015, the CICIG investigated 200 cases and brought charges against approximately 200 former and current government officials, including two former presidents, a handful of ministers, police chiefs, military officers, prosecutors, and judges. Charges of customs fraud, racketeering, and bribery came as a result of 89,000 wiretapped phone calls, which revealed that the president had collected US$3.8 billion in bribes between May 2014 and April 2015 alone.

Guatemala still has a long way to go in overcoming entrenched corruption. Its ranking in TI's Corruption Perceptions Index has barely budged in the decade since the CICIG's creation (though the country has very likely been penalized for the heightened perception of corruption that, as we've mentioned previously, often accompanies anticorruption crackdowns).

To find an externally triggered crackdown that led to more decisive results, we need to go back a little further in history, to the British decision to clean up corruption in Hong Kong in the 1970s. At the time, Hong Kong residents had to pay "tea money" for just about any government service— tea money for an ambulance to get to the hospital, and tea money to get a glass of water or a bedpan from an orderly once there. There was a thriving trade in gambling and prostitution, protected by a deeply corrupted police force.

The British government was pressed to confront these problems after a high-ranking police officer, Peter Godber, slipped out of the colony while under investigation for accepting hundreds of thousands of dollars in bribes, to the outrage of Hong Kong's frustrated residents. Colonial authorities responded to the Godber affair with the creation of Hong Kong's Independent Commission Against Corruption (ICAC) in 1974. The ICAC was endowed with extraordinary powers, including the right to arrest officials suspected of corruption and bribery without a warrant. Their investigative efforts were aided by leads from Hong Kong residents, who were able to report on suspected corruption to the ICAC without fear of reprisal. As a result of these efforts, hundreds of police officers were prosecuted for corruption between 1974 and 1977. (The ICAC also worked to bring about changes in social awareness and attitudes, instituting educational campaigns in schools to increase the moral burden of participation in corrupt activities.)

The ICAC-led crackdown successfully resulted in a rapid and permanent decline in corruption—Hong Kong is considered one of the world's least corrupt nations today.[23]

Even Italy's Clean Hands investigation involved important external triggers. In addition to the obvious catalyst provided by the collapse of the Soviet Union, which freed anticommunist voters in Italy to switch their allegiance from the ruling Christian Democrats, a less noticed but arguably just as important external factor was judicial. Thanks to 1990 changes to Switzerland's penal code enacted to prevent money laundering—which were themselves the result of prodding by international judicial authorities—Swiss officials aided the Italian justice system by providing banking records of politicians suspected of corruption. The Clean Hands judges thereby finally obtained crucial evidence from their Swiss counterparts for use in their investigations.

The potential importance of an external actor in inducing a change in equilibrium is inherent to the very concept of equilibrium: in equilibrium, no one wants to change her behavior, given the status quo, so an external jolt may be needed in order to bring about change. In both Guatemala and Hong Kong, outside authorities had the independence and credibility to intervene quickly; when they moved in on corrupt networks, the public was happy to cooperate in exposing and sanctioning corruption.

8.5 How can political leadership reduce corruption?

Citizens do not always need to wait around for an external force to trigger the fight against corruption. Sometimes government simply moves on its own. This is what happened in the Republic of Georgia, which was, according to perception surveys, the most corrupt post-Soviet republic after the collapse of the Soviet Union in 1991. In addition to suffering from a rotten government, Georgia also served as a locus for organized crime, which, many believed, involved parts of the police and security forces. Popular protest against the regime's growing authoritarianism produced the 2003 Rose Revolution, which installed former justice minister Mikheil Saakashvili as president. Elected in part on an anticorruption platform, Saakashvili began immediately with a radical restructuring of the police. Within the first two years of his presidency, more than 60 percent of the country's 25,000 police were dismissed. In some units, including the highway patrol, every single officer was fired, and a handful then carefully and selectively rehired. The government was determined to demonstrate its commitment to fighting corruption to a population that had grown accustomed to endemic street-level malfeasance by police officers. Saakashvili provided substantial pay increases to new members of the reorganized police force and improved recruitment, training, and performance evaluation procedures. Suspected corrupt officials elsewhere in government were aggressively prosecuted, the government was restructured (in large part with the aim of bringing the security forces under control), and various governmental responsibilities were reassigned. For instance, a new agency was created to distribute digital identity cards, which could be used in a newly consolidated government office. As a result, instead of dealing with multiple offices, each of which had discretion to extort bribes, citizens dealt with a single office that was centrally monitored for corruption.

The reforms were remarkably successful, leading to a large decline in corruption by low-level government officials, including the police. In 2000, 17 percent of a sample of residents in the country's capital city, Tbilisi, reported having paid a bribe to a public official; the figure was only 3.8 percent for the country as a whole five years later. Georgians now trust and have confidence in their police. Reforms in other governmental institutions—business licensing and regulation, for instance—while not as dramatic as for the police, have also made the country a poster child of effective post-Soviet anticorruption efforts. In the TI rankings, Georgia has experienced dramatic improvements, moving from 133rd least corrupt in 2003 to 68th least corrupt in 2010, and then 50th in 2014.[24]

Whatever reservations we may have about the validity of TI's survey data for across-year comparisons, such a dramatic change clearly reflects something real.

Yet this new anticorruption regime proved politically unstable. Reports of human rights abuses and creeping authoritarianism fueled a shift in voter support from the government, and Saakashvili lost his bid for reelection in 2012. He subsequently left the country rather than face what he claimed were politically motivated charges of human rights violations and embezzlement. Regardless of how we parse the story, one moral is that it can be very difficult for democratic regimes to go after corruption effectively, even when they are determined to do so. Vested interests are powerful, and efforts at taking them on may be crippled—unless the regime is prepared to sacrifice civil liberties and the rule of law.

In autocratic regimes, where voters are unable to eject officials from public office even if they want to, there are also cases of leaders who take it upon themselves to clean up the government. This seems to have been the story in Singapore, when Lee Kuan Yew committed himself—and the country—to a zero-tolerance policy. Lee was one of the founders of the People's Action Party (PAP), which first entered the electoral arena in 1957 on a platform focused on curbing corruption. He became Singapore's first prime minister when Britain's colony was granted self-rule in 1959. Upon assuming power, the PAP introduced a comprehensive anticorruption policy, consisting of improved enforcement, harsher penalties, and stronger investigative authority to anticorruption officials. In the 1980s, after the economy had improved, Singapore also raised salaries and improved working conditions for civil servants. The latter was intended to reduce incentives for corruption, whereas the first set of tactics—the harsher judicial penalties and greater monitoring and enforcement—was meant to reduce opportunities.[25]

Singapore emerged as one of the world's least corrupt nations, despite a long history of widespread corruption while under British rule. In general, if an autocratic regime is truly committed to reducing corruption, it is more likely than a democracy to have the means to succeed. But as this discussion suggests, major policy shifts by autocrats are, by definition, quite arbitrary, and we have no way to know when or why an unelected leader will decide to spring a genuine anticorruption campaign on his country. Relatively enlightened leaders who decide to commit their countries to strong economic growth and low-corruption are rare; far more common are autocrats who regularly steal public funds and ship them out of the country. Overall, then, autocracies hold few lessons for anticorruption reformers: either autocrats use their authority to steal from the state, or they clean up corruption in ways that are unpredictable and likely hard to replicate in a freer democratic society.

8.6 What did we learn in chapter 8?

- There are two main reasons that voters reelect corrupt politicians:
  - because they lack *information* on politicians' illicit behavior;
  - because they fail to *coordinate* their efforts to give up individual vote-buying or patronage benefits for the collective benefit of cleaner government.

- As a result of the need to coordinate, common knowledge about candidates (and expectations about how others will vote as a result) is likely important to getting voters to eject corrupt politicians.
- Precisely because corruption is a stable equilibrium, external forces may be needed to jump-start anticorruption reform.
- Anticorruption reform can come from government leadership itself, but top-down anticorruption regimes are extremely rare and their actions implemented arbitrarily.

9

WHAT CAN BE DONE TO REDUCE CORRUPTION?

Much as we might like to think otherwise, unless humans turn into angels, corruption won't be eradicated any time soon, and even incremental improvements are hard to come by. That shouldn't discourage us from attacking the problem—reducing corruption holds the potential to improve the lives of billions of citizens in high-corruption countries.

In this chapter, we discuss a host of oft-mentioned strategies for fighting corruption. We begin by evaluating some policy measures—including high pay for bureaucrats, establishing a dedicated anticorruption agency, and others—that governments implement in order to reduce corruption. Our goal is to assess how useful each is likely to be (and under what conditions) in curbing corruption. We then confront the question of whether a government should introduce these policies incrementally (one at a time, or perhaps rolled out gradually across cities or states), or whether it is more useful for a government to concentrate its efforts in a major, multipart "big bang" approach.

To this point in the chapter, our focus will have been on government institutions. But as we've argued often throughout the book, citizens play a critical role in driving reform. We thus consider next the tools that individual anticorruption reformers—whether inside the government or acting as private citizens—might be able to access, including social media and technological fixes. We conclude by returning to the question that serves as the foundation of our entire book: how a high-corruption equilibrium can be changed, whether by political leaders or by anticorruption activists.

There are no easy fixes for a problem that has been around for millennia. We hope that our small contribution provides anticorruption forces with some insights and ideas that will make their hard work a bit more likely to bear fruit.

9.1 What government policies reduce corruption?

There is a standard set of policy instruments that government officials often look to in their anticorruption efforts. In the next sections, we review some of the most important: higher salaries for public employees, the establishment of a dedicated anticorruption agency, greater transparency, and more monitoring and enforcement. We will explore whether and how these efforts might be successful, and also discuss some of the unintended consequences they've produced in the past.

Do higher government salaries reduce corruption?

Raising civil servants' salaries is on any list of anticorruption strategies. This prescription most often brings to mind the image of a well-meaning civil servant who can't afford to feed his kids or pay their school fees on his formal salary of, say, $100 a month. To make ends meet, he needs to supplement his government paycheck through bribes.

There is surely some truth to this view. In much of the world, bribe taking is so well established and so deeply ingrained that both government officials and citizens accept that bribe income is a necessary supplement to formal salaries (in the same way that restaurant patrons in the United States accept that a tip is required after a meal if waitstaff are to make a decent living). Thus, wages stay low because everyone understands that officials receive bribes, and officials in turn must resort to bribery because their salaries are so low. Without excusing their behavior, the public may at least find it to be understandable. Who, for example, would expect police constables in Sierra Leone to survive on less than US$100 a month, which was their salary until 2014. (Their wages were increased that year, along with those of select other civil servants, as part of a donor-funded project to—you guessed it—curb corruption.)

The raw correlation between government salaries and corruption is negative.[1] In other words, across the many countries in the world for which data are available, those with higher government salaries also exhibit lower rates of corruption. The extreme cases seem to further support this relationship—in addition to the fact that civil servants in many highly corrupt countries are paid too little to survive (making it all but certain they will take bribes), proponents of the higher-wages-as-anticorruption strategy often point to Singapore, where top officials earn salaries in excess of a million dollars—and run a squeaky-clean government.

These casual empirical observations still leave us a long way from having any real confidence that raising salaries reduces corruption. Furthermore, when we look into the details of specific instances of government pay hikes, we find that their track record is rather mixed. For example, a 2008 study by economists Prachi Mishra, Arvind Subramanian, and Petia Topalova looked at the effects of a pay reform in India, which raised customs officials' salaries by up to 100 percent in 1997. Mishra and her coauthors found that the reform had no impact on tariff evasion at all, leading to the conclusion that officials kept taking bribes at the same rate after receiving their pay increase.

The study used what is now a well-established method for measuring evasion, based on the gap between reported exports and imports. Here's the basic idea: there are rarely tariffs at the country of origin on exports. So companies have no incentive to lie on their export declarations. But when the same shipment arrives in India, you need to pay duties on the declared shipment. An importer of, say, bottles of soda faced a tariff in 1997 of well over 100 percent, which created a potentially enormous increase in profits if officials could be bribed to underreport the value of soda shipments.[2]

In the Indian case, the evidence shows that if customs agents were taking bribes to look the other way when high-tariff shipments came in, they did it just as much even after their salaries doubled. Mishra et al. suggest that, given the very high import tariffs at the time, there was so much money to be made through corruption that the salary increase was of little consequence. One retired Indian official we spoke to went even further, claiming that customs officials' higher salaries allowed them to lead outwardly more lavish lifestyles, which might even have made them *more* inclined to engage in corruption. Before the salary increase, officials feared raising suspicions by spending too much on home renovations, cars, jewelry, and other visible forms of consumption. With their higher salaries, they could do so more freely without drawing the attention of neighbors or government auditors.

This misfire shouldn't lead us to conclude that salary hikes are useless in fighting corruption. But evidence like this certainly forces us to take a step back to consider more carefully the theory on how salary increases work to reduce corruption. The model we described at the outset—and the one that most of us have in mind in assuming higher salaries mean lower corruption—is that honesty is what economists call a "normal good." That is, individuals "consume" more honesty as their incomes increase. When applied to corruption, this presumes that the individual in question suffers emotionally from having to take bribes, and will indulge her conscience in being an honest public servant when she can afford to do so. But it's not clear that this model accurately describes a society where bribery has long been the norm. Public officials may have become so inured to taking bribes that they no longer suffer pangs of guilt as a result, and instead rationalize their behavior as appropriate to the circumstances. If this is the case, then raising government salaries in places where bribery is the norm may result in richer—but equally corrupt—civil servants.

Something more may thus be needed to make a salary hike an effective anticorruption tool. Perhaps at a minimum, pay raises need to be combined with genuine efforts at changing permissive attitudes toward corruption. In other words, norm change may need to accompany salary increases if the latter are to have the intended effect. We take up the issue of how this might be accomplished later in this chapter—but bribe-taking officials need to feel censured or socially sanctioned if, once they can afford not to, they continue in their corrupt ways.

By similar reasoning, enforcement also provides a crucial addition to our thinking about the salary-corruption connection. Think back to the cop in Sierra Leone earning perhaps US$100 per month. If he loses his job because a motorist reports him for demanding a bribe, it's not such a big deal—there are other jobs where he can earn just as much if he lives off the official salary alone. But double his pay to US$200, and he'll have trouble finding anything as remunerative if he's fired. Will the higher salary keep him honest? It depends on whether he thinks that bribe taking actually increases his odds of getting fired. If it doesn't, there's no reason to expect any change in behavior. In this view of the world, higher salaries and improved anticorruption enforcement are complementary tools in fighting corruption: each works better in the presence of the other.[3] This was exactly the conclusion of a study of a crackdown on corruption in public hospital procurement in Buenos Aires, conducted by Argentine economists Rafael Di Tella and Ernesto Schargrodsky.[4] They find that higher wages result in hospitals paying lower prices for basics like hydrogen peroxide and ethyl alcohol, which they interpret as evidence that higher pay reduced the kickbacks that procurement officers were demanding from suppliers. But this pattern *only* appeared following an anticorruption crackdown.[5] The study thus supports the view that higher wages are most likely to work in reducing corruption if they are accompanied by more monitoring and enforcement.

If low salaries may tempt officials to take bribes, there is also a compelling argument that setting public-sector salaries too high may also increase corruption. In fact, serious scholars—not to mention the founding fathers of the United States—have argued that government salaries should be low or even nonexistent precisely for the purpose of reducing corruption. Their argument is based on the self-selection of citizens who enter public service. Who will be most apt to serve selflessly and look out for the public's interests? Those with motivations other than money. Financially motivated individuals will be more likely to seek public office if the pay is good relative to that of other comparable occupations, and financially motivated individuals are also those who are most likely to try to profit by whatever means available once elected or appointed. This worry led Benjamin Franklin to propose that holders of public office receive no pay, lest the government be taken over by "men of strong passions and indefatigable activity in their selfish pursuits."[6] To this day, the state of New Hampshire provides no salary to its state legislators, lest they be corrupted by even a token payment.

The study we described in chapter 6, which showed that Danish college students who said they wanted jobs in government were more honest than ones destined for private sector employment, also supports the view that setting salaries too high can backfire. Less honest students with private sector employment ambitions said they'd be more likely to look for a job in government if only the pay were better.[7]

In summary, reformers need to recognize that raising salaries can have multiple, possibly counteracting, effects on corruption—effects that are dependent on making complementary reforms, possibly a change in norms or improved legal enforcement.

There is a bigger lesson to the preceding discussion: we should resist the notion that there's a silver bullet that will end corruption, or even that a given intervention, like raising salaries, will have the same effect when applied in different circumstances. Transparency, enforcement, cultural change, higher wages—they're all potentially important tools in fighting corruption, but they interact with one another in complex ways and their effects depend on preexisting circumstances. Double a policeman's salary leaving norms unchanged, and he might just breathe a sigh of relief and steal more; change what citizens expect of him as well, and he might finally lift his head and become honest.

Can better monitoring and enforcement eradicate corruption?

Perhaps the most obvious way of changing an individual's decision to give or pay bribes is to make it more costly to do so, by improving monitoring or enforcement. In the previous section, we saw how this can complement the effects of a salary increase. But why not just focus exclusively on more regular enforcement and harsher punishments as the primary means of combating corruption?

The problem is that, in a country where corruption is pervasive, the officials who are meant to monitor bureaucrats and enforce the law may be willing to take bribes themselves to look the other way. In the words of the Roman poet Juvenal, "Who will guard the guards themselves?"[8] Five hundred years earlier, Plato had expressed the same worries in his *Republic*, but came to an optimistic conclusion: leaders will be well trained to serve the public trust. Given the epic scale of corruption in the ancient world, Plato's confidence in the ruling class may have been misplaced.[9] And in our modern context, why would we expect enforcers to be above reproach if they're drawn from a society mired in a culture of corruption?

One frequently proposed solution is to recruit an elite class of enforcers and cordon them off from the culture and norms that dominate a government in need of reform. These independent anticorruption authorities (ACAs) are meant to be insulated from retribution and to have broad latitude to investigate and punish violators. They're kept honest through careful selection and the cultivation of a culture of independence and integrity. Paying high salaries helps to ensure that good candidates apply, and that they stay clean in order to keep their high-paying jobs.[10]

When supported by political officials at the highest levels, enforcement authorities have seen tremendous successes. The corruption crackdown in China, launched by President Xi Jinping on taking office in December 2012, has taken down high-level officials in just about every branch of government.[11]

The city of Hong Kong, which was returned to China in 1997 by the British government, is also often cited as an illustration of the potentially transformative role of an anticorruption authority. Its Independent Commission Against Corruption (ICAC), which we described near the end of chapter 8, is credited with turning a deeply corrupted government into one that is, according to Transparency International's rankings, now among the least corrupt in the world.

To understand why it's been so hard for other ACAs to pull off the same trick, it's instructive to look at the recent experiences of the ICAC's counterpart in Kenya, the Ethics and Anti-Corruption Commission (EACC). The predecessor to the EACC, the Kenyan Anti-Corruption Commission (KACC), was founded by President Mwai Kibaki when he came to power in 2003 on a corruption-fighting platform. The KACC was created in much the same spirit as Hong Kong's ICAC—independent and autonomous. It was to be run by the muckraking journalist John Githongo, a man respected for his integrity.[12]

However, it turned out that Kibaki's commitment to honest government was little more than an election ploy. After a year or so as anticorruption czar, Githongo started to catch wind of the same kinds of shady deals he had dug up as a reporter, including transfers of public funds to nonexistent companies and overpriced contracts.[13] When he raised these concerns with senior officials, he was told to back off. When he chose to continue his investigations, Githongo was chased into exile, less than two years after taking up his post.[14]

Recall that Hong Kong's ICAC answered to the colony's governor, who in turn answered to the British Parliament and, ultimately, to the Queen. In other words, the ICAC was backed by an institution that was external to domestic politics, had a historical commitment to good governance, and was far removed from the influence and norms of local bureaucrats and even local colonial officers. (We emphasized the importance of these external pressures in our discussion in chapter 8.) The KACC, by contrast, reported to domestic political leaders who were thoroughly corrupted themselves. Setting up an independent anticorruption agency that will work may require top-level political authorities to be genuinely committed to its success. Juvenal, it would seem, was raising a critical concern for anticorruption reformers—how can we enforce reforms if the reformers themselves can't be trusted?

It would be a disservice to the hard work and successes of a handful of ACAs to lump them all in with the KACC. In a series of eight case studies, lawyer Gabriel Kuris illustrates how ACAs, confronted with similar cultural challenges and antagonism from high-level officials, have nonetheless made progress in combating corruption.[15] All of the ACAs he examined ultimately developed strong internal controls to ensure that, at least within the anticorruption organization itself, the enforcers remained honest. More intriguingly, like Githongo, nearly all "face[d] resistance from powerful beneficiaries of domestic corruption networks, who perceive the new institution as adverse to their interests." These ACAs succeeded, however, when they were able to "outflank their antagonists by building alliances with citizens, state institutions, media, civil society, and international actors."[16] Even with ACAs, then, corruption reform may ultimately depend on the active support of everyday citizens—and certainly they must rely on bottom-up support if the country's leading political authorities are not fully committed to the enterprise.

Does greater government transparency reduce corruption?

Is sunlight, as Justice Louis Brandeis once claimed, the best of disinfectants? Given his view that "publicity is justly commended as a remedy for social and industrial diseases," Justice Brandeis would surely have been pleased to see the results of an experiment in transparency run by the World Bank in collaboration with the government of Uganda in the 1990s. Two World Bank researchers, Ritva Reinikka and Jakob Svensson, had conducted a survey of school funding in the early 1990s, and had found an astonishing "leakage" rate of 80 percent—for each dollar the central government sent to school districts, only 20 cents arrived.[17] More than 50 percent of schools received no transfers at all—local bureaucrats charged with disbursing the funds kept everything. And the problem was worse in low-income school districts—a doubling of local incomes increased the fraction of funds that reached their destination by 30 percentage points.

After documenting this tragic misappropriation of resources—essentially theft from the most vulnerable—the Ugandan government set about publicizing the findings. The impact of the publicity campaign was dramatic. Between 1996 and 2001, leakage fell from 80 to 20 percent. Some schools benefited more than others. Consistent with the "sunlight as disinfectant" hypothesis, the areas that saw the largest declines in leakage were the ones with closer access to newspaper distributors, one of the main outlets through which leakage results were publicized. And this, in turn, had an effect on how well the schools served their students—schools in areas exposed to leakage information had higher increases in enrollment between 1996 and 2001, and even saw improvements in students' test scores.

There is some caution in order if we think about the extent to which Uganda's school fund success story can be repeated. In targeting school funding, the Ugandan government focused attention on the corruption of a government service that's most apt to elicit an emotional response in parents, given their strong interest in seeing their children succeed. The public's attention was captured by the storyline of corrupt bureaucrats benefiting at the expense of the country's next generation. And in directing the publicity campaign, the central government made clear that it stood behind reform efforts. Moreover, the public was alerted to the theft of school funds in a way consistent with the theory of successful cultural change that we advanced in chapter 8: everyone not only received new information but also knew that everyone else knew as well. Finally, the public was empowered to respond. The same cannot be said of citizens wishing to stop coruption in Suharto's Indonesia or Putin's Russia.

None of this is to diminish the astonishing effects of Uganda's public campaign against school fund theft. But it's worth keeping in mind that sunlight only helps to detect corruption. Citizens must also be willing and able to act upon what's uncovered.

9.2 Does gradual reform work as well as a "big bang" approach?

Governments have many policy instruments at their disposal to fight corruption. They might employ them all at once, or focus on a small subset of reforms at any one time. They might roll out changes nationwide, or start with just a few cities or regions. Change can occur in just a single bureaucracy—the police or education—or take place across all branches of government. Is it preferable to move slowly or take a "big bang" approach?

We are not the first to argue in favor of the "big bang."[18] There are many reasons to think that, if possible, moving simultaneously on multiple fronts is likely to be more effective than incremental reform. Gradual reform allows vested interests time to strategize and react by changing how they steal from government or rig contracts. Likewise, the big bang approach changes expectations more fully. Let's return to the example, discussed in chapter 8, of police reform in the Republic of Georgia. Firing the entire highway patrol, as well as a majority of other police units, certainly disrupted expectations in a radical way. Whereas in the past, everyone knew that they would have to bribe their way out of a traffic ticket, with an entirely new police force, no one knew what to expect when pulled over for speeding. It also afforded the chance to create norms of integrity and honesty among new police recruits, who weren't saddled by the corrupt culture of their predecessors. The wholesale dismissal of the police was effective in changing the equilibrium. Georgians used to be deeply distrustful of their police, and now they trust them to behave honestly and honorably. The police, in turn, adhere to these new expectations.

The example of Georgian policing illustrates the benefits of sudden, drastic, and thorough change: it shakes up expectations and allows a new norm to emerge. But big bangs are expensive and difficult to orchestrate—there are many moving parts, and the failure to deliver on one dimension can undermine the whole enterprise (recall, for example, the limited impact of raising salaries without improving enforcement). They require not only a sudden infusion of funds but also the authority of government to change policies dramatically and implement these changes effectively. At the same time, sudden change risks creating so much social and political blowback or upheaval as to make things even worse. What if the fired Georgian police had retained their service revolvers and conspired together to overthrow the democratically elected government? Even if they hadn't succeeded, in a country still recovering from a civil war, a police uprising would surely have had negative political and economic consequences.

This makes the big bang an uncomfortable path for a reform-minded government to tread. But we would argue that, given the need to shift norms to make any significant headway against corruption, the choice is largely between rapid change versus no change at all.

9.3 What tools are most effective in combating corruption?

Is there a technological solution to the problem of corruption?

In *To Save Everything, Click Here: The Folly of Technological Solutionism*, Evgeny Morozov argues that the techno-utopians of Silicon Valley (and to some extent the rest of us) have deluded themselves into thinking that technology—"Big Data," "Smart Devices," "the Internet"— will:

> [conquer] obesity, insomnia, and global warming ... politics, finally under the constant and far-reaching gaze of the electorate, is freed from all the sleazy corruption, backroom deals, and inefficient horse trading.... Lobbyists of all stripes have gone extinct as the wealth of data about politicians—their schedules, lunch menus, travel expenses—are posted online for everyone to review.... Even those who never bothered to vote in the past ...rush to use their smartphones to "check in" at the voting booth.[19]

Although Morozov has faith in the abilities of tech entrepreneurs to build apps and devices that change the way we live and interact—whether through analyzing sleep patterns or monitoring the political process—he's skeptical of their ability to solve underlying social ills. By making it so easy and stress-free to vote, will we create a more active electorate or a more complacent one? And when it comes to corruption, will technological solutions merely shift problems elsewhere? If every smartphone-wielding citizen helps to ensure that politicians don't get bribed with fancy meals or fancy watches, maybe they'll just get bought off in ways that prove even less visible and more elusive.

The truth, as always, probably lies somewhere between the two extremes, a point driven home by the story of India's biometric identification program. While the program's hard-won successes illustrate the potential of technology to reduce corruption, some of the challenges highlight the fact that technology alone will not be our salvation.

India is a long-standing and stable democracy, but a notoriously corrupt one. As a result of its democratic commitments to a deeply impoverished population, the country has undertaken many ambitious welfare and public assistance schemes. All too often, these efforts have been undermined by the misdirection or outright theft of funds. Take the Mahatma Gandhi National Rural Employment Guarantee Act (NREGA), which the Indian government adopted in 2005 to give any rural adult a guaranteed 100 days of employment at a minimum daily wage of anywhere between 194 and 240 rupees (approximately US$2–$3).[20] Its history is indicative of the problems that have afflicted many Indian social programs. A 2012 World Bank study found that NREGA was failing to accomplish its primary goal: many individuals who expressed a desire to find employment were never reached by the program, and unmet need was greatest in the country's poorest states.[21] As an exposé by the *Indian Express* found, in place of impoverished Indians, the NREGA employment rolls were filled with the ineligible—doctors and teachers, along with "ghost" workers who didn't exist at all. The *Indian Express* reported, for example, that in one village in the state of Gujarat with only 338 registered voters, there were 1,145 NREGA beneficiaries, including "some long dead, family members who had two separate job cards made in their names, government officials and some who never even stayed in this village."[22] A 2013 study found that when NREGA increased its daily wage, workers reported no change in the monies they received, indicating that officials administering the program were skimming the entire increase off the top.[23]

NREGA faces the standard trade-off between giving local authorities enough freedom to implement the program effectively while still maintaining sufficient accountability to keep them from exploiting it. The evidence shows that during the first half-dozen years of NREGA's existence, officials used their discretion to enrich themselves and their friends rather than benefit those in need. Enter the Smartcard, India's ambitious biometric identification system. Under the Smartcard plan, each Indian was to be enrolled using biometric data (typically all ten fingerprints) along with a digital photograph. All registered citizens were then to receive a physical Smartcard that included an embedded electronic chip storing biographic, biometric, and bank account details. To receive payment via the Smartcard for a program like NREGA, an eligible individual would have to go to a point-of-service device to have her fingerprints verified and, if appropriate, receive payment along with a receipt.

Registering the population for Smartcards was an immense undertaking, with a number of hiccups in implementation before the program gathered momentum. Although the first Smartcard was issued in 2006, relatively few had been handed out by 2010, when a team of economists arranged with the state government of Andhra Pradesh to study the effects of Smartcards on the effectiveness of NREGA as well as on the distribution of pension benefits. While every resident of Andhra Pradesh was to get a Smartcard eventually, the government agreed to randomize the staging of enrollment campaigns, which gave the researchers an opportunity to clearly identify the effects of Smartcards on program performance. Eight districts (with combined populations of nineteen million) were chosen for the study, and within each district a subset of several hundred subregions (referred to as "mandals") was assigned to either be "treated" with Smartcards in 2010 or 2011, or left as "controls" for later rollout.

How does this help us measure the effect of Smartcards? Think about two mandals, Kundurpi and Kambadur, in the

Anantpur district at the southwest corner of the state. The two rural mandals sit next to each other on the state's western edge, with similar numbers of inhabitants and comparable literacy rates. Kundurpi was picked at random to receive Smartcards in 2010, while Kambadur wasn't, and would thus only receive Smartcards somewhat later. Any differences that emerge in the performance of the NREGA program in Kambadur and Kundurpi in 2011 and 2012 can plausibly be attributed to Smartcards rather than some other factor like local politics or education, or to a statewide anticorruption campaign that might happen to coincide with the Smartcard rollout.

In this case, technology won the day. Relative to control mandals, NREGA participants in Smartcard-treated mandals reported receiving 25 percent higher wages, had their payments arrive 30 percent faster after a day's work, and spent 20 percent less time dealing with payment logistics. The researchers estimate that "leakage" through ghost workers and other ruses to profit illegally from NREGA dropped by more than 40 percent. They found similar improvements in the disbursement of social security pensions in "treated" mandals relative to control ones.[24]

Technology in the form of Smartcards may thus help put Indian welfare programs on track to greater efficiency and less corruption, and force them to serve the country's poor rather than its bureaucratic elite. But that shouldn't make Indians complacent, or lead them to think that technology will make their corruption problems vanish. Smartcards create winners—the intended participants of NREGA and other programs—as well as losers. Scammers who previously benefited from putting multiple cousins on the NREGA payroll, as well as bureaucrats who skimmed wages off the top, have every interest in derailing the Smartcard program. These groups will not sit quietly by and watch their illicit incomes disappear. In fact, one of the authors of the NREGA study told us that government officials had been set to end the disbursement of NREGA payments via Smartcards under the pretense of needless complication. The compelling results of the study—combined with grassroots support from the NREGA participants who benefited from higher wages—convinced them otherwise.[25]

Would-be reformers should take a lesson from a program that linked Indian Smartcards to subsidies for liquid propane gas (LPG). This story doesn't have as happy an ending. Like NREGA, LPG subsidies target India's poorest citizens, who use LPG as their primary source of cooking fuel. It's an enormous program, providing over US$8 *billion* in subsidies in the 2013–2014 fiscal year, amounting to 11.5 percent of the national government's budget (by comparison, NREGA cost US$5.5 billion that year). And as with NREGA, the LPG subsidies were notoriously corrupted through theft by officials, as well as use by ineligible households and fictitious "ghost" beneficiaries. A thriving black market also arose from the trade in ill-gotten subsidized propane.

When a Ph.D. student at Columbia University, Prabhat Barnwal, studied the rollout of Smartcard-linked fuel subsidies, he found many of the same benefits that had appeared in the NREGA program: less disappearance of funds and less government waste—it cut the cost of the subsidy program by 11 percent, or about a billion dollars.[26] Despite this spectacular savings of government money, the use of Smartcards for fuel distribution was unexpectedly dropped in the run-up to national elections in 2014. Immediately, leakage and costs went right back to where they were in the pre-Smartcard era.

Why cancel a money-saving program that allowed the government to better serve its citizens? Powerful interests had a lot to lose from a less corrupted LPG subsidy program, and were thus well motivated to try to abolish the program. Black marketeers weren't happy to lose access to subsidized fuel, and given the resulting shortage in cheap gas, black market prices went through the roof, upsetting their customers. After the program's unexpected demise, black market prices dropped by about 15 percent, pleasing the special interests that, one presumes, had lobbied for a return to corruption in fuel subsidies. The best technology that India's engineers can offer won't help much if governments don't use them.[27]

We provide one final illustration of how technological solutions to corruption may be sabotaged by those who stand to lose from their introduction. One of us, working with political science Ph.D. students Joseph Asunka, Sarah Brierley, Eric Kramon, and George Ofosu, studied electoral fraud in the 2012 presidential elections in Ghana, the first elections there to use biometric identification machines to verify voter identities. The technology was new and unpracticed, and about 17 percent of machines broke down at some point on election day. This delayed the vote and allowed some voters to cast ballots on the basis of the paper registry rather than—as required by the Electoral Commission—having their identity verified biometrically. In the polling stations without neutral, trained domestic election observers standing by to help prevent electoral irregularities, however, the rate of breakdown was double that of the polling places under daylong observation. Furthermore, in these polling stations, rates of election fraud were also higher.[28]

Technology, in short, holds great promise for tackling corruption and improving accountability. However, technological fixes require ongoing human oversight and vigilance to ensure that no one sabotages their operation, or simply presses the "off" button. Precisely because of their promise in reducing corruption, new technologies can be expected to encounter resistance and political threats of being discontinued. And when they are allowed to proceed, they encourage the corrupt to invent new methods of evasion to escape detection, which may be even more difficult to expose than their predecessors.

How useful is the press and traditional media in fighting corruption?

As the Uganda school funds experiment that we discussed earlier in this chapter suggests, the media can play an essential role in broadcasting information on government theft. A thieving-but-smart official will recognize this possibility and work to ensure that the press never gets in the business of exposing corruption. From his perspective, better that the government control what journalists choose to report. That can help to explain why, in so many countries, the media is directly owned by the government, by families connected to the party in power, or by political parties themselves.

A 2003 study on media ownership provides a number of instructive examples.[29] The fourth-largest daily in Kenya, the *Kenya Times*, is owned by the Kenyan African National Union Party. In Kazakhstan, the president's daughter and son-in-law own seven of the country's twelve media outlets, while in Saudi Arabia, the royal family owns two of the five most popular dailies. Then there are the many cases where governments skip the middleman and just own the media directly. In Myanmar, the largest TV station is owned by the Ministry of Information and Culture; the second largest, by the military. (Many cases of government ownership appear more innocuous. The British Broadcasting Corporation (BBC) is government-owned, but we know of no accusations of government favoritism there, at least not in how it reports the news. Rather, it's a case of government funding to prop up a cultural institution that can't pay its own way. In contrast to the case of Myanmar and comparable media organizations in the Ivory Coast, Malaysia, and elsewhere, the BBC, the Canadian Broadcasting Corporation, the U.S. Public Broadcasting Service, and other government-funded media organizations in low-corruption environments tend to have a high degree of operational autonomy.)

Overall, the study finds that state media ownership and influence is far higher under autocratic governments—regimes where the press is likely used as a means of propagandizing and controlling the population. If an authoritarian regime decides to make a priority of fighting corruption, as is currently the case in China, perhaps state ownership of the media can act as one tool for exposing corrupt officials. More often, as the researchers write, state ownership of the media acts to "suppress public oversight of the government and facilitate corruption."[30] Indeed, they find that state media ownership is also associated with higher corruption.

Independent media operating outside of the safe umbrella of government protection can face potentially fatal risks. Russian journalists are particularly familiar with the dangers of digging up dirt on the government. One recent casualty, the late Boris Nemtsov, was an outspoken critic of Russian president Vladimir Putin. In a 2013 report, Nemtsov claimed that as much as US$30 billion had been stolen from funds allocated for the 2014 Winter Olympics in Sochi. Nemtsov was shot four times in the back on a bridge near the Kremlin in February 2015. There is a Wikipedia page devoted to murdered Russian journalists, and it comprises a lengthy list. According to the Committee to Protect Journalists, a third of the victims covered the corruption beat.

A softer attack was allegedly launched by the Indian government against the newsmagazine *Tehelka*, after journalists conducted a sting operation capturing on film defense ministry officials accepting bribes (we discussed the sting in chapter 2). The company was targeted with government investigations and arrests in 2003 that, according to Tarun Tejpal, one of its founders, "bogged us down with a lot of legal nonsense."[31]

Yet as we learned in chapter 3, the efforts of courageous muckraking journalists can bear fruit. Recall the case of Vladimiro Montesinos, Peru's director of intelligence, who kept many of the country's politicians, judges, and media owners on his payroll. A single television station, Canal N, refused to be bought. And when Canal N got its hands on tapes of Montesinos buying the support of opposition politicians and the judiciary, it was enough to bring down the government of Alberto Fujimori.

Because the media can be so powerful, it is hard to keep it out of the hands of thieving dictators. The exposés from

Canal N, *Tehelka*, and others give us a glimpse of the enormous impact that an independent media can have in bringing about reform. The importance of an independent media is twofold: it conveys accurate information that citizens might not otherwise receive, and it creates a community of knowledge, one in which everyone knows that everyone else in the country has the same information.[32] Whether people are willing or able to act on the information is a separate matter, but without it, the public cannot respond to corruption.

What are the roles of social media in reducing corruption?

For citizen oversight of police brutality, March 3, 1991, represents a turning point. That evening, after a high-speed car chase, Los Angeles cops apprehended taxi driver Rodney King, ordered him to the ground, and beat him senseless. Unbeknown to the police, much of the scene was captured on tape by George Holliday, who witnessed the beating from his nearby balcony. Handheld video recorders, which had been widely available for just a few years, shifted police behavior into the public domain, providing evidence where it had previously been a cop's word against that of an accused felon.

The brutal treatment of Rodney King was seen well beyond the courtroom, with Holliday's footage broadcast worldwide. Today, we don't need to lug around bulky camcorders that cost nearly a thousand dollars—anyone with a smartphone can record the misdeeds of police, or indeed of public officials more generally. Nor do we need to rely on broadcast news: we have YouTube, Facebook, and other websites where video or images can go viral.

There is no doubt that this has had an impact on the conspicuous excesses of public officials in some countries. Rolex-wearing Chinese officials are far rarer these days; it's even possible that citizen documentation of the cars and jewelry of public officials pushed the government to launch the anticorruption crackdown that we mentioned earlier in this chapter. It is less helpful in countries where the government is immune to public pressure. Vladimir Putin's spokesman, Dmitry Peskov, created social media waves when he appeared wearing a US$670,000 18k gold watch at his wedding in 2015. A year later, as we write this, he is still in office and still wearing the watch.[33] Furthermore, we do not know the extent to which such "gotcha" images just push officials to take bribes in less conspicuous forms, like numbered Swiss bank accounts instead of gold watches.

Social media has also been put forward as a means of crowdsourcing information on officials' bribe demands, which, it was assumed, would then force a response from the authorities. This was the premise of ipaidabribe.com, an Indian website launched in August 2010 by the nonprofit organization Janaagraha. The website gave citizens of Bangalore, India's third-largest city, the opportunity to report the details of bribe demands online, including the amount requested and the name of the official involved. The initial response was enormous, with the site receiving over 5,000 bribe reports in its first six months. ipaidabribe.com basked in the glow of worldwide media attention, with profiles appearing in the *New York Times*, *The Economist*, and numerous Indian papers. The site reported two quick successes in eliciting government responses as well, with reforms to property registration and the driver's licensing process. Similar websites sprang up around the world: Colombia, Sri Lanka, and Ghana, to name just a few, now have citizen bribe-reporting platforms.

By 2010, though, interest in the site fizzled. Traffic to the site slowed and, more important, it reported no further successes in influencing policy. This disillusioned potential whistle-blowers even more—why go through the bother and risk of reporting if nothing comes of it? Furthermore, all crowdsourced information suffers from the common challenge of credibility: if reports can be made freely and anonymously, what's to stop a bitter driver from retaliating against an honest ticket-issuing cop by reporting him for bribery?[34] Social media can spread misinformation, fail to aggregate information accurately, and get hijacked for private vendettas. Inaccurate reports can ruin careers and lives.

Where social media offers greater promise is in allowing ordinary people to communicate with one another and to coordinate their efforts in fighting corruption. In the 2011 Arab Spring that swept countries such as Egypt, Tunisia, Morocco, and Jordan, social media—notably, Twitter and Facebook—proved important in generating protest cascades; thus digital social technology was instrumental in coordinating protest activities.

Throughout this volume, we have stressed the value of information, and in particular, the importance of common knowledge: not what people know per se, but of what they know others know and what others know they know. Social media may prove extremely valuable in creating common knowledge and allowing people to know that expectations are changing. We don't want to exaggerate the importance of social media—after all, protests and revolutions have occurred for centuries without it. But it might very well allow for the creation of networks of common knowledge more quickly and more broadly than used to be possible.

9.4 How does norm change occur?

Throughout this volume, we have framed corruption as an equilibrium. And to change an equilibrium, we need to change expectations. In this final section, we examine two ways that norm change occurs: through inspired political leadership and from the bottom up.

As we saw in our discussion of culture in chapter 6, it's possible for two otherwise identical groups or societies to end up with very different levels of corruption.[35] This can result from some accident of history that leads one population to have a culture of bribe paying and taking, and the other to have a norm of following the letter of the law. Though initially identical, each has settled into a distinct equilibrium, with different beliefs about what happens, say, when a traffic cop stops a driver for speeding: demand and offer a bribe in one society; collect and pay the fine in the other. Mismatched expectations lead to trouble for one or both parties involved.

One might be tempted to think that it should be easy enough to nudge the corrupt group toward behaving like the law-abiding one. After all, there seems to be little other than custom and convention to distinguish the two. But, as we have also emphasized, that would be a mistake. Once entrenched, norms can be very hard to change, even if everyone agrees that change would be a good thing. If we think about a culture of corruption as a societal equilibrium, with mutually consistent beliefs about how others will behave, it doesn't only matter whether you are for or against corruption. How you'll act depends on how you think *everyone else* will behave—it's painful to be the one honest individual while everyone else pays bribes to skip to the front of the line.

To reform a culture of corruption, then, we need somehow to change *everyone's* beliefs about how to behave all at once.

How can political leadership change a culture of corruption?

By some measure, norm change defines the role of a great leader. (If it were anything less, we'd have a lot more success stories to fill this book.) The eccentric architect of one of the great anticorruption reforms in modern history can give us some insights into how this might be done.

In 1994, Antanas Mockus was a professor of math and philosophy at the Universidad Nacional de Colombia in Bogotá. The previous year he had resigned as university president after mooning an auditorium full of unruly students. He defended his actions to the press, stating, "Innovative behavior can be useful when you run out of words."[36] Two years later, he was mayor of Bogotá, elected in a landslide.

The city at the time was still reeling from the legacy of Pablo Escobar and the drug wars that had left the streets in chaos and the murder rate higher than in any other urban center outside of a war zone. The election of Professor Mockus—an "antipolitician" by his own reckoning—was the result of Bogotanos' disillusionment with the political establishment. It was now Mockus's job to bring order to chaos.

To say that Mockus brought his own brand of innovative behavior to addressing the city's ills is an understatement. In an early (and now much-recounted) act as mayor, Mockus hired theater students to dress as mimes to mock jaywalking pedestrians. The mimes were also armed with cards printed with a "thumbs down" picture on them to flash, soccer referee–style, at offending pedestrians or drivers that ran red lights. (The multipurpose cards could be flipped to reward good citizens with a thumbs up.)

If you think it crazy to imagine that silent, white-faced theater students could reform the lawless streets of Bogotá, it's worth pausing to consider what the approach might have going for it. It *is* gimmicky, but that gave it the shock value and attention that more traditional interventions would never have gotten. (When their university president pulled down his pants in front of a thousand Colombian college students, there was indeed silence—that gimmick worked as well.) Mockus himself was convinced that image-conscious Bogotá residents would respond more to shaming than to police citations or fines—and as we'll see, for all his eccentricities, he had a genius for understanding what made his people tick.

Punishment through mockery has at least a couple of other advantages over, for example, sending more cops into the streets to issue more tickets for jaywalking. Recall that Mockus came to office with a decisive majority, winning 70 percent of the popular vote. So when Mockus—a candidate who clearly represented a break from politics as usual—came into office, everyone knew that *everyone else* (or at least 70 percent of everyone else) was also looking to shake up the system. The issuing of a traffic violation is, by its nature, a private transaction. The mime-shaming of offenders brought a postmodern form of street theater to busy downtown intersections, attracting the attention of thousands. Mockus cleverly deployed the mimes to allow "audience participation" in the spectacle, through the "thumbs down" cards handed out to passersby. That way, regular citizens could visibly signal their support for change by themselves shaming lawbreakers.

Also in contrast to a traditional enforcement crackdown, the mimes were bribe-proof. Imagine what you'd do if, crossing against the lights, a clown appeared behind you, holding a sign with "INCORRECTO" printed in bright red lettering. Somehow pulling out your wallet to offer a few pesos to get him to stop doesn't fit into the picture. In some ways, an enforcement crackdown might have worked in the other direction—a police force acculturated to corruption might have exploited the crackdown to extract even more bribes from civilians (while still collecting enough fines to satisfy their superiors).

And why jaywalking? It's a highly visible transgression, so it is perfect for communicating that changes were afoot. The social consequences are also limited, making it a great starting point for raising awareness of a shift in norms of legal compliance. You couldn't have solved Bogotá's enormous problems of theft or murder via mockery—Bogotá's residents wouldn't have stomached gimmicky responses to such grave concerns, and odds are Bogotá's murderous thugs would have pummeled or killed off the mimes.[37]

The mimes provided an immediate win for Mockus's government. Pedestrian compliance with traffic laws tripled in a matter of weeks. Other crimes were slower to decline. But within a few years, murders had dropped by 70 percent and the city was bursting with pride.

There was more to the Mockus success story than mimes. Early in his tenure, 2,000 traffic cops were fired to try to clean out the corrupt culture that permeated the police force. A gun buy-back program that got firearms off city streets surely also contributed to the drop in violent crime.

If you ask Mockus, he'll tell you that reforming rules and culture worked together in bringing about the city's transformation. His understanding of corruption and rule-following as a coordination problem—where how I behave depends on how I think everyone else will—may have been a critical component to his success.

What is the lesson of Bogotá's anticorruption success story? It is emphatically not about the transformative power of mimes or mockery. (It's unfortunate that a number of copycat cities tried mime-based policing after observing their impact in Bogotá.) Instead, it's about the importance of shifting societal beliefs about the right way to behave, a process where the mimes played a pivotal role.[38]

What can I do if I live in a highly corrupt country?

What if you live in a highly corrupt country that isn't blessed with a Mockus-equivalent on hand to change expectations from the top down? In this final section, we aim to speak more directly to readers who are forced to deal with corruption directly and what they can do about it. Perhaps you were asked for a bribe last week when you drove to work or to school. Perhaps your family had to pay a cash supplement to the doctor caring for your uncle. Perhaps you have an idea for a business but are discouraged by the paperwork and multiple government offices you will have to go to, each of which is likely to ask you—illegally—for a bribe to have your application considered (or considered anytime this year).

You may know that corruption is wrong, and you may not want to pay bribes. But if that's how things work, what's to be done? That is, what can *you* do?

We want to encourage you to use what you learned from this book and to think about how it may apply to your own situation. We have stressed that corruption constitutes an equilibrium, or a set of shared expectations about how to behave. Reducing corruption requires changing those expectations.

And doing this requires creating new beliefs and changing common understanding about how to behave, which in turn means that effective anticorruption activities involve groups of people operating in public, rather than individual moralism.

Transparency International has an *Anti-Corruption Kit: 15 Ideas for Young Activists* available at https://www.transparency.org/whatwedo/tools/anti_corruption_kit_15_ideas_for_young_activists/3/. It offers a list of specific anticorruption activities that ordinary people can undertake.[39] TI's list consists in part of the following:

- monitor government spending;
- audit government benefits and services;
- write citizen report cards;
- crowdsource information;
- protest;
- petition;
- ask candidates or voters to commit to election pledges.

All of these ideas are attractive and, in some settings, feasible. Some are activities that even a small group of individuals could start on their own. We hope that you'll be able to connect the suggestions from TI (or elsewhere) to the ideas we've presented in this book to better appreciate how to apply them (and which ones best apply) in your particular circumstances.

As you do so, we'd encourage you to keep your eye on the overarching goal: changing social expectations. In other words, you want to contribute to the creation of a shared understanding about corruption—where everyone knows that everyone else knows that paying bribes and selling votes isn't how things work and, indeed, that it is no longer how things *will* work in your country. This requires attracting public attention for your efforts—you need others in your community to know what you are doing. It requires that you collectively speak out. This requires courage—there is safety in numbers once there is a broader acceptance that corruption is a problem to be addressed—but it's always costly and possibly dangerous to go against prevailing social norms.

In a village or other close-knit community, attracting attention might be as easy and as obvious as putting together a public gathering among like-minded friends and agreeing not to pay bribes for some government service. Word will travel fast. In larger cities and towns, however, a communication strategy is surely going to be an important element to effecting change.

Both of us writing this book came of age long before the advent of social media platforms, which present the enticing possibility that the next generation of anticorruption crusaders will have more effective tools at their disposal. In the preceding sections we discussed some of social media's early successes, and also its limitations. However, it is still early days for this particular technology, which holds enormous potential as a means of coordinating social actions and beliefs. This promise was made clear by the way Twitter and Facebook helped reformers organize Arab Spring protests, another multiple equilibrium setting where you only want to go to a demonstration if you know you won't be the only one facing down government forces. Social media may yet prove similarly helpful in coordinating anticorruption efforts by shifting beliefs about what's expected of public officials (and, critically, how many others hold the same beliefs).

There is yet another effect of social media and improved informational flows: even the world's most remote villager now has access to a lot more information about how people behave, and ought to behave, in law-abiding, developed democracies. Maybe it is the norm to ply the traditional leader with baskets of goodies, or to vote as he instructs. Those customary practices collide head-on with what villagers see on television, hear on the radio, read in the newspaper, or review on their cell phones. New information is not sufficient for changing beliefs about how village politics operate, but it is necessary. There is almost no regime left in the world that can isolate its citizens from the message that public officials are supposed to behave in the public interest, laying bare the shortcomings of corrupt officials.

9.5 Can political corruption ever be entirely eradicated?

In this chapter thus far, we've provided a smattering of prominent ideas that have been put forth over the years to end corruption. Idealists and reformers have a much longer list, running the full gamut of plausibility. In *Corruption in America*, legal scholar Zephyr Teachout gives the example of a nineteenth-century Chicago journalist who saw the problem of American corruption as being specific to Washington, D.C., a city where "the paramount, overshadowing occupation of the residents, is office-holding and lobbying, and the prize of life is a grab at the contents of UNCLE SAM's till ...[which] makes the city a great festering, unbearable sore on the body politic. No healthy public opinion can reach down here to purify the moral atmosphere of Washington."[40]

The correspondent's solution to Washington's rotten culture was to move the nation's capital to New York where, removed from the corrupting inflences that engulfed legislators in Washington, civic virtue could thrive. Observers of Wall Street culture and the Great Recession of 2008 might question the Chicago correspondent's judgment. But the idea that the seat of government's location might affect corruption finds support in a recent study by economists Filipe Campante and Quoc-Anh Do.[41] They show that, within the United States, states with capitals that are isolated from the populations they serve tend to have relatively high rates of corruption, because they are too far removed from the voters and activists who would hold them accountable. According to this theory, the state of New York might indeed do well to consider moving its legislature from Albany to New York City.

Is it realistic to imagine that, with some creativity, experimentation, and hard work, schemes such as these will eventually come together to end corruption? Not unless human beings turn into angels, or we end up with incorruptible robots as overlords. For the foreseeable future, there will be an ongoing need to create and enforce laws to constrain officials' behavior. Sociologist Max Weber famously described bureaucracy as an "iron cage"—rigid and dehumanizing. If this cage is necessary to prevent bureaucrats from exploiting their positions of power, it can also demotivate and keep them from exercising appropriate judgment. So we need to balance rules with discretion. We can hope that, for the most part, those entrusted with public office exercise discretion with virtue and integrity. But some will not. That's a cost of relying on trust instead of rules alone.

The goal of a corruption-free world also does a disservice to the connivers and con artists of the world. As reformers find ways of keeping them honest, those intent on subverting the rule of law just as surely search for new avenues of corruption. The problem of anticorruption crusaders (and law enforcement officials more generally) is reminiscent of the ubiquitous carnival game whack-a-mole. Small furry creatures stick their heads out of their burrows, and your task is to use your mallet to whack them back into their holes as quickly as possible. But the moment you knock one down, another appears. You can never defeat the moles completely, just smack them on the heads as quickly as possible when and where they pop up. You just hope that the new ways of embezzling funds or paying bribes that appear are more costly and difficult than the ones that came before—and hence that fewer scoundrels succeed.

None of this is to suggest that anticorruption efforts are ill-spent. The problem would be much worse without the many activists and reformers that have devoted their lives to honest government. And the petty costs and hassles experienced by most of the world's inhabitants—not to speak of the billions of dollars diverted from government coffers into the pockets of politicians— make a compelling case that we're still a long way from worrying about whether we've gone too far in fighting corruption.

9.6 What did we learn in chapter 9?

- Increasing government salaries will more plausibly reduce corruption if accompanied by stricter enforcement or efforts at changing permissive norms.
- Fighting corruption through stricter monitoring and enforcement raises the question of how to ensure monitors and enforcers will not themselves be corrupted. Dedicated and autonomous anticorruption authorities have shown promise in fighting corruption when accompanied by popular support, even in high-corruption settings.
- Technologies such as biometric identification hold promise for limiting the corruption of government programs and elections. But technologies can be undermined by those who stand to lose as a result.
- A free press is useful in exposing corruption and catalyzing support for reform. But in much of the world, the media is owned directly or otherwise controlled by the government.
- Social media holds particular promise as a technology for creating common knowledge and coordinating anticorruption efforts from the bottom up.
- Effective leadership can be very important for driving change in corruption norms from the top down, serving to coordinate the further efforts of ordinary citizens.

NOTES

1. J. C. Scott, *Comparative Political Corruption* (Englewood Cliffs, N.J.: Prentice-Hall, 1972).
2. S. Rose-Ackerman, *Corruption: A Study in Political Economy* (New York: Academic Press, 1978).

Chapter 1. Introduction

1. One objection to this line of reasoning is that, if there were no corruption, the process of bidding for government contracts would become a lot more competitive. The reason is that when public contracting is corrupted, firms that are not able to offer bribes cannot hope to compete with bribe-paying firms. As a result, the latter group effectively monopolizes the industry, and bribery serves as a barrier to entry against honest competitors. In addition, in the presence of corruption, firms can often save money by reducing the quality of the work they provide—erecting schools that collapse in earthquakes, for instance—thereby profiting from lower costs rather than higher prices paid by the government. But this objection returns us to a point we made earlier: where it's commonplace, corruption distorts markets in such profound ways that it's difficult to know what the world would look like without it. Overall, we would argue that these distortions favor industry insiders, but not the community of prospective business owners overall.
2. T. C. Schelling, *Micromotives and Macrobehavior* (New York: W. W. Norton, 1978).
3. The first wave of research into corruption, which occurred during an intense period of decolonization and newly won independence

by less developed nations, reveals a very different picture of what ordinary people thought about corruption. Writing in the 1960s and 1970s, political scientists and economists such as Samuel Huntington, Nathaniel Leff, and James C. Scott depicted voters in newly independent nations as eager participants in corrupt transactions, often due to sheer ignorance about the proper roles and responsibilities of public officials. Today, however, voters in even the world's poorest nations are typically more sophisticated, with greater awareness of democratic norms and acute sensitivity to breaches of public duty. For the older view, see S. P. Huntington, *Political Order in Changing Societies* (New Haven: Yale University Press, 1968); N. H. Leff, "Economic Development through Bureaucratic Corruption," *American Behavioral Scientist* 8(2) (1964): 8–14; and J. C. Scott, *Comparative Political Corruption* (Englewood Cliffs, N.J.: Prentice-Hall, 1972).

4. We draw the bribe-benefit line as eventually sloping downward, since the payoff to bribery likely falls when there is fierce competition from other bribers.

5. Or, more accurately, understanding this is a major intellectual challenge on which no completely satisfactory work exists but which we expect many are seeking to solve.

6. This anecdote comes from R. Fisman and T. Sullivan, *The Org: The Underlying Logic of the Office* (Princeton: Princeton University Press, 2013).

7. More recently, M. Gladwell, *The Tipping Point: How Little Things Can Make a Big Difference* (Boston: Little, Brown, 2002) popularized the concept of the tipping point. For a graphical presentation of the "threshold model" pioneered by Schelling, see M. Humphreys, *Political Games: Mathematical Insights on Fighting, Voting, Lying, and Other Affairs of State* (New York: Norton, 2016), item 43.

8. Our depiction of modernization theory has been informed in particular by S. M. Lipset, *Political Man: The Social Bases of Politics* (expanded ed.) (Baltimore: Johns Hopkins University Press, [1963] 1981); and also by the amended variant espoused by S. P. Huntington, *Political Order in Changing Societies* (New Haven: Yale University Press, 1968).

9. Economist Anne Krueger coined the term "rent-seeking" in a classic 1974 paper. See A. O. Krueger, "The Political Economy of the Rent-Seeking Society," *American Economic Review* 64(3) (1974): 291–303.

10. We refer readers here to the view of democracy as competition between teams of political elites articulated by J. A. Schumpeter, *Capitalism, Socialism, and Democracy* (New York: Harper & Row, 1962), and to the theory of retrospective voting introduced in M. P. Fiorina, *Retrospective Voting in American National Elections* (New Haven: Yale University Press, 1981); and subsequently formalized by J. Ferejohn, "Incumbent Performance and Electoral Control," *Public Choice* 50(1–3) (1986): 5–25.

11. For an accessible presentation of their arguments, see D. Acemoglu and J. A. Robinson, *Why Nations Fail: The Origins of Power, Prosperity, and Poverty* (New York: Crown Publishing, 2012).

12. Our understanding of democratic institutions as self-enforcing (in the sense that people *choose* to follow formal rules) draws in part on A. Przeworski, "Selfenforcing Democracy," in B. R. Weingast and D. Wittman, eds., *Oxford Handbook of Political Economy*, Oxford Handbooks of Political Science (New York: Oxford University Press, 2008); and J. D. Fearon, "Self-enforcing Democracy," *Quarterly Journal of Economics* 126(4) (2011): 1661–708.

Chapter 2. What Is Corruption?

1. See http://www.transparency.org/what-is-corruption#define, accessed December 4, 2016.

2. The TI definition incorporates a great many other types of abuse, including sexual abuse of children by religious authorities. This involves the utterly immoral abuse of entrusted power, but extending the definition to be so broadly inclusive dilutes its usefulness, in our view.

3. A study by Italian economists Stefano Gagliarducci and Marco Manacorda shows that, when a politician is elected, local businesses are more likely to employ workers who share the politician's last name. Gagliarducci and Manacorda take this as evidence that jobs to relatives are being used by firms to reward the politician instead of cash. See S. Gagliarducci and M. Manacorda, "Politics in the Family: Nepotism and the Hiring Decisions of Italian Firms," unpublished paper, 2016.

4. Our example of vote buying in nineteenth-century upstate New York draws on the work of G. W. Cox and J. M. Kousser, "Turnout and Rural Corruption: New York as a Test Case,"

American Journal of Political Science 25(4) (1981): 646–63. Recent
research documenting voter intimidation in Hungary is I. Mares
and L. E. Young, "The Core Voter's Curse: Coercion and
Clientelism in Hungarian Elections," unpublished paper, 2016.

5. J. C. Scott, *Comparative Political Corruption* (Englewood Cliffs,
   N.J.: Prentice-Hall, 1972), chap. 1.

6. For more details on the Agnelli case, see M. Faccio, "Politically
   Connected Firms," *American Economic Review* 96(1) (2006): 369–86.

7. The results of the study are reported in M. G. Findley, D. Nielson,
   and J. Sharman, *Global Shell Games: Experiments in Transnational
   Relations, Crime, and Terrorism* (New York: Cambridge University
   Press, 2014).

8. See, for example, "Panama Papers Reveal Wide Use of Shell
   Companies by African Officials," *New York Times*, July 25, 2016,
   http://www.nytimes.com/2016/07/25/world/americas/
   panama-papers-reveal-wide-use-of-shell-companies-by-african-
   officials.html?_r=0. More details on the Panama Papers are
   available at the website set up by the International Consortium of
   Investigative Journalists: https://panamapapers.icij.org/,
   accessed December 7, 2016.

9. Legal prosecutions, although not reliable as measures of the
   overall frequency of corruption, might be useful in other ways,
   however. For instance, if the judiciary behaves in fairly standard
   ways across regions within a country—as when corruption
   investigations are handled by federal authorities—then
   prosecutions could be a reasonable measure of how corruption
   varies among states or provinces within that country. Examples of
   studies that use prosecutorial measures of cross-state corruption
   for the United States include J. E. Alt and D. D. Lassen, "Political
   and Judicial Checks on Corruption: Evidence from the American
   States," *Economics & Politics* 20(1) (2008): 33–61; and R. Fisman
   and R. Gatti, "Decentralization and Corruption: Evidence from
   U.S. Federal Transfer Programs," *Public Choice* 113(1) (2002):
   25–35.

10. The World Bank produces a similar measure, also based on other
    organizations' surveys. The particular indices underlying the CPI
    and the World Bank's Control of Corruption index differ a bit, as
    does the mathematics used to calculate them, but in practice they
    are virtually interchangeable. Because many survey respondents
    are businesspeople, measures like the CPI and the World Bank's

index tend to reflect corrupt relationships between business and government. The nature of these surveys thus makes it even more useful to restrict our definition of corruption to activities that are illegal: businesspeople are exquisitely sensitive to whether they are under pressure to pay bribes to do business, though perhaps less concerned with or even knowledgeable about whether public officials are behaving in a manner that the general public might consider untoward. So although the surveys that underpin TI's and other similar measures do not specifically refer to illegality, the general context in which most survey respondents operate makes bribery of public officials in exchange for government contracts or fixing some regulatory process the most likely point of reference for their answers. Our understanding of these types of measures has been especially influenced by C. Arndt and C. Oman, *Uses and Abuses of Governance Indicators* (Paris: OECD, 2006), which provides a detailed critique of many aspects of perceptual measures. Another useful reference for thinking about problems with indices is B. Høyland, K. Moene, and F. Willumsen, "The Tyranny of International Index Rankings," *Journal of Development Economics* 97(1) (2012): 1–14.

11. M. Razafindrakoto and F. Roubaud, "Are International Databases on Corruption Reliable? A Comparison of Expert Opinion Surveys and Household Surveys in Sub-Saharan Africa," *World Development* 38(8) (2010); 1057–69.

12. It's possible that experts overestimate the frequency of corruption because they implicitly have in mind bribes that are paid by businesses in addition to those paid by ordinary people, despite the wording of the questions they were asked. It's also possible that businesses are extorted more often for bribes than ordinary people, if only because businesses interact with government officials more frequently. It's more likely, though, that the experts' perceptions are simply conforming to a global consensus on corruption rankings, since the experts' responses are highly correlated with those from other expert surveys administered worldwide.

13. The interested reader may find a primer on forensic economic research in E. Zitzewitz, "Forensic Economics," *Journal of Economic Literature* 50(3) (2012): 731–69.

14. M. A. Golden and L. Picci, "Proposal for a New Measure of Corruption, Illustrated with Italian Data," *Economics and Politics* 17(1) (2005): 37–75.

15. "Making a Killing on Contracts: How Italy's Mafia Has Plundered EU Building Funds," *The Daily Telegraph*, October 20, 2012, http://www.telegraph.co.uk/news/worldnews/europe/italy/ 9622553/Making-a-killing-on-contractshow-Italys-Mafia-has-plundered-EU-building-funds.html, accessed August 10, 2016.

16. Note that our distinction between bureaucratic and political corruption hinges on the perpetrator of corruption. The pathbreaking study by S. Rose-Ackerman, *Corruption: A Study in Political Economy* (New York: Academic Press, 1978), distinguishes "legislative" from "bureaucratic" corruption, a focus that involves the arena of the activity rather than the perpetrator. Rose-Ackerman defines legislative corruption as influence peddling and the buying of votes in the making of laws, and bureaucratic corruption as illegal activities in administering the laws. Much of what she defines as legislative corruption is not necessarily illegal and falls instead under what we would call special interest politics.

17. While a majority of incumbents choose to recontest in every democracy we are familiar with, there is considerable variation across countries in the extent to which incumbents tend to run for office and, relatedly, their chances of winning if they do. For example, in the United States, almost all politicians at the national level choose to stand for reelection, and enjoy a considerable incumbency advantage when they do. In India, the number of recontesting incumbents is more like 70 or 80 percent (though rising), with incumbents suffering a possible electoral *disadvantage*. On the incumbency advantage of U.S. members of Congress, see A. Gelman and G. King, "Estimating Incumbency Advantage without Bias," *American Journal of Political Science* (1990): 1142–64. For a discussion of the incumbency disadvantage of politicians in India and elsewhere, see M. Klašnja, "Corruption and the Incumbency Disadvantage: Theory and Evidence," *Journal of Politics* (forthcoming). The question of a possible incumbency disadvantage has generated an interesting debate; see A. Fowler and A. B. Hall, "No Evidence of Incumbency Disadvantage," unpublished paper, 2016.

18. This view is supported in an analysis conducted by L. Iyer and A. Mani, "Traveling Agents: Political Change and Bureaucratic Turnover in India," *Review of Economics and Statistics* 94(3) (2012): 723–39.

19. The Pulitzer Prize-winning story of Walmart's misdeeds in Mexico, by *New York Times* reporter David Barstow, may be found at http://www.nytimes.com/interactive/business/walmart-bribery-abroad-series.html, accessed July 12, 2016.

20. See the information available at http://www.publicintegrity.org/2003/01/06/3160/most-favored-corporation-enron-prevailed-federal-state-lobbying-efforts-49-times, accessed February 24, 2016.

21. See, for example, the results of a 2015 Gallup poll, where 75 percent of Americans responded affirmatively to the question "Is corruption widespread throughout the government in this country, or not?" Discussion of the survey may be found at http://www.gallup.com/poll/185759/widespread-government-corruption.aspx, accessed July 11, 2016.

22. D. Igan, P. Mishra, and T. Tressel, "A Fistful of Dollars: Lobbying and the Financial Crisis" (National Bureau of Economic Research [NBER], Working Paper No. 11085), 2011.

23. The related problem that elected officials may become prisoners of information provided by the longer-serving bureaucrats they supervise was raised by Max Weber. This is different from the issue of influence peddling by business, but it stems from the same source: the lack of policy and technical expertise by elected politicians. See M. Weber, *Economy and Society*, ed. G. Roth and C. Wittich (Berkeley: University of California Press, 1978).

24. M. Bertrand, M. Bombardini, and F. Trebbi, "Is It Whom You Know or What You Know? An Empirical Assessment of the Lobbying Process," *American Economic Review* 104(12) (2014): 3885–920.

25. Another study that examines the revenues of lobbying firms that employ former staffers of senators and members of Congress reports that a lobbyist's revenues plummet when their former employer retires from government. The study's authors argue that the reason companies are willing to pay for a lobbyist's services is their government connections rather than their expertise. See J. Blanes i Vidal, M. Draca, and C. Fons-Rosen, "Revolving Door Lobbyists," *American Economic Review* 102(7) (2012): 3731–48.

26. Reported in a Washington Post–ABC News poll, Feb. 17, 2010, http://www.washingtonpost.com/wp-dyn/content/article/2010/02/17/AR2010021701151.html, accessed June 7, 2016.

27. An embarrassing illustration of how partisan payback can distort the legitimacy of patronage appointments comes from George Tsunis, President Barack Obama's 2013 nomination for ambassador to Norway. Tsunis showed a dismaying ignorance of all things Norwegian during his congressional confirmation hearings. Evidently, he had been picked for the job because of his effectiveness as an Obama fundraiser rather than his qualifications—for instance, he had never previously been to Norway.

28. V. O. Key Jr., "Methods of Evasion of Civil Service Laws," *Southwestern Social Science Quarterly* 15(4) (1935): 337–47.

29. These examples are taken from M. A. Golden, "Electoral Connections: The Effects of the Personal Vote on Political Patronage, Bureaucracy and Legislation in Postwar Italy," *British Journal of Political Science* 33(2) (2003): 189–212.

30. R. Burgess, R. Jedwab, E. Miguel, A. Morjaria, and G. Padró i Miquel, "The Value of Democracy: Evidence from Road Building in Kenya," *American Economic Review* 105(6) (2015): 1817–51, 1825.

31. S. C. Stokes, T. Dunning, M. Nazareno, and V. Brusco, *Brokers, Voters, and Clientelism: The Puzzle of Distributive Politics* (New York: Cambridge University Press, 2013).

32. A. Diaz-Cayeros, F. Estévez, and B. Magaloni, *The Political Logic of Poverty Relief: Electoral Strategies and Social Policy in Mexico* (New York: Cambridge University Press, 2016).

33. M. A. Golden and L. Picci, "Pork Barrel Politics in Postwar Italy, 1953–1994," *American Journal of Political Science* 52(2) (2008): 268–89.

34. Useful material about electoral fraud is available in F. E. Lehoucq, "Electoral Fraud: Causes, Types, and Consequences," *Annual Review of Political Science* 6(1) (2003): 233–56; and A. Schedler, "The Menu of Manipulation," *Journal of Democracy* 13(2) (2002): 36–50.

35. Electoral fraud is measured differently than other types of corruption, and is not included in the perceptual indices that are used to capture most corruption. The available measures of electoral fraud—like survey-based corruption indices in general—are often quite impressionistic, usually collected by foreign observers who come to monitor elections.

36. R. Hausmann and R. Rigobón, "In Search of the Black Swan: Analysis of the Statistical Evidence of Electoral Fraud in Venezuela," *Statistical Science* 26(4) (2011): 543–63.

Chapter 3. Where Is Corruption Most Prevalent?

1. The link between corruption and poverty doesn't depend on our choice of the particular measures we use here—any other measure of corruption (or income) that we might have selected would have produced a similarly striking pattern. Other studies, such as M. Johnston, *Syndromes of Corruption: Wealth, Power, and Democracy* (Cambridge: Cambridge University Press, 2005), utilize more complex ways of sorting countries.

2. For a more detailed account of Haiti's disappearing railroads, and other shocking tales of corruption, see E. Abbott, *Haiti: The Duvaliers and Their Legacy* (New York: Touchstone Books, 1991).

3. See P. Mauro, "Corruption and Growth," *Quarterly Journal of Economics* 110(3) (1995): 681–712.

4. This is essentially what the modernization hypothesis, which we mentioned in chapter 1, argues.

5. For a pathbreaking presentation of the role of randomized trials in improving policies for economic development (including those related to corruption and governance), see A. Banerjee and E. Duflo, *Poor Economics: A Radical Rethinking of the Way to Fight Global Poverty* (New York: Public Affairs Press, 2011).

6. This is separate from the practical matter of finding a government willing to collaborate on such a study. First, higher public servants' salaries in the "treatment" group would come out of public revenues, making it a very expensive experiment to run. Second, it would be difficult—and perhaps impossible—to keep the salary hike of those benefiting from the wage increase secret from those whose salaries stayed stagnant. At a minimum, this might lead the two groups to contaminate each other—for example, the behavior of disgruntled employees might become even worse out of resentment due to inequitable treatment. Worse still, these employees might direct their wrath toward the government itself.

7. Concerns of external validity apply to nonexperimental findings as well—even if you believe that higher government salaries are an important element in Singapore's success in fighting corruption, you wouldn't necessarily want to start raising officials' salaries in southern Italy without giving careful consideration to whether the two settings are sufficiently similar.

8. To explore issues of external validity, the organization Evidence in Governance and Politics (EGAP) has designed and implemented

parallel experiments in different countries. Information on these efforts (labeled *Metaketa*, after the Basque word for "accumulation," as in "accumulation of knowledge") may be found at http://egap.org/metaketa, accessed December 7, 2016.

9. Nobel laureate Amartya Sen has been particularly influential in bringing attention to Kerala's achievements. See, for example, J. Dreze and A. Sen, *Indian Development: Selected Regional Perspectives* (New York: Oxford University Press, 1997). For a broader discussion of the non-income aspects of development, see A. Sen, *Development as Freedom* (New York: Oxford University Press, 1999).

10. See, for instance, Amol Sharma, "It's Not the Economy, Stupid, It's the Free Blenders and Sheep," *Wall Street Journal*, April 11, 2011, http://www.wsj.com/articles/ SB10001424052748703280904576246722341966968.

11. A well-researched, on-the-ground study detailing this is A. Gupta, *Red Tape: Bureaucracy, Structural Violence, and Poverty in India* (Durham, NC: Duke University Press, 2012).

12. There is a surprising dearth of research in recent years that systematically studies the histories of how once-corrupt nations have become less corrupt. For one exception, see the collection of essays included in E. L. Glaeser and C. Goldin, eds., *Corruption and Reform: Lessons from America's Economic History* (Chicago: University of Chicago Press, 2006). Perhaps because it is more easily measured using historical data, there is more research showing how electoral fraud was reduced with the introduction of the secret ballot; see, for instance, J.-M. Baland and J. A. Robinson, "Land and Power: Theory and Evidence from Chile," *American Economic Review* 98(5) (2008): 1737–65; and I. Mares, *From Open Secrets to Secret Ballots: The Adoption of Electoral Reforms Protecting Voters against Intimidation* (New York: Cambridge University Press, 2015). An overview of the decline of clientelism is presented in S. C. Stokes, T. Dunning, M. Nazareno, and V. Brusco, *Brokers, Voters, and Clientelism: The Puzzle of Distributive Politics* (New York: Cambridge University Press, 2013), chap. 8. The focus of this last study is on vote buying by political parties, which historically was not illegal; interestingly, the factors that Stokes et al. identify as important for the demise of vote buying in Britain and the United States—industrialization,

electoral scale, and rising per capita income—overlap only in part
with macro-level factors that seem important for reducing
corruption more broadly. This suggests that in the developed
world, the causes of the decline of corruption may be distinct
from the causes of the decline of vote buying. Clearly, much more
historical research is called for.

13. For more details on this period in American history, see
R. Hofstadter, *The Age of Reform: From Bryan to FDR* (New York:
Vintage, 1955).

14. Independently of overall economic conditions, raising the salaries
of public servants is a common prescription for anticorruption
efforts, building most prominently on Singapore's success in
rooting out corruption under Lee Kuan Yew, who—among other
reforms that he implemented—drastically increased civil
servants' wages. We will discuss this very common policy
recommendation in much greater detail in chapter 9, along with
the many complications in its application.

15. N. Quian and J. Wen, "The Impact of Xi Jinping's
Anti-Corruption Campaign on Luxury Imports in China,"
unpublished paper, 2015.

16. Reported in Naomi Larsson, "Anti-Corruption Protests around
the World—in Pictures," *Guardian*, March 18, 2016, http://www.
theguardian.com/global-development-professionals-network/
gallery/2016/mar/18/anti-corruption-protests-around-
the-world-in-pictures, accessed June 12, 2016.

17. See the analysis by L. Picci, "The Supply Side of International
Corruption: A New Measure and Critique," unpublished paper,
2016.

18. Recall that we discussed experiential measures of corruption in
greater detail in the last chapter. We observed that their coverage
is too spotty and subject to their own difficulties in interpretation
to provide a reliable benchmark for changes over time.

19. The Suharto family denies allegations of corruption to this day,
and sued *Time Asia* over a 1999 exposé that pegged the family's
wealth at US$15 billion, a figure that many believe to be an
underestimate. See http://edition.cnn.com/ASIANOW/time/
asia/magazine/1999/990524/cover1.html, accessed July 26, 2016.

20. We are in good company. *The Economist* recently made the same
argument; see http://www.economist.com/news/leaders/

21699917-more-visible-scandals-may-mean-country-becoming-
less-corrupt-cleaning-up?force=scn/tw/te/pe/ed/cleaningup,
accessed June 5, 2016.

21. Montesinos was in fact known for his political savvy. Fujimori
had been a political novice when he came to power in 1990, and
many believe that he was simply a puppet, with Montesinos
running things behind the scenes. The latter reportedly boasted
that Fujimori was "completely malleable: he does nothing at all
without my knowing it." See J. McMillan and P. Zoido, "How to
Subvert Democracy: Montesinos in Peru," *Journal of Economic
Perspectives* 18(4) (2004): 70. In most tapes, Montesinos is seen
informing bribe-takers that the proceedings were being taped
(or telling recipients after the fact that a camera was running).
He similarly ensured that the cash handoff was clearly captured
on film. The tapes thus provided a threat that he could use
against anyone who might turn against him—including Fujimori,
whose presidency would be destroyed by the tapes'
release.

22. Our knowledge and understanding of the bribes paid by
Montesinos comes from the remarkable study by J. McMillan and
P. Zoido, "How to Subvert Democracy: Montesinos in Peru,"
Journal of Economic Perspectives 18(4) (2004): 69–92.

23. Evan Osnos, "Born Red: How Xi Jinping, An Unremarkable
Provincial Administrator, Became China's Most Authoritarian
Leader since Mao," *The New Yorker*, April 6, 2015,
http://www.newyorker.com/magazine/2015/04/06/born-red.

24. Xi would be hardly the first to have used the excuse of cleaning
up government to get rid of political enemies: in recent years
anticorruption campaigns in Zambia and Kenya have turned out
to be ruses by presidents for consolidating power.

25. Reported on January 26, 2016, in Ryan Lenora Brown,
"Is Nigeria's Anti-Corruption Crusade Aimed at Clean-Up or
Political Opponents?" *Christian Science Monitor*,
http://www.csmonitor.com/World/Africa/2016/0126/
Is-Nigeria-s-corruption-crusade-aimed-at-clean-up-
or-political-opponents, accessed December 7, 2016.

26. B. Nyhan and M. M. Rehavi, "Tipping the Scales? Political
Influence on Public Corruption Prosecutions," unpublished
paper, 2016.

27. For a deeper understanding of interest group politics, we refer readers to G. M. Grossman and E. Helpman, *Special Interest Politics* (Cambridge: MIT Press, 2001).

Chapter 4. What Are the Consequences of Corruption?

1. N. H. Leff, "Economic Development through Bureaucratic Corruption," *American Behavioral Scientist* 8(2) (1964): 8–14.
2. From chapter 2, book IV, of *The Wealth of Nations* (emphasis added).
3. For a modern formulation of this argument, see R. Lipsey and K. Lancaster, "The General Theory of Second Best," *Review of Economic Studies* 24(1) (1956): 11–32. Given the timing of its publication, Nathaniel Leff would have been familiar with the "second best" argument by the time he wrote "Economic Development through Bureaucratic Corruption."
4. S. P. Huntington, *Political Order in Changing Societies* (New Haven: Yale University Press, 1968).
5. In A. V. Banerjee, "A Theory of Misgovernance," *Quarterly Journal of Economics* 112(4) (1997): 1289–332, the very definition of red tape is bureaucracy that goes beyond what's necessary for government to do its job.
6. P. Mauro, "Corruption and Growth," *Quarterly Journal of Economics* 110(3) (1995): 681–712.
7. S. Djankov, R. La Porta, F. Lopez-de Silanes, and A. Shleifer, "The Regulation of Entry," *Quarterly Journal of Economics* 117(1) (2002): 1–37.
8. For a contrast between regulatory rules versus actual regulatory practices based on the Business Climate Survey, see M. Hallward-Driemeier and L. Pritchett, "How Business Is Done in the Developing World: Deals versus Rules," *Journal of Economic Perspectives* 29(3) (2015): 121–40.
9. A discussion of regulations that serve the sole purpose of extracting bribes appeared as early as 1968 in Gunnar Myrdal's *Asian Drama*, an epic three-volume treatise on the politics and economics of poverty in India and Pakistan. Myrdal quotes the Santhanam Committee, formed in 1962 to investigate Indian corruption, which observed in its 1964 report: "We have no doubt that quite often delay is deliberately contrived so as to obtain some kind of illicit gratification," i.e., a bribe. See G. Myrdal,

Asian Drama: An Inquiry into the Poverty of Nations (London: Allen Lane/Penguin Press, 1968), 952.

10. D. Kaufmann and S.-J. Wei, "Does 'Grease Money' Speed up the Wheels of Commerce?" (National Bureau of Economic Research [NBER], Working Paper No. 7093), 1999.

11. See https://www.bloomberg.com/news/articles/2013-04-25/ -suddenly-the-floor-wasn-t-there-factory-survivor-says, accessed December 4, 2016.

12. R. Fisman and Y. Wang, "The Mortality Cost of Political Connections," *Review of Economic Studies* 82(4) (2015): 1346–82.

13. "Coal Miners Pay with Their Lives for Cronyism in China," *Hindustan Times*, August 11, 2005.

14. See Dan Barry, "Courthouse That Tweed Built Seeks to Shed Notorious Past," available at http://www.nytimes.com/ 2000/12/12/nyregion/courthouse-that-tweed-built-seeks-to-shed-notorious-past.html, accessed July 27, 2016.

15. As with public construction, military procurement is reputedly rife with graft, bid-rigging, and inflated prices—and for similar reasons. Owing to their technical complexity, fighter jet contracts can't be evaluated by the general public. Even if they could, military purchases are often subject to security considerations, so the relevant information may not be available.

16. The results were published as B. Olken, "Monitoring Corruption: Evidence from a Field Experiment in Indonesia," *Journal of Political Economy* 115(2) (2007): 200–49.

17. One effort to study the costs of corruption in road building on a larger scale comes from researchers Jonathan Lehne, Jacob Shapiro, and Oliver Eynde. The trio examine what happens to road contracts in India when a state-level politician is narrowly elected. They find that after his election, companies owned by individuals who share the politician's surname are more likely to get road building contracts. They further show that the cost of roads built by "related" businesses are higher and the quality lower. See J. Lehne, J. N. Shapiro, and O. V. Eynde, "Building Connections: Political Corruption and Road Construction in India," unpublished paper, 2016.

18. N. Ambraseys and R. Bilham, "Corruption Kills," *Nature* 469(7329) (2011): 153–55.

19. S. Gupta, H. Davoodi, and R. Alonso-Terme, "Does Corruption Affect Income Inequality and Poverty?" *Economics of Governance* 3(1) (2007): 23–45.

20. J. Hunt, "Bribery in Health Care in Uganda," *Journal of Health Economics* 29(5) (2010); 699–707.

21. J. Botero, A. Ponce, and A. Shleifer, "Education, Complaints, and Accountability," *Journal of Law and Economics* 56(4) (2013): 959–96.

22. C. J. Anderson and Y. V. Tverdova, "Corruption, Political Allegiances, and Attitudes toward Government in Contemporary Democracies," *American Journal of Political Science* 47(1) (2003): 91–109.

23. A. Chong, A. L. De La O, D. Karlan, and L. Wantchekon, "Does Corruption Information Inspire the Fight or Quash the Hope? A Field Experiment in Mexico on Voter Turnout, Choice and Participation," *Journal of Politics* 77(1) (2015): 55–71.

24. A. Shleifer and R. W. Vishny, "Corruption," *Quarterly Journal of Economics* 108 (1993): 599–617.

25. B. A. Olken and P. Barron, "The Simple Economics of Extortion: Evidence from Trucking in Aceh," *Journal of Political Economy* 117(3) (2009): 417–52.

26. Olken and Barron's paper also looks at other aspects of Indonesian trucker extortion, such as whether bribes increase the closer the driver gets to his destination, and whether gun-wielding soldiers extract higher payments than more lightly armed ones.

27. Reported in Tracy Wilkinson, "In Honduras, Rival Gangs Keep a Death Grip on San Pedro Sula," *Los Angeles Times*, December 17, 2013, http://www.latimes.com/world/la-fg-c1-honduras-violence-20131216-dto-htmlstory.html, accessed July 11, 2016.

28. On the concept of protection, see D. Gambetta, *The Sicilian Mafia: The Business of Private Protection* (Cambridge, MA: Harvard University Press, 1993).

29. The *Planet Money* episode that discusses the plight of Honduran bus drivers may be found at http://www.npr.org/sections/money/2014/12/12/370350849/episode-589-hello-i-m-calling-from-la-mafia, accessed December 7, 2016.

30. The question of just how responsive individual effort is to tax rates is a much-debated question among labor and public finance economists, but not one we will take up here.

31. Government policy can be fraught with uncertainty as well. Governments come, governments go. Some lower taxes; others raise them. There is also a good deal of research on the effects of government policy uncertainty on investment, and we refer readers in particular to D. Rodrik, "Policy Uncertainty and Private Investment in Developing Countries," *Journal of Development Economics* 36(2) (1991): 229–42. But as we will see shortly, whatever impact there might be from policy uncertainty is likely swamped by the risk posed by bribe-demanding bureaucrats.

32. S.-J. Wei, "How Taxing Is Corruption on International Investors?" *Review of Economics and Statistics* 82(1) (2000): 1–11.

33. S.-J. Wei, "Why Is Corruption So Much More Taxing Than Tax? Arbitrariness Kills" (National Bureau of Economic Research [NBER, Working Paper No. 6255), 1997.

34. In one recent example of the consequences of contractual ambiguity, the United States Supreme Court heard a case on the country's Affordable Care Act, which was being challenged on the basis of the Act's wording that health insurance exchanges were to be "established by the state." The government argued that the intent of the language was that the federal government (i.e., the state) mandated the creation of health insurance exchanges, whereas the Act's challengers argued that the language indicated that each of the fifty states of the Union were to decide for themselves whether to provide insurance exchanges. While the court sided with the federal government, just a few words out of an 11,000-page document nearly proved the Act's undoing.

35. Victor Mallet, "Thais Make a Mess of Their Muddling," *Financial Times*, June 22, 1993.

36. This quote comes from an INSEAD teaching case, Ulla Fionna and Douglas Webber, *Manulife in Indonesia*, rev. ed. (Feb. 26, 2015).

37. There is almost no evidence documenting this claim, and results from a study conducted by political scientist Laura Paler suggest that the truth is probably not quite so stark. Paler conducted a public awareness campaign, combined with a series of tax experiments, in Indonesia. As expected, she found that when citizens saw their own money at stake, they were more likely to hold incumbent politicians to account. But she also found that citizens were not indifferent to how public monies were spent

even when derived from resource windfalls. See L. Paler, "Keeping the Public Purse: An Experiment in Windfalls, Taxes, and the Incentives to Restrain Government," *American Political Science Review* 107(4) (2013): 706–25.

38. For a discussion of various theories of the resource curse (as well as additional references), see M. L. Ross, "The Political Economy of the Resource Curse," *World Politics* 51(2) (1999): 297–322. In addition to the corruption-related theories we focus on here, Ross discusses the role of "Dutch disease," in which a country invests excessively in a single sector. It is named after Holland's single-minded investment in tulips in the sixteenth century, as a result of what was, in retrospect, an obvious bubble. The Dutch economy went bust as a result, since it hadn't diversified into other areas. Similarly, countries that overinvest in oil or diamond production are exposed to boom-bust commodity cycles.

39. J. D. Sachs and A. M. Warner, "Natural Resource Abundance and Economic Growth" (National Bureau of Economic Research [NBER], Working Paper No. 5398), 1995.

40. M. L. Ross, "The Political Economy of the Resource Curse," *World Politics* 51(2) (1999): 297–322.

41. There is a body of evidence which shows that countries that are generally ranked as more corrupt are also those with higher deforestation rates and less success in biodiversity conservation. Of course, causality probably goes both ways.

42. P. O. Cerutti and L. Tacconi, "Forests, Illegality, and Livelihoods: The Case of Cameroon," *Society and Natural Resources* 21(9) (2008): 845–53.

43. For material describing these criminal activities, see C. Nellemann and INTERPOL Environmental Crime Program (Eds.), "Green Carbon, Black Trade: Illegal Logging, Tax Fraud and Laundering in the World's Tropical Forests," A Rapid Response Assessment, United National Environmental Programme, 2012.

44. We refer readers to her classic work, E. Ostrom, *Governing the Commons: The Evolution of Institutions for Collective Action* (New York: Cambridge University Press, 1990).

45. One way to mitigate corruption in natural resources is simply to pay people to conserve, but that is not a practical solution in many instances. An interesting study along these lines is S. Jayachandran, J. de Laat, E. F. Lambin, and C. Y. Stanton, "Cash for Carbon: A Randomized Controlled Trial of Payments for

Ecosystem Services to Reduce Deforestation" (National Bureau of
Economic Research [NBER], Working Paper No. 22378), 2016.
46. One of the very few experimental studies of corruption and
conservation shows this; see A. Sundström, "Corruption and
Violations of Conservation Rules: A Survey Experiment with
Resource Users," *World Development* 85 (2016): 73–83.

Chapter 5. Who Is Involved in Corruption, and Why?

1. This was, until recently, a more controversial assertion than you
might imagine. The dominant school of thought held that
individuals responded to greater wealth by adjusting their
"reference" level of consumption to their new level of prosperity:
if you were happy to drive a moped, once you get a car life seems
empty without one; and once you've made enough to buy a
Mercedes, driving a Toyota leaves you in a state of existential
despair. According to this view, a person will be happier only
temporarily after a rise in income, with the effect quickly
dissipating as they acclimate to their new level of prosperity.
Economists Betsy Stevenson and Justin Wolfers, using happiness
and income data over many years from many countries, have
largely disproven this hypothesis. Their research shows that
greater income continues to improve happiness, at least over the
incomes earned by their survey respondents, which range as high
as US$100,000. See B. Stevenson and J. Wolfers, "Economic
Growth and Subjective Well-Being: Reassessing the Easterlin
Paradox" (National Bureau of Economic Research [NBER],
Working Paper No. 14282), 2008.
2. Mahmoud Bahrani, "The Economics of Crime with Gary Becker,"
Chicago Maroon, May 25, 2012, http://chicagomaroon.com/2012/
05/25/the-economics-of-crime-with-gary-becker/, accessed
September 10, 2015.
3. O. Bandiera, A. Prat, and T. Valletti, "Active and Passive Waste in
Government Spending: Evidence from a Policy Experiment,"
American Economic Review 99(4) (2009): 1278–1308.
4. It is notoriously difficult to distinguish between corruption and
mere inefficiency, laziness, and stupidity. The researchers who
studied Consip's introduction attributed most of the initial waste
to lazy rather than corrupt officials.
5. See A. V. Banerjee, "A Theory of Misgovernance," *Quarterly
Journal of Economics* 112(4) (1997): 1289–332 for an economic
model of how bureaucratic discretion leads to bribe taking.

6. For a quantitative assessment of the economic consequences of bid rigging in Quebec government procurement, see R. Clark, D. Coviello, J.-F. Gauthier, and A. Shneyerov, "Bid Rigging and Entry Deterrence: Evidence from an Anticollusion Investigation in Quebec," unpublished paper, 2015.

7. Olson in turn quoted Edward Banfield's study of southern Italy as inspiring his analysis of roving versus stationary bandits: "Monarchy is the best kind of government because the King is then owner of the country. Like the owner of a house, when the wiring is wrong, he fixes it." For the record, Olson felt that a well-functioning democracy was better still than even a forward-looking dictator. The Banfield quote appears in M. Olson, "Dictatorship, Democracy, and Development," *American Political Science Review* 87(3) (1993): 567–76, 567.

8. Some material in this section is drawn from one of the author's columns in *Slate*, which may be accessed at http://www.slate.com/articles/business/the_dismal_science/2012/04/how_corrupt_are_politicians_in_india_at_least_being_in_parliament_doesn_t_pay_.html, accessed December 7, 2016.

9. R. Fisman, F. Schultz, and V. Vig, "Private Returns to Public Office," *Journal of Political Economy* 122(4) (2014): 806–62.

10. In practice, we use what is called a "regression discontinuity design" to study the benefits of winning. If you are interested in this type of statistical analysis, we recommend you consult T. Dunning, *Natural Experiments in the Social Sciences: A Design-Based Approach* (New York: Cambridge University Press, 2012), chap. 3.

11. We also show in our analysis that former ministers who are elected—but don't serve again as ministers because their party isn't in office—don't see their assets grow particularly fast. This argues against the "smart minister" hypothesis.

12. On the returns to political office in Sweden see, for example, H. Lundqvist, "Is It Worth It? On the Returns to Holding Political Office" (IEB Working Paper No. 2013/014), 2013; on the United Kingdom, A. Eggers and J. Hainmuller, "MPs for Sale? Returns to Office in Postwar British Politics," *American Political Science Review* 103(4) (2009): 319–42; and on the United States, P. Querubín and J. M. Snyder Jr., "The Control of Politicians in Normal Times and Times of Crisis: Wealth Accumulation by U.S.

Congressmen, 1850–1880," *Quarterly Journal of Political Science* 8(4) (2013): 409–50.

13. From Madison's speech at the Virginia Ratifying Convention, June 20, 1788. Taken from Z. Teachout, *Corruption in America: From Benjamin Franklin's Snuff Box to Citizens United.* (Cambridge: Harvard University Press, 2014), 52.

14. Our information on this is drawn from S. Kernell and M. P. McDonald, "Congress and America's Political Development: The Transformation of the Post Office from Patronage to Service," *American Journal of Political Science* 43(3) (1999): 792–811.

15. The employees at Brazil's state oil company, Petrobras, who organized the kickback scheme that came to light in the Petrobras scandal were largely patronage appointments. These employees benefited personally, but so did their political benefactors: hundreds of millions of dollars in kickbacks were used to fund political campaigns for the ruling Workers' Party.

16. M. Callen and J. D. Long, "Institutional Corruption and Election Fraud: Evidence from a Field Experiment in Afghanistan," *American Economic Review* 105(1) (2015): 354–81.

17. R. Wade, "The System of Administrative and Political Corruption: Canal Irrigation in South India," *Journal of Development Studies* 18(3) (1982): 287–328.

18. Recounted in T. Gong, "Dangerous Collusion: Corruption as a Collective Venture in Contemporary China," *Communist and Post-Communist Studies* 35 (2002): 85–103, 94–97.

19. "Fighting Corruption," *The Economist*, April 29, 2004, http://www.economist.com/node/2643440, accessed July 14, 2016.

20. This is what led the great libertarian economist Milton Friedman to pen an influential 1970 essay, "The Social Responsibility of Business Is to Increase Its Profits," (published as M. Friedman, "The Social Responsibility of Business Is to Increase Its Profits," *New York Times Magazine*, 1970, 32–33, 122–24). Friedman argued that free market capitalism, guided by price signals and the self-interested motivations of consumers and producers alike, led to the best (or at least most efficient) of all possible worlds. Any deviation from profit maximization—by, say, paying workers "too much," or keeping rivers cleaner than required by law—would lead to value-destroying distortions to the market.

Friedman suggested that if we wanted cleaner rivers or better-paid employees than were dictated by profit maximization, that was the role of the government, which would need to set more stringent rules. It wasn't the role of business executives to circumvent democracy and make such decisions themselves, in his view. Nearly half a century later, Friedman's essay remains highly controversial. In any event, corruption lies outside the bounds of his arguments, as he explicitly advocated that companies maximize profits within the constraints imposed by law.

21. The corporation as a profit-maximizing black box is a useful starting point for understanding why companies pay bribes. However, it is necessarily an incomplete one. Just as a government is composed of individual bureaucrats and politicians, a company is made up of owners and employees, each of whom is in turn a collection of selfish motivations bundled with a conscience, just like the rest of us. They're all subject to the same social pressures, conform to whatever cultural norms they're immersed in, and engage in the same rationalizations. We defer the discussion of these issues to chapter 6, which focuses on cultures of corruption.

22. N. Ufere, S. Perelli, R. Boland, and B. Carlsson, "Merchants of Corruption: How Entrepreneurs Manufacture and Supply Bribes," *World Development* 40(12) (2012): 2440–53.

23. Ibid., 2444.

24. This section draws heavily on R. Fisman and E. Miguel, *Economic Gangsters: Corruption, Violence, and the Poverty of Nations* (Princeton: Princeton University Press, 2010), chap. 2.

25. R. Fisman, "Estimating the Value of Political Connections," *American Economic Review* 91(4) (2001): 1095–102.

26. In fact, Suharto's ill health turned out to be good news for a handful of less connected companies, as investors saw that they might have a better chance at securing government contracts and licenses once Suharto and his cronies were out of the way. This points to how well entrenched crony capitalism had become in Indonesia at the time.

27. If you examine Figure 5.1, you'll notice another curious pattern in Bimantara Citra's stock price. Recall that the government announced Suharto's German medical trip on July 4, 1996. But in the two days before the announcement, Bimantara's stock was

already in a fairly steep slide, down about 5 percent from its earlier levels. The collective wisdom of investors seems to have foreseen that Suharto would seek German medical attention a full two days before it was announced. How could that be? A lot of money was on the line. If you had known on July 2 that Bimantara's price would start its free fall on July 4, you could have sold your shares for a much higher price than what you would have gotten for the same shares just two days later. Certainly Suharto's doctors knew about the upcoming trip, so you can guess they were dumping any Bimantara shares they held personally, driving its price down ahead of the official announcement. The same could be said of those lucky investors who were friends with Suharto's medical team or inner circle. These pre-event movements don't figure into our 25 percent calculation above. If we incorporate them, the value of connections we generate is somewhat higher. The early decline that we observe in Bimantara's stock price cannot directly be linked to illegal insider trading, but it is, let us say ... suggestive.

28. We have discussed a pair of papers in chapter 2 which show that lobbying firms' fortunes are directly linked to their government connections. For example, a lobbying firm that employs a former staff member of a United States senator sees its revenues decline when that senator leaves office. See M. Bertrand, M. Bombardini, and F. Trebbi, "Is It Whom You Know or What You Know? An Empirical Assessment of the Lobbying Process," *American Economic Review* 104(12) (2014): 3885–920; and J. Blanes i Vidal, M. Draca, and C. Fons-Rosen, "Revolving Door Lobbyists," *American Economic Review* 102(7) (2012): 3731–48.

29. For details see note 7 of chapter 2.

30. In estimating the value of connections, Faccio also looks at how the market responds to unexpected announcements of politicians receiving appointments to corporate boards.

31. For a graphical presentation of the prisoners' dilemma, see M. Humphreys, *Political Games: Mathematical Insights on Fighting, Voting, Lying, and Other Affairs of State* (New York: Norton, 2016), item 1.

32. These countries had very little tolerance for corruption on their own soil, but permitted their businesses to pay bribes to officials in other countries—and even to receive a tax deduction for bribes paid as a business expense.

33. For a sense of the scope of cross-border corruption globally, see L. Escresa and L. Picci, "A New Cross-National Measure of Corruption," World Bank Policy Research Working Paper, (7371), July 2015.

34. Reported in European Commission, "Corruption," Special Eurobarometer 397, February 2014, http://ec.europa.eu/public_opinion/archives/ebs/ebs_397_en.pdf, accessed July 15, 2016.

35. The study is available at http://www.pewglobal.org/files/2014/11/Pew-Research-Center-Country-Problems-and-Institutions-Report-FINAL-November-6-2014.pdf, accessed December 7, 2016.

36. This is documented across the various "barometer" surveys conducted in different regions of the world by R. Rose and C. Peiffer, *Paying Bribes for Public Services: A Global Guide to Grass-Roots Corruption* (New York: Palgrave Macmillan, 2015).

37. R. Di Tella, R. Perez-Truglia, A. Babino, and M. Sigman, "Conveniently Upset: Avoiding Altruism by Distorting Beliefs about Others' Altruism," *American Economic Review* 105(11) (2015): 3416–42.

Chapter 6. What Are the Cultural Bases of Corruption?

1. For research based on his experiences, see J. J. Cooper, "How Robust Is Institutionalized Extortion? A Field Experiment with Truck Drivers in West Africa," unpublished paper, 2015.

2. If you're interested in digging up some of these stories yourself (including videos of those caught in the act), Liberman suggests googling, "extranjero trata de sobornar a carabinero" ("foreigner tries to bribe a Chilean police officer").

3. R. Fisman and E. Miguel, "Corruption, Norms, and Legal Enforcement: Evidence from Diplomatic Parking Tickets," *Journal of Political Economy* 115(6) (2007): 1020–48.

4. A. Ichino and G. Maggi, "Work Environment and Individual Background: Explaining Regional Shirking Differentials in a Large Italian Firm," *Quarterly Journal of Economics* 115(3) (2000): 1057–90.

5. An experiment conducted by Abigail Barr and Daniela Serra with students at Oxford University was explicitly designed to get at questions of culture and cultural change in a laboratory experiment. The researchers found that among undergraduate

subjects at Oxford University, those from very corrupt countries were more likely to "bribe" other subjects, relative to undergraduates from cultures where corruption was not tolerated, though the effect partially dissipated with exposure to the norms of the United Kingdom. Reported in A. Barr and D. Serra, "Corruption and Culture: An Experimental Analysis," *Journal of Public Economics* 90 (2010): 862–69.

6. The quote is taken from the 1973 film, *Serpico*, starring Al Pacino.

7. R. Hanna and S.-Y. Wang, "Dishonesty and Selection into Public Service: Evidence from India" (National Bureau of Economic Research [NBER], Working Paper No. 19649), 2015.

8. This experimental method was devised by U. Fischbacher and F. Föllmi-Heusi, "Lies in Disguise—An Experimental Study on Cheating," *Journal of the European Economic Association* 11(3) (2013): 525–47.

9. See S. Barfort, N. Harmon, F. Hjorth, and A. L. Olsen, "Sustaining Honesty in Public Service: The Role of Selection," unpublished paper, 2016.

10. It is difficult to compare the overall cheating rate between the two countries, since the Danish experiment was run online whereas the Indian experiment was conducted in-person in a computer lab.

11. The quote is from a review of J. T. Noonan, *Bribes* (Berkeley: University of California Press, 1984), in D. H. Lowenstein, "Review: For God, for Country, or for Me?" *California Law Review* 74(4) (1986): 1479–1512.

12. See, for example, M. M.-h. Yang, *Gifts, Favors, and Banquets: The Art of Social Relationships in China* (Ithaca: Cornell University Press, 1994), for a discussion of the fine line between a gift and a bribe in China.

13. M. Mauss, *The Gift: The Form and Reason for Exchange in Archaic Societies*, Routledge Classics Series (New York: Routledge, 1990).

14. N. R. Buchan, R. T. Croson, and R. M. Dawes, "Swift Neighbors and Persistent Strangers: A Cross-Cultural Investigation of Trust and Reciprocity in Social Exchange," *American Journal of Sociology* 108(1) (2002): 168–206.

15. The experiment was devised in J. Berg, J. Dickhaut, and K. McCabe, "Trust, Reciprocity, and Social History," *Games and Economic Behavior* 10(1) (1995): 122–42.

16. J. T. Noonan, *Bribes* (Berkeley: University of California Press, 1987).

17. M. Granovetter, "The Social Construction of Corruption," in
    V. Nee and R. Swedberg (Eds.), *On Capitalism* (Stanford: Stanford
    University Press, 2007).
18. The student is now a well-regarded finance professor, and still
    sending presents.
19. E. M. Uslaner, "Trust and Corruption," in J. G. Lambsdorff,
    M. Taube, and M. Schramm (Eds.), *The New Institutional Economics
    of Corruption* (London: Routledge, 2004).
20. Researchers have run the same investment game with high school
    students in Palermo, Sicily. They find lower trust among students
    from neighborhoods historically run by the Mafia. As any viewer
    of *The Godfather* films knows, favors from mob bosses are often of
    the "offer you can't refuse" variety, with a dreaded quid pro quo
    sometime in the future. See S. Meier, L. Pierce, and A. Vaccaro,
    "Trust and In-Group Favoritism in a Culture of Crime,"
    unpublished paper, 2014.
21. "ISIS Crucifies One of Its Own in Syria for Corruption," *Al
    Arabiya*, June 27, 2014, http://english.alarabiya.net/en/
    News/middle-east/2014/06/27/ISIS-crucifies-one-of-its-own-
    in-Syria-for-corruption-.html, accessed July 29, 2016.
22. R. Gatti, S. Paternostro, and J. Rigolini, "Individual Attitudes
    toward Corruption: Do Social Effects Matter?" *World Bank Policy
    Research Working Paper*, (3122), 2003.
23. D. Treisman, "The Causes of Corruption: A Cross-National
    Study," *Journal of Public Economics* 76(3) (2000): 399–457.
24. H. Tajfel, M. G. Billig, R. P. Bundy, and C. Flament, "Social
    Categorization and Intergroup Behaviour," *European Journal of
    Social Psychology* 1(2) (1971): 149–78.
25. Tajfel's work has been replicated and extended in the years since,
    and was even preceded by a nonscientific experiment run well
    before the Klee-Kandinsky study. Some readers may be familiar
    with the exercise run by schoolteacher Jane Elliott on the day after
    Martin Luther King's assassination in 1968, in which she grouped
    her class based on eye color, quickly leading to hostilities between
    previously friendly blue- and brown-eyed students.
26. Where there wasn't interethnic animosity initially, colonial
    powers sometimes fomented hostilities to "divide and conquer"
    the local population.
27. See A. Alesina, A. Devleeschauwer, W. Easterly, S. Kurlat, and
    R. Wacziarg, "Fractionalization," *Journal of Economic Growth* 8(2)

(2003): 155–94; for a discussion, see J. D. Fearon, "Ethnic and Cultural Diversity by Country," *Journal of Economic Growth* 8(2) (2003): 195–222.

28. A. Alesina et al., "Fractionalization."

29. A similar correlation was observed by economist Paolo Mauro, using a coarser measure of fractionalization, in his important study of corruption and economic growth; P. Mauro, "Corruption and Growth," *Quarterly Journal of Economics* 110(3) (1995): 681–712.

30. See A. Banerjee and R. Pande, "Parochial Politics: Ethnic Preferences and Politician Corruption" (Kennedy School of Government Working Paper No. RWP07-031), Centre for Economic Policy Research, 2007.

31. See J. Habyarimana, M. Humphreys, D. N. Posner, and J. M. Weinstein, *Coethnicity: Diversity and the Dilemmas of Collective Action* (New York: Russell Sage Foundation, 2009).

32. For a discussion of Botswana's economic success, see J. A. Robinson, D. Acemoglu, and S. Johnson, "An African Success Story: Botswana," in D. Rodrik (Ed.), *In Search of Prosperity: Analytic Narratives on Economic Growth* (Princeton: Princeton University Press, 2003).

Chapter 7. How Do Political Institutions Affect Corruption?

1. Put more technically, this means that if you know a country's per capita GDP and you guess how corrupt it is on that basis, the variance of the error in your guesses will be 60 percent smaller than if you simply guess that the country has an average level of corruption.

2. We say this on the basis of aggregate, cross-national data that is not able to show any significant advantage for democracy in the provision of public services or public goods. In recent work that analyzes electricity provision using satellite data, Brian Min documents that democracies are more effective in delivering this particular service, especially for rural, impoverished populations. See B. Min, *Power and the Vote: Elections and Electricity in the Developing World* (New York: Cambridge University Press, 2015).

3. A. Przeworski, M. E. Alvarez, J. A. Cheibub, and F. Limongi, *Democracy and Development: Political Institutions and Well-Being in the World, 1950–1990* (New York: Cambridge University Press, 2000).

4. In B. F. Jones and B. A. Olken, "Do Leaders Matter? National Leadership and Growth since World War II," *Quarterly Journal of Economics* 120(3) (2005): 835–64, economists Benjamin Jones and Benjamin Olken document that, while there is no difference in economic growth on average, dictatorships are more prone to stop-start growth. That is, they tend to either grow very rapidly under "pro-growth" dictators like Lee Kuan Yew of Singapore and Augusto Pinochet of Chile, or to experience economic collapse under chaotic kleptocracies (the list of which is too lengthy to include here).

5. Some contemporary political scientists avoid using the term "dictatorship" because there is an assortment of nondemocratic systems, only some of which are controlled by a single dictatorial figure.

6. Sometimes a few other regime types are added, such as oligarchies—rule by an elite few—but these are the main ones.

7. A newspaper story from 2016 described Mr. Nguema's son, also named Teodoro, thus: "It's hard to imagine a public official with more toys than Teodoro Nguema Obiang Mangue, who spent $300 million on Ferraris, a Gulfstream jet, a California mansion and even Michael Jackson's 'Thriller' jacket. The buying spree is all the more remarkable since this scion of the ruling family of Equatorial Guinea, one of Africa's smallest countries, bought all this while on an official salary of $100,000 a year." Reported in Leslie Wayne, "Wanted by U.S.: The Stolen Millions of Despots and Crooked Elites," *New York Times*, February 16, 2016.

8. See "Mozambique Is Floundering Amid Corruption and Conflict," *The Economist*, March 18, 2016, http://www.economist.com/news/middle-east-and-africa/21695203-scandals-and-setbacks-gas-and-fishing-industries-darken-mood-mozambique, accessed August 3, 2016.

9. See, for example, D. Treisman, "What Have We Learned about the Causes of Corruption from Ten Years of Cross-National Empirical Research?" *Annual Review of Political Science* 10 (2007): 211–44.

10. In principle, fielding more honest candidates isn't even necessary. If voters discipline corrupt incumbents by ejecting them from office, eventually even politicians who would prefer to steal or take bribes will learn that they will soon be out of office if they do, and rein in their behavior. As we show in the next chapter, however, voters are usually unable to get rid of corrupt

politicians. For a general treatment of the issues, see T. Besley, *Principled Agents? The Political Economy of Good Government* (Oxford: Oxford University Press, 2006).

11. The distinction between voice and exit, along with a discussion of its many implications, may be found in A. O. Hirschman, *Exit, Voice, and Loyalty: Responses to Decline in Firms, Organizations, and States* (Cambridge, MA: Harvard University Press, 1970).

12. Quoted in E. Kramon, "Vote Buying and Electoral Turnout in Kenya," in M. Bratton (Ed.), *Voting and Democratic Citizenship in Africa* (Boulder, CO: Lynne Rienner, 2013), 106.

13. An interesting discussion of relevant phenomena and cases is E. L. Gibson, *Boundary Control: Subnational Authoritarianism in Federal Democracies* (New York: Cambridge University Press, 2013).

14. D. Treisman, "What Have We Learned about the Causes of Corruption from Ten Years of Cross-National Empirical Research?" *Annual Review of Political Science* 10 (2007): 211–44, 232.

15. A thoughtful attempt to surmount these kinds of problems comes from T. Persson and G. Tabellini, *The Economic Effects of Constitutions* (Cambridge, MA: MIT Press, 2003).

16. There are, of course, exceptions to this general observation. See, for example, the fascinating study of local unelected leaders in Zambia documented in K. Baldwin, *The Paradox of Traditional Chiefs in Democratic Africa* (New York: Cambridge University Press, 2015).

17. On one hand, a cross-national study by Daniel Treisman finds that, all else equal, federal states are more corrupt than centralized polities. See D. Treisman, "The Causes of Corruption: A Cross-National Study," *Journal of Public Economics* 76(3) (2009): 399–457. This is at least somewhat at odds with the finding of another study, reported in R. Fisman and R. Gatti, "Decentralization and Corruption: Evidence from U.S. Federal Transfer Programs," *Public Choice* 113(1) (2002): 25–35), which shows that countries are less corrupt if local or state governments control a greater share of financial resources than central governments. These two sets of findings indicate, at the very least, the complexities of the relationship between decentralization and corruption (and also the limits of what we can likely learn from national-level cross-country analyses).

18. Reported in P. Bardhan and D. Mookherjee, "Pro-Poor Targeting and Accountability of Local Governments in West Bengal," *Journal of Development Economics*, 79(2) (2006): 303–27.

19. One of our students studied the allocation of infrastructure for communal water provision—wells and pumps—in Tanzania and also found evidence of local political distortions. Tanzania is a nominally democratic but effectively one-party political system that, due to its poverty, receives considerable foreign aid. In recent years, a lot of aid has gone to trying to improve access to clean water in rural areas, where infrastructure dating back to the country's socialist era had fallen into disrepair. Using detailed budget data and maps that showed the location of every water access point in the country, Ruth Carlitz found that the allocation of financial resources for water provision was fairly equitable. So the national government was doing pretty much what it ought to have been doing in improving access to clean water. But within local government authorities, Carlitz identified clear patterns of political favoritism: local politicians allocate new water points to the communities in their constituencies that support them electorally and punish areas whose voters are less supportive. There may be nothing illegal or corrupt in this, but it suggests that political favoritism does not cease just because politicians are nominally closer to their voters. The research is reported in R. Carlitz, "Money Flows, Water Trickles: Explaining the Disconnect between Spending and Improved Access to Clean Water in Tanzania," (PhD thesis, University of California at Los Angeles, 2016).

20. One recent study in Indonesia provided villagers with better information on a rice subsidy program whose implementation was controlled by local leaders. Merely providing this information to citizens on the benefits they were entitled to was enough to increase the subsidies received by beneficiaries by over 25 percent. See A. Banerjee, R. Hanna, J. C. Kyle, B. A. Olken, and S. Sumarto, "The Power of Transparency: Information, Identification Cards and Food Subsidy Programs in Indonesia" (National Bureau of Economic Research [NBER], Working Paper No. 20923), 2015.

21. C. Ferraz and F. Finan, "Electoral Accountability and Corruption: Evidence from the Audits of Local Governments," *American Economic Review* 101(4) (2011): 1274–311.

22. D. Coviello and S. Gagliarducci, "Tenure in Office and Public Procurement," unpublished paper, 2015.
23. Our knowledge about campaign financing regulations draws on the data available in the Political Finance Database of the International Institute for Democracy and Electoral Assistance; see the description in M. Ohman, "Political Finance Regulations around the World: An Overview of the International IDEA Database," Stockholm, 2012.

Chapter 8. How Do Countries Shift from High to Low Corruption?

1. See the review by C. E. de Vries and H. Solaz, "The Electoral Consequences of Corruption," *Annual Review of Political Science* 20 (2017).
2. See the interesting analysis by B. Nyblade and S. R. Reed, "Who Cheats? Who Loots? Political Competition and Corruption in Japan, 1947–1993," *American Journal of Political Science* 54(4) (2008): 926–41.
3. In a study using survey experiments, two political scientists found that voters in low-corruption Sweden never tolerated corruption—probably because it was not considered normatively acceptable and voters were never pressured into corrupt behavior—whereas in high-corruption Moldova, voters reacted against corruption only when the economy was performing badly. Reported in M. Klašnja and J. A. Tucker, "The Economy, Corruption, and the Vote: Evidence from Experiments in Sweden and Moldova," *Electoral Studies* 32(3) (2013): 536–43.
4. See S. Djankov, C. McLiesh, T. Nenova, and A. Shleifer, "Who Owns the Media?" *Journal of Law and Economics* 46(2) (2003): 341–82.
5. C. Ferraz and F. Finan, "Exposing Corrupt Politicians: The Effect of Brazil's Publicly Released Audits on Electoral Outcomes," *Quarterly Journal of Economics* 123(2) (2008): 703–45.
6. A. V. Banerjee, D. P. Green, J. McManus, and R. Pande, "Are Poor Voters Indifferent to Whether Elected Leaders Are Criminal or Corrupt? A Vignette Experiment in Rural India," *Political Communications* 31(3) (2014): 391–407.
7. See A. Chong, A. L. De La O, D. Karlan, and L. Wantchekon, "Does Corruption Information Inspire the Fight or Quash the Hope? A Field Experiment in Mexico on Voter Turnout, Choice and Participation," *Journal of Politics* 77(1) (2015): 55–71.

8. R. Weitz-Shapiro and M. S. Winters, "Discerning Corruption: Information Credibility, Political Sophistication, and the Punishment of Politicians in Brazil," *Journal of Politics* (forthcoming).

9. M. S.-Y. Chwe, *Rational Ritual: Culture, Coordination, and Common Knowledge* (Princeton: Princeton University Press, 2013).

10. Less obviously networked products may also fit with Chwe's notion of common knowledge—if I know everyone else in America saw the cool Nike ad, I know everyone will think I'm cool if I wear Nike sneakers.

11. The term is due to B. Magaloni, *Voting for Autocracy: Hegemonic Party Survival and Its Demise in Mexico* (New York: Cambridge University Press, 2006).

12. K. Bidwell, K. Casey, and R. Glennerster, "Debates: Voting and Expenditure Responses to Political Communication" (Stanford Center for International Development, Working Paper No. 563), 2016.

13. But more work is needed to know whether the benefits of common knowledge serve to keep politicians honest in a wider set of countries and circumstances. Results from work in progress have been mixed. An interrelated set of studies coordinated by Evidence in Governance and Politics in different countries has produced weak support of the common knowledge theory, although analysis is still underway as we write this. The plan for the studies is laid out in T. Dunning, G. Grossman, M. Humphreys, S. Hyde, C. McIntosh, C. Adida, and N. Sircar, "Political Information and Electoral Choices: A Pre-Meta-Analysis Plan," unpublished pre-analysis plan, 2015. For some preliminary results, see C. Adida, J. Gottlieb, E. Kramon, and G. McClendon, "How Coethnicity Moderates the Effect of Information on Voting Behavior: Experimental Evidence from Benin," unpublished paper, 2016.

14. The interested reader may see Mackie's original paper; G. Mackie, "Ending Footbinding and Infibulation: A Convention Account," *American Sociological Review* 61(6) (1996): 999–1017. The material is also covered in K. A. Appiah, *The Honor Code: How Moral Revolutions Happen* (New York: W. W. Norton, 2010).

15. We document this more rigorously in E. C. Chang, M. A. Golden, and S. J. Hill, "Legislative Malfeasance and Political Accountability," *World Politics* 62(2) (2010): 177–220.

16. Some readers will recognize the resemblance of this situation to the classic game theoretic problem of the prisoners' dilemma. The prisoners in the standard version of this problem are forced to decide simultaneously whether to confess, so they can't condition their decision on the confessions of others. See the discussion of the structure of the prisoners' dilemma in chapter 5.

17. R. S. Katz and P. Ignazi, "Introduction," in R. S. Katz and P. Ignazi (Eds.), *Italian Politics: The Year of the Tycoon*, vol. 10, *Italian Politics: A Review* (Boulder, CO: Westview, 1996), 22.

18. R. Katz, "Electoral Reform and the Transformation of Party Politics in Italy," *Party Politics* 2(1) (1996): 31–53, 47.

19. Reported in M. J. Bull and J. L. Newell, *Italian Politics: Adjustment under Duress* (Cambridge: Polity, 2005), Table 6.1, 112.

20. R. Asquer, "Media Coverage of Corruption and Incumbent Renomination in Italy" (PhD thesis, University of California at Los Angeles, 2015).

21. See A. Del Monte and E. Papagni, "The Determinants of Corruption in Italy: Regional Panel Data Analysis," *European Journal of Political Economy* 23 (2007): 379–96.

22. Reported in A. Acconcia and C. Cantabene, "A Big Push to Deter Corruption: Evidence from Italy," *Giornale degli Economisti e Annali di Economia* 67(1) (2008): 75–102, Figs. 1 and 2, 80.

23. Our account is based on the research reported in M. Manion, *Corruption by Design: Building Clean Government in Mainland China and Hong Kong* (Cambridge, MA: Harvard University Press, 2004), chap. 2.

24. For the Republic of Georgia's fight against corruption, we draw on M. Light, "Police Reforms in the Republic of Georgia: The Convergence of Domestic and Foreign Policy in an Anti-Corruption Drive," *Policing and Society* 24(3) (2004): 318–45.

25. Our understanding of Singapore's success in bringing down corruption comes from J. S. Quah, "Controlling Corruption in City-States: A Comparative Study of Hong Kong and Singapore," *Crime, Law & Social Change* 22 (1995): 391–414.

Chapter 9. What Can Be Done to Reduce Corruption?

1. See C. Van Rijckeghem and B. Weder, "Bureaucratic Corruption and the Rate of Temptation: Do Wages in the Civil Service Affect Corruption, and by How Much," *Journal of Development Economics* 65(2) (2001): 307–31.

2. This information is reported in P. Mishra, A. Subramanian, and P. Topalova, "Tariffs, Enforcement, and Customs Evasion: Evidence from India," *Journal of Public Economics* 92(10) (2008): 1907–25.

3. This is a variant of the efficiency wage theory in economics. See C. Shapiro and J. E. Stiglitz, "Equilibrium Unemployment as a Worker Discipline Device," *American Economic Review* (1984): 433–44.

4. R. Di Tella and E. Schargrodsky, "The Role of Wages and Auditing during a Crackdown on Corruption in the City of Buenos Aires," *Journal of Law and Economics* 46 (2003): 269–92.

5. The study found no relationship between wages and prices paid when the crackdown was at its height. The authors argue that procurement officers would have been so closely monitored at that time that none—regardless of salary—risked soliciting kickbacks.

6. Taken from Franklin's speech, "Dangers of a Salaried Bureaucracy," delivered to the Constitutional Convention in Philadelphia in 1787.

7. The study in question is S. Barfort, N. Harmon, F. Hjorth, and A. L. Olsen, "Sustaining Honesty in Public Service: The Role of Selection," unpublished paper, 2016.

8. Juvenal used the phrase in concerns over marital infidelity, but the idea is similar.

9. These observations are taken from Leonid Hurwicz's 2007 Nobel address. To hear a recorded version, go to http://www.nobel prize.org/nobel_prizes/economic-sciences/laureates/2007/ hurwicz-lecture.html, accessed December 7, 2016.

10. Anticorruption authorities have their own association and associated website, http://www.acauthorities.org/, where you can find further information, accessed December 7, 2016.

11. It is interesting that China's ranking on TI's Corruption Perceptions Index actually worsened between 2012 and 2014, lending credence to the view that corruption perceptions may be driven as much by public exposure of corruption as the underlying problem itself.

12. For a detailed account of Githongo's attempts at fighting corruption in Kenya, see M. Wrong, *It's Our Turn to Eat: The Story of a Kenyan Whistle-Blower* (New York: Harper Perennial, 2010).

13. Many of these schemes aimed to benefit Kibaki's Kikuyu tribe. The reader may recall from chapter 6 that Kibaki used his power as president to reward members of his own ethnic group.

14. One of those targeted by Githongo, energy minister Kiraitu Murungi, alleges that Githongo was a British spy. This accusation has not been substantiated.

15. An overview and summary of these cases may be found at https://successfulsocieties.princeton.edu/publications/ underdogs-watchdogshow-anti-corruption-agencies-can-hold- potent-adversaries, accessed December 7, 2016.

16. Gabriel Kuris, "From Underdogs to Watchdogs: How Anti-Corruption Agencies Can Hold Off Potent Adversaries," Innovation for Successful Societies, Princeton University Working Paper 3, 2014.

17. The study results were reported in R. Reinikka and J. Svensson, "Fighting Corruption to Improve Schooling: Evidence from a Newspaper Campaign in Uganda," Journal of the European Economic Association 3(2–3) (2005): 259–67.

18. B. Rothstein, "Anti-Corruption: The Indirect 'Big-Bang' Approach," Review of International Political Economy 18(2) (2011): 228–50.

19. See E. Morozov, "To Save Everything, Click Here: The Folly of Technological Solutionism," New York: Public Affairs (2014): ix.

20. The NREGA guaranteed wage rate varies by state. The figures are as of 2016.

21. S. Dutta, "Power, Patronage and Politics: A Study of Two Panchayat Elections in the North Indian State of Uttar Pradesh," South Asia: Journal of South Asian Studies 35(2) (2012): 329–52.

22. Report available at http://archive.indianexpress.com/news/ nregs-lootdead-men-walking-as-ghost-workers/711901/, accessed December 7, 2016.

23. P. Niehaus and S. Sukhtankar, "The Marginal Rate of Corruption in Public Programs: Evidence from India," Journal of Public Economics 104 (2013): 52–64.

24. K. Muralidharan, P. Niehaus, and S. Sukhtankar, "Building State Capacity: Evidence from Biometric Smartcards in India," American Economic Review (forthcoming).

25. Private communication with Sandip Sukhtankar.

26. P. Barnwal, "Curbing Leakage in Public Programs with Biometric Identification Systems: Evidence from India's Fuel Subsidies," unpublished paper, 2015.

27. Some of our information comes from Prabhat Barnwal "Curbing Leakage in Public Programs with Direct Benefit Transfers," unpublished working paper, https://assets.publishing. service.gov.uk/media/57a08986ed915d622c00026f/89111_ barnwal2014leakage.pdf, accessed December 4, 2016.

28. These results are reported in M. A. Golden, E. Kramon, G. Ofosu, and L. Sonnet, "Biometric Identification Machine Failure and Electoral Fraud in a Competitive Democracy," unpublished paper, 2015.

29. S. Djankov, C. McLiesh, T. Nenova, and A. Shleifer, "Who Owns the Media?" *Journal of Law and Economics* 46(2) (2003): 341–82.

30. Ibid., 367.

31. Tejpal was arrested for rape in 2013. The case is still pending at the time of writing, so we cannot yet say for certain whether he used his authority to victimize women in addition to exposing public deceit. Tejpal could be guilty of sexual assault and nonetheless himself be a victim of government harassment related to other matters.

32. The importance of shared information in building a sense of national community and identity is stressed in B. Anderson, *Imagined Communities: Reflections on the Origin and Spread of Nationalism* (London: Verso, 1983).

33. Peskov claimed it was a wedding present from his bride, though he had been spotted wearing it months before their marriage.

34. Similar websites were less successful than the original. Most notably, the Chinese version fizzled very quickly. Political scientist Yuen Yuen Ang argued that this was the result of long-term repression of NGOs by the Chinese government, which left such organizations without the professionalism and autonomy to replicate the Indian version. See Y. Y. Ang, "Authoritarian Restraints on Online Activism Revisited: Why 'I-Paid-A-Bribe' Worked in India but Failed in China," *Comparative Politics* 47(1) (2014): 21–40.

35. This section borrows some material from R. Fisman and E. Miguel, *Economic Gangsters: Corruption, Violence, and the Poverty of Nations* (Princeton: Princeton University Press, 2010).

36. Simon Romero, "A Maverick Upends Colombian Politics," *New York Times*, May 7, 2010, A8.

37. We're often asked why the mimes weren't beaten up or killed for mocking jaywalkers. Recall again that there was a general sense among the citizenry of a desire for change. We conjecture that a

mime attack might have elicited a mob of vigilantes protecting the mimes.

38. A pair of documentaries have been made about Mockus and the transformation of Bogotá. One of them, part of the series *Cities on Speed*, is freely available online at https://www.youtube.com/watch?v=4lOkLNIT3gI, accessed December 7, 2016.

39. Anticorruption icon Robert Klitgaard coauthored a how-to manual that is freely available online as well, titled *Corrupt Cities: A Practical Guide to Cure and Prevention*. You can download a copy at http://documents.worldbank.org/curated/en/2000/01/693273/corrupt-cities-practical-guide-cure-prevention, accessed December 7, 2016. There is some overlap between his suggestions and those we discuss below, though his prescriptions focus more on policymakers than individual citizens.

40. Z. Teachout, *Corruption in America: From Benjamin Franklin's Snuff Box to Citizens United* (Cambridge, MA: Harvard University Press, 2014), 12.

41. F. R. Campante and Q.-A. Do, "Isolated Capital Cities, Accountability and Corruption: Evidence from US States (National Bureau of Economic Research [NBER], Working Paper No. 19027), 2013.

INDEX